RETURN TO THE LITTLE KINGDOM

STEVE JOBS,
THE CREATION OF APPLE,
AND HOW IT CHANGED THE WORLD

Also by Michael Moritz (with A. Barrett Seaman)

Going for Broke: The Chrysler Story

RETURN TO THE
LITTLE KINGDOM

STEVE JOBS,
THE CREATION OF APPLE,
AND HOW IT CHANGED THE WORLD

MICHAEL MORITZ

THE OVERLOOK PRESS
New York

This edition published in the United States in hardcover in 2009 by

The Overlook Press, Peter Mayer Publishers, Inc.
141 Wooster Street
New York, NY 10012
www.overlookpress.com

The author gratefully acknowledges *Fortune* for permission
to reprint content included in the Prologue here.

This book, excluding the Prologue and Epilogue,
was previously published in a slightly different form under
the title *The Little Kingdom: The Private Story of Apple Computer*
(William Morrow & Co, 1984).

Cataloging-in-Publication Data is available from
the Library of Congress

Book Design by Bryce Schimanski
Printed in the United States of America
First Edition
1 3 5 7 9 8 6 4 2
ISBN 978-1-59020-281-4

For the best additions since
the first edition:

HCH JWM WJM

TABLE OF CONTENTS

ACKNOWLEDGMENTS

Dozens of people agreed to be interviewed for this book. Many did not. I hope that those who opened their doors and interrupted more profitable pursuits don't feel they wasted their time. Others kindly let me rummage through filing cabinets and peer at photograph albums while the editors of the *San Jose Mercury News* made me welcome in their morgue. Dick Duncan, *Time's* chief of correspondents, tolerated another of my disruptive excursions and gave me a leave of absence. Ben Cate, *Time's* West Coast Bureau chief, provided the unwavering support that those who have worked for him will understand. Catazza Jones improved a first draft, Julian Bach took care of business, and Maria Guarnaschelli applied a deft and graceful touch.

—MICHAEL MORITZ
Potrero Hill
Spring 1984

PROLOGUE

When *Time* engages in its annual ritual of announcing the selection for its person of the year, I am inevitably reminded of an occasion, almost thirty years ago, when a similar bulletin caught me in its crosshairs. At the dawn of 1982, while I was on leave from my position as a correspondent in *Time*'s San Francisco bureau, the magazine's editors decided to nominate the computer as its "person" of the year. Buried inside this issue was a profile, to which I had contributed, of Apple's co-founder Steve Jobs. It was there that my troubles began.

It was hard to say who was more incensed by *Time*'s story—Jobs or me. Steve rightly took umbrage over his portrayal and what he saw as a grotesque betrayal of confidences, while I was equally distraught by the way in which material I had arduously gathered for a book about Apple was siphoned, filtered, and poisoned with a gossipy benzene by an editor in New York whose regular task was to chronicle the wayward world of rock-and-roll music. Steve made no secret of his anger and left a torrent of messages on the answering machine I kept in my converted earthquake cottage at the foot of San Francisco's Potrero Hill.

He, understandably, banished me from Apple and forbade anyone in his orbit to talk to me.

The experience made me decide that I would never again work anywhere I could not exert a large amount of control over my own destiny or where I would be paid by the word. I finished my leave; published my book, *The Little Kingdom: The Private Story of Apple Computer*, which I felt, unlike the unfortunate magazine article, presented a balanced portrait of the young Steve Jobs; honored my obligation to *Time* and, at the first opportunity, fled to become, at the outset, half of the entire workforce of a specialty publishing business that many years later—long after I had entered the venture capital field—was acquired by Dow Jones.

In the three decades since, I have sometimes wondered about the quirks of fate that have connected me with Steve. Had I not been in my twenties, *Time* would probably never have posted me to San Francisco, where I happened to be of the same generation that was starting computer, software and biotech companies. Had I not met Steve, I would not have encountered Don Valentine, the founder of Sequoia Capital, and an original investor in Apple. Had I not met Don, I would never have found myself interviewing to become the lowest man on Sequoia Capital's short totem pole. Had I not written about Apple, where I became obsessed with the then-unchronicled tale of its very early days, I would never have thought hard about the traits and accidents that shape a company. Had I not started learning the ropes of the venture trade in the mid 1980s, I would never have had the good luck that has flowed my way. And, had I not met Steve and Don, I would never have understood why it's best not to think like everyone else.

I'm sure that when Steve was a teenager, growing up in Los Altos, California, he could never have imagined that some day he would be at the helm of a company whose headquarters, according to Google maps, is three street turns and 1.6 miles from the front gate of his high school, that has sold over 200 million iPods, a billion iTunes songs, 26 million iPhones, and over 60 million computers since 1996; or that his face would have adorned the front cover of *Fortune* on twelve occasions; or that, almost as a sideline, he would single-handedly finance and help shape Pixar, the computer animation company that has rung up more than $5 billion in cumulative box office sales from ten immensely popular movies. He might wonder too about those twists and turns that helped make him what he is: the fact that his boyhood was spent in an area that, back then, had not even been labeled Silicon Valley; that Apple's co-founder, Stephen Wozniak, was a boyhood chum; that he worked one summer as a lab technician at Atari, the maker of Pong, the first popular arcade video game; that Atari's founder, Nolan Bushnell, had raised money from Don Valentine; and that Nolan was one of the people who steered Steve towards Don. Such are the haphazard breadcrumbs strewn along the trail of life.

These days, thanks to the rough and tumble experiences of almost twenty-five years in the venture capital business, I have developed what I hope is a more refined perspective on the extraordinary accomplishments of Steve's business life—one that deserves to be ranked amongst the greatest of any American, living or dead.

Steve is the CEO of Apple but, much more importantly (even though his business card does not say this), he is a founder of the company. As the history of Apple shows, there is no greater distance known to man than the single footfall that separates a CEO from a founder. CEOs are, for the most part, products of educational and institutional breeding. Founders or, at least, the very best of them, are unstoppable, irrepressable forces of nature. Of the many founders I've encountered, Steve is the most captivating. Steve, more than any one other person, has turned modern electronics into objects of desire.

Steve has always possessed the soul of the questioning poet—someone a little removed from the rest of us who, from an early age, beat his own path. Had he been born at a different time, it's easy to see how he would have hopped freight cars and followed his star. (It is not a coincidence that he and Apple helped underwrite Martin Scorcese's *No Direction Home*, the absorbing biopic of Bob Dylan.) Steve was adopted and raised by well-meaning parents who never had much money. He was attracted by Reed College, a school that exerts an unusual appeal for bright and thoughtful teenagers, and which, in the 1970s, was tailor-made for any child who wished he had been at Woodstock. It was there that a calligraphy class sharpened his sense of the aesthetic—that influence is still apparent in all Apple products and advertising.

Jobs's critics will say he can be willful, obdurate, irascible, temperamental, and stubborn—but show me someone who has achieved anything meaningful who, from time to time, doesn't display these characteristics, who is not a perfectionist. There is also the mischievous, calculating, suspicious twinkle of the souk about Steve. He is an insistent, persuasive and mesmerizing salesman—about the only man I know with the audacity to adorn bus shelters nationwide with advertisements for a product as mundane as a wireless mouse. But he is also a man who, decades ago, was kind enough make visits to a hospital to visit a CEO felled by a stroke and who, recently, in an avuncular fashion, has offered younger Silicon Valley CEOs generous advice.

About the time I entered the venture business, Apple's board fired Steve in favor of a man from the East who was a creature of convention. Characteristically, Steve sold all but one share of his holdings in the company and, at Sequoia Capital, we shook our heads as we watched him shape the company that he came to call NeXT. He raised money from investors (including Ross Perot) at a massive valuation and I remember visiting its headquarters, which bore all the hallmarks of a fiasco-in-waiting. There was a logo designed by Paul Rand and a floating staircase in the lobby— echoes of which are visible in the staircases that you can see today in many Apple stores.

NeXT took Steve out of his natural milieu. He was trying to sell computers to large companies—entities not swayed by products with visceral appeal. It also meant he was removed from the fray of the consumer business at a time when computer companies were beginning to demonstrate that, thanks to their edge with software and silicon, they had a natural advantage over consumer companies struggling to become computer companies. Steve persisted at NeXT when weaker beings would have thrown in the towel, but eventually when the death rattle started to emanate from the company, it appeared that he too would be consigned to occupy a footnote in history.

It's hard now, twelve years later, to appreciate the dire straits that Apple was in after it bought NeXT at the end of 1996 in a desperate effort to revivify itself. The Silicon Valley cynics chuckled at the way Steve was able to sell NeXT for more than $400 million even though it only had sold about 50,000 computers. Steve returned to Apple hardened by years of commercial adversity.

Many are familiar with the re-emergence of Apple. They may not be as familiar with the fact that it has few, if any parallels. When did a founder ever return to the company from which he had been rudely rejected to engineer a turnaround as complete and spectacular as Apple's? While turnarounds are difficult in any circumstances they are doubly difficult in a technology company. It is not too much of a stretch to say that Steve founded Apple not once but twice—And the second time he was alone.

For anyone who would like to gain a better sense of Steve, I suggest going to YouTube and watching the commencement speech he gave at Stanford in 2005—which must rank as one of the more forthright and meaningful addresses ever given to a collection of young people. Among the sentiments he conveyed was the opportunity we all have to make our mark, do something special and, above all, follow our own path. He ended that talk with the admonition, borrowed from the final edition of the Whole Earth Catalog, to "Stay Hungry. Stay foolish." This, I have discovered, also happens to be wonderful advice for anyone who wants to spend their life investing in young companies.

— Michael Moritz,
San Francisco, 2009

INTRODUCTION

Writing about companies can be a perilous occupation. For like people, companies are never what they seem to be. Both share a natural impulse to put their best foot forward but companies, particularly large ones, spend a lot more time and money on appearances than do most individuals. Advertisements are designed to portray the corporation and its products in the most appealing light. Public-relations agencies are retained to issue press releases, deal with reporters, and cope with uncomfortable issues. Security analysts, bankers, and brokers are sedulously courted to make sure that stock exchanges give proper attention to the company's shares.

There is then some charm about businesses that have not stepped into the public light. They don't have to worry about the strictures of federal agencies or shareholders who appreciate only a cultivated notoriety. Their founders and managers tend to speak with fewer inhibitions than executives at larger organizations, and they guard their secrets with less anxiety. During their first few years most companies are content with whatever publicity they can get. But the stories that appear in large newspapers and magazines tend, by virtue of the subject, to be short and usually gloss over many aspects of a young company's progress while the appeal of novelty tends to soften criticism. Yet by the time corporate histories are commissioned the details of those early stages are often lost. Myths spring up about life in the good old days and even the best-intentioned efforts turn from fact to fiction. Nostalgia, as the wise man said, isn't what it was. So there's much to be said for writing about a company before its founders and early employees die or lose details in a gin-mottled fog.

While they remain small, companies are easy enough to describe but once they outgrow a garage or an office suite they become increasingly opaque. As employees are scattered in factories and warehouses across the country or overseas, one is left to deal with impressions that have to be recorded with the dots and dabs of pointillism. If sheer size is one obstacle there are also more mechanical obstructions. For trying to figure out the tone and nature of a large American corporation is a bit like charting the affairs of Gorki. Some stories can be gleaned from bitter refugees but a closer inspection is more hazardous. It's difficult to obtain a tourist visa, simple to discover the official line, impossible to move around without being followed, and all too easy to get expelled.

Sad to say, small businesses in a particular corner of California have an irritating habit of turning into large corporations. During the past thirty years the orchards between San Jose and San Francisco have been mowed down to make way for dozens of companies which now form Silicon Valley. Most of these make their money from some connection with electronics and have grown so fast that it's easy to believe that the prunes and apricots shed some fertile residue. During the last decade, as developments in microelectronics have moved from the missile cone to the tabletop, these companies have attracted the usual parasitic herd of politicians, management consultants, and journalists eager to uncover a cure for the ills that have bothered other industries.

To some extent the popular conception of these companies has been formed by contrived illusion. They are supposed to conduct their business in novel ways. They are considered to be informal and relaxed places to work, where unusual minds can be kept entertained. Their founders are supposed to share the wealth, while hierarchy and bureaucracy, the curses of conventional corporations, have somehow been abolished. The heads of companies, we are told, let employees wander into their offices and are reluctant to fire anyone but thieves and bigots. To listen to the publicity merchants these companies are started by people with daring imaginations and a yen for risk. They seem to introduce new products with the predictable certainty with which Henry Kaiser once launched Liberty ships and the development of a new chip or a faster computer is invariably portrayed as the result of the march of destiny. They are rarely discussed without some invocation of God, country, or the pioneering spirit.

There is no better example of all this than Apple Computer, Inc., which is Silicon Valley's most precocious child. Within eight years it has gone from a living room to a yearly sales rate of more than $1 billion while the stock market has placed a value of more than $2.5 billion on its shares. It took less time to reach the *Fortune* 500 than any other start-up in the history of the index and it stands a good chance of falling among the one hundred largest U.S. industrial corporations before its tenth birthday. Two of its stockholders are said to be among the four hundred wealthiest people in the United States and well over one hundred of its employees have become millionaires. By most conventional standards Apple has dwarfed the accomplishments of any company born in Silicon Valley. It is larger than enterprises founded decades earlier, it has designed and introduced new products, and it hasn't had to seek help from a corporate sugar daddy.

When I started to think about writing this book, Apple was already a large company. It was perched between the great success brought by the Apple II personal computer and the twin challenges of building and introducing a new round of machines and competing with the Juggernaut from Armonk, IBM. Apple's early days were fast slipping into the stuff of folksong and legend and the personal-computer industry was maturing fast. Small companies that had managed to survive the early days were beginning to fall by the wayside. A few had emerged as leaders and Apple was one.

I thought that I could learn more about Silicon Valley, the start of a new industry, and life at a young company by focusing on one firm rather than by trying to come to grips with many. I was interested in whether image matched reality and whether public statements corresponded with private actions. I wanted to concentrate on the years before Apple became a publicly held company, examine the atmosphere that nourished the founders, and find out how their personalities came to affect the company. To a lesser extent I also wanted to come to terms with the conventional questions: Why? when? and how? "In the right place at the right time" clearly explains part of Apple's success but dozens, if not hundreds, of other people who started microcomputer companies have failed.

For some months I enjoyed a carefully circumscribed freedom at Apple. I was allowed to attend meetings and watch progress on a new computer. But the company I saw in 1982 was very different from the little business that filled a garage in 1977. Consequently, I have scattered these corporate snapshots throughout the book. This isn't an authorized portrait of Apple Computer nor was it ever supposed to be a definitive history. Apart from documents that were leaked, I had no access to corporate papers. The name of one character who appears briefly in the narrative, Nancy Rogers, has been changed, and some of the people mentioned in the text have either left the company or assumed different titles. I discovered quickly enough that writing a book about a growing company in an industry that changes with dizzying rapidity has at least one similarity to the production of a computer. Both could always be better if every new and enticing development were included. But like an engineer I had to bolt down and ship. So this is about Apple's road to its first one billion dollars.

"Can we ship your party?" Jobs asked.

A large set of French windows rinsed the California sun. The filtered light, which had the long wash of fall, played along a rumpled line of suitcases, garment bags, backpacks, and guitar cases. The owners of the luggage were seated around a stone fire-place in generous crescents of straight-backed chairs. Most of the sixty or so faces fell into that blind gap that camouflages those between their late teens and early thirties. About a third were women. Most wore androgynous uniforms of jeans, T-shirts, tank tops, and running shoes. There were a few paunches, some occasional patches of gray hair, and more than the average run of spectacles. Some cheeks were unshaven and a few were still swollen with sleep. Several blue-brimmed polyester baseball caps carried the silhouette of an apple with a bite gouged out of the side and, in black lettering, the words MACINTOSH DIVISION.

At the front of the group, sitting on the edge of a steel table, was a tall, slight figure in his late twenties. He was dressed in a checked shirt, bleached jeans, and scuffed running shoes. A slim digital watch ran around his left wrist. His long, delicate fingers had nails that were chewed to the quick, while glossy black hair was carefully shaped and sideburns crisply trimmed. He blinked a pair of deep, brown eyes as though his contact lenses were stinging. He had a pale complexion and a face divided by a thin, angular nose. The left side was soft and mischievous while the right had a cruel, sullen tint. He was Steven Jobs, chairman and co-founder of Apple Computer and general manager of the Macintosh Division.

The group waiting for Jobs to speak worked for Apple's youngest division. They had been bused from the company's headquarters in Cupertino, California, across a range of pine-covered hills for a two-day retreat at a resort built for weekenders on the edge of the Pacific. Sleeping quarters were wooden condominiums with stiff-necked chimneys. The wood had been bleached gray by the wind and the spray and the buildings were set among sand dunes and spiky grass. Collected together in the clear morning light, the group formed the footloose confection typical of a young computer company. Some were secretaries and laboratory technicians. A few were hardware and software engineers. Others worked in marketing, manufacturing, finance, and personnel. A couple wrote instruction manuals. Some had recently joined

Apple and were meeting their colleagues for the first time.
Others had transferred from a division called Personal Computer
Systems, which made the Apple II and Apple III computers.
A few had once worked for the Personal Office Systems Division,
which was preparing to introduce a machine called Lisa that
Apple intended to sell to businesses. The Macintosh Division was
sometimes called Mac but the lack of an official-sounding name
reflected its uncertain birth. For the computer code-named Mac
was, in some ways, a corporate orphan.

Jobs began speaking quietly and slowly. "This," he said, "is
the cream of Apple. We have the best people here and we must do
something that most of us have never done: We have never shipped
a product." He walked with a springy step to an easel and pointed
to some plain mottos written in a childish hand on large, creamy
sheets of paper. These he converted into homilies. "It's Not Done
Until It Ships," he read. "We have zillions and zillions of details
to work out. Six months ago nobody believed we could do it.
Now they believe we can. We know they're going to sell a bunch
of Lisas but the future of Apple is Mac." He folded back one of
the sheets of paper, pointed to the next slogan, and read: "Don't
Compromise." He mentioned the introduction date planned for
the computer and said, "It would be better to miss than to turn
out the wrong thing." He paused and added, "But we're not going
to miss." He flipped another page, announced, "The Journey Is
the Reward," and predicted, "Five years from now you'll look
back on these times and say, 'Those were the good old days.' You
know," he mulled in a voice that rose half an octave, "this is the
nicest place in Apple to work. It's just like Apple was three years
ago. If we keep this kind of pure and hire the right people, it'll still
be a great place to work."

Jobs pulled a torn white plastic bag along the table, dangled
it by his knee, and asked in the tone of someone who knows what
the answer will be: "Do you want to see something neat?" An
object that looked like a desk diary slipped from the plastic bag.
The case was covered in brown felt and fell open to reveal a mock-
up of a computer. A screen occupied one half and a typewriter
keyboard the other. "This is my dream," said Jobs, "of what we'll
be making in the mid- to late eighties. We won't reach this on Mac
One or Mac Two but it will be Mac Three. This will be the culmi-
nation of all this Mac stuff."

Debi Coleman, the division's financial controller, was more interested in the past than the future and, much like a child hoping for a familiar bedtime tale, asked Jobs to tell the newcomers how he had silenced the founder of Osborne Computers whose portable computer had been putting a dent in Apple's sales. "Tell us what you told Adam Osborne," she implored. With a reluctant shrug Jobs waited for the anticipation to build before embarking on the story. "Adam Osborne is always dumping on Apple. He was going on and on about Lisa and when we would ship Lisa and then he started joking about Mac. I was trying to keep my cool and be polite but he kept asking, 'What's this Mac we're hearing about? Is it real?' He started getting under my collar so much that I told him, 'Adam, it's so good that even after it puts your company out of business, you'll still want to go out and buy it for your kids.'"

The group alternated between the indoor sessions and alfresco sessions on a bank of sun-parched grass. Some foraged in a cardboard box and donned T-shirts that had the computer's name racing across the chest in a punky script. The retreat seemed a cross between a confessional and a group-encounter session. There was a nervous, slightly strained, jocularity but the old-timers who had attended previous retreats said the atmosphere was relaxed and low-key. A couple of the programmers muttered that they would have preferred to stay and work in Cupertino, but they lounged on the grass and listened to briefings from other members of the group.

Some picked at bowls of fruit, cracked walnuts, and crumpled soft-drink cans while Michael Murray, a dark-haired marketing man with dimples and mirrored sunglasses, rattled through industry charts and projected sales rates and market share. He showed how Mac would be introduced between the more expensive office computers made by competitors like IBM, Xerox, and Hewlett-Packard and the cheaper home computers sold by companies like Atari, Texas Instruments, and Commodore. "We've got a product that should be selling for five thousand dollars but we have the magic to sell for under two thousand. We're going to redefine the expectations of a whole group of people." He was asked how sales of Mac would affect Apple's office computer, Lisa, which was a more elaborate computer but built around the same principles.

"There is one disaster scenario," Murray admitted. "We could say Lisa was a great exercise for Apple. We can put it down to experience and sell ten."

"Lisa is going to be incredibly great," Jobs interjected firmly. "It will sell twelve thousand units in the first six months and fifty thousand in the first year."

The marketing sorts talked of ploys to boost sales. They discussed the importance of trying to sell or donate hundreds of Macs to universities with gilded reputations.

"Why not sell Mac to secretaries?" asked Joanna Hoffman, a perky woman with a faint foreign accent.

"We don't want companies to think the machine is a word processor," Murray retorted.

"There's a way to solve that problem," Hoffman countered. "We could say to the secretaries: 'Here's your chance to grow into an area associate.'"

There was a discussion of improving sales overseas. "We have the kind of hi-tech magnetism that can attract the Japanese," Hoffman mentioned. "But there's no way they can succeed here while we're here and we're going to succeed there regardless."

"We were very big in Japan until recently," Bill Fernandez, a beanstalk-thin technician, observed in a pinched staccato.

Chris Espinosa, manager of the writers who prepared the computer's instruction manuals, slopped in his sandals to the front of the group. He had just turned twenty-one, and as he pulled some notes from a small red backpack he announced, "You all missed a great party."

"I heard there was free acid," somebody piped up.

"It was for sale outside," Espinosa chortled.

"Can we ship your party?" Jobs asked sharply.

Espinosa blanched and settled down to business. He told his colleagues that he was having difficulties hiring qualified writers, that his staff needed more Mac prototypes to work with, and that Apple's graphics department wasn't geared to cope with some of his demands. "We want to make books that are gorgeous," he said, "that you read once and then keep on your shelf because they look so great."

* * *

The work sessions were broken up by coffee breaks and by walks along the beach, some Frisbee games on the grass, a few scattered poker games, and a fuchsia sunset. Though dinner was served at long canteen tables, it bore no hint of the mess hall. Clutches of Zinfandels, Cabernets, and Chardonnays stood on every table but the breadsticks disappeared more quickly. After dinner someone who looked like a demure orthodontist, with thinning silver hair and owl-eyed spectacles, performed what, in computer circles, amounted to a cabaret act. The figure wearing a Mac T-shirt over a long-sleeved dress shirt was Ben Rosen. He had turned a reputation gained as a Wall Street electronics analyst, the industrious publisher of an informative, sprightly newsletter, and host of annual personal-computer conferences into a career as a venture capitalist. Before he started investing in computer companies his comments had been sought as much as his ear.

For the Mac group Rosen worked from a casual script of observations, wisecracks, tips, and industry gossip. He gave a brief survey of some of Apple's competitors and dismissed Texas Instruments as "a company for the case studies of business schools," though by way of an afterthought he added: "They are supposed to announce their IBM almost-compatible computer in three weeks."

"What price?" Jobs asked.

"Twenty percent under the comparable price," Rosen replied.

He talked about low-priced home computers and mentioned Commodore: "I have a few notes about Commodore that I can tell in polite company. The more you know about the company the more difficult it is to be sanguine."

Some of the frivolous rustle disappeared when Rosen started to talk about IBM whose personal computer had been providing severe competition for Apple. "One of the fears about Apple," Rosen noted, "is IBM's future." He admitted to being impressed by a recent visit to IBM's Personal Computer Division in Boca Raton and described what he thought were its plans for three new personal computers. Then he looked around the room and said: "This is the most important part of Apple Computer. Mac is your most offensive and defensive weapon. I haven't seen anything that compares to it." He quizzically mentioned another industry rumor: "One of the things going around Wall Street is an IBM-Apple merger."

"IBM already said they weren't for sale," Randy Wigginton, a young blond programmer, shot back.

Members of the Mac group started to ask questions. One wanted to know how Rosen thought Apple's stock would perform. Another was eager to find out when a personal-computer software company would turn a $100 million in sales, while one with a strategic inclination wondered how Apple could ensure that computer dealers would make room on their increasingly crowded shelves for Mac.

"We have a crisis looming," Jobs told Rosen, from the back of the room. "We've got to decide what to call Mac. We could call it Mac, Apple IV, Rosen I. How's Mac strike you?"

"Throw thirty million dollars of advertising at it," Rosen said, "and it will sound great."

Rosen was the one interlude in a string of presentations by every manager of a department at Mac. They provided an abbreviated tour of a computer company and numbed everyone with a welter of facts. The snappy presentations were interrupted every now and again by applause at some piece of good, or unexpected, news. The engineering manager, Bob Belleville, a soft-spoken engineer who had just come to Apple from Xerox, said, "At Xerox we used to say it was important to get a little done every day; at Mac it's important to get a lot done every day." The main hardware engineer, Burrell Smith, blushed fiercely, said he didn't have enough material to last ten minutes, and played his guitar. The designer of the computer case lit some candles, sat in a chair with his back to the others, and played his remarks from a cassette tape. Others told about problems meeting the standards for electronic devices set by the FCC.

The programmers relayed their progress on the software. Matt Carter, a burly man with a beleaguered look, who was responsible for part of the manufacturing, rattled through a quick course in factory layout and showed a film of what Apple's new production line for Mac would look like. He talked about carousels and bins, automatic inserters and linear belts, prototype builds and pricing commitments. Another manufacturing man told about defect rates, improvements in output per person per day, and material handling. The last prompted Jobs to promise: "We're going to come down real hard on our vendors. We're going to come down on 'em like never before." Debi Coleman, the financial controller, gave her version of Accounting 101, explaining differences between direct and indirect labor costs, inventory control, fixed-asset tracking systems, tooling analysis, inventory valuation, purchase price variance, and break-even levels.

At the tag end of the retreat, Jay Elliot, a tall man from Apple's human resources department, introduced himself. "I'm a human-resources manager," he said. "I really appreciate being here. Thank you for being here. At human resources we try to leverage top performers—"

"What does that mean in English?" Jobs snapped.

"Human resources," Elliot stumbled, "is typically viewed as a bureaucratic, bullshit organization . . ."

Once Elliot recovered, he suggested ways of coping with the need for recruitment. The projected organization chart for the Mac Division was dotted with little boxes filled with the initials TBH. These stood for "To Be Hired." Elliot said his department was swamped with fifteen hundred résumés a month and suggested panning recruits from the names of Apple's owner-warranty cards.

"Nobody any good sends in their warranty card," Jobs said. He leaned over the back of his chair and addressed Andy Hertzfeld, one of the programmers. "Andy, did you send in your warranty card?"

"The dealer filled it in," Hertzfeld said.

"See?" said Jobs, swiveling around in his seat.

"We could put ads on ARPANET," Hertzfeld suggested, referring to the government-funded computer network that links universities, research establishments, and military bases. "There would be legal problems with that but we could ignore them."

"We could put ads in newspapers but the catch factor is kind of low," volunteered Vicki Milledge who also worked in the human resources department.

"What we should do," Jobs said, "is send Andy out to the universities, let him hang out in the labs and find the red-hot students."

After Elliot finished, Jobs embarked on a soliloquy. He fingered a gray, glossy folder that contained a summary of progress on Mac and warned everyone to carefully guard all company documents. "One of our salespeople in Chicago," he said, "was offered a complete sales introduction plan on Lisa from somebody at IBM. They get everywhere." He returned to the easel and a final flip chart that carried the picture of an inverted pyramid. At the bottom a band was labeled MAC and succeeding layers carried the Words FACTORY, DEALERS, SUPPLIERS, SOFTWARE HOUSES, SALES FORCE, and CUSTOMERS. Jobs explained the triangle and pointed to the succession of bands: "We have a major opportunity to influence where Apple is going. As every day passes, the work fifty people are doing here is going to send a giant ripple through the universe. I am really impressed with the quality of our ripple." He paused. "I know I might be a little hard to get on with, but this is the most fun thing I've done in my life. I'm having a blast." A trace of a smile appeared on his face.

BOOMTOWN BY THE BAY

Bulldozers and steam shovels lurched about the quarry, tearing tawny scars across a cheek of the hillside. The machines sent plumes of dust into the air above the southern end of San Francisco Bay. Large wooden placards declared that the equipment and quarry belonged to the Kaiser Cement Company. The earth in the dumpsters was going to form the substance of the towns that were being built on the plain that spread below the quarry. The trucks rumbled by rolls of barbed wire, coasted past signs that warned of a steep incline, tested their brakes, rolled onto a country lane, and negotiated the thin bends and chuckholes that led toward Cupertino, a village that was trying hard not to become a town. From the quarry gates, on those weekday mornings in the mid-fifties, the position of the crossroads that formed the center of Cupertino was revealed by the cylindrical shapes of some clay-colored feed and grain silos.

In the fifties the Santa Clara Valley was still predominantly rural. In places the greenery was broken by splotches of buildings. From a distance it looked as if someone had spilled small loads of garbage that had then been smeared and raked across parts of the valley floor to form a string of small towns that worked along the plain between San Jose and San Francisco: Los Gatos, Santa Clara, Sunnyvale, Mountain View, Los Altos, Palo Alto, Menlo Park, Redwood City, San Carlos, Hillsborough, Burlingame, and South San Francisco.

Most of the towns still had the manners and style of the thirties. The buildings rarely rose over two stories. The automobiles could park at raked angles on Main Street. Corners were frequently decorated with a State Farm Insurance office, a gas station, a branch of the Bank of America, and an International Harvester franchise, and in towns like Cupertino there had been, not so long before, concerted campaigns to lure a permanent dentist and doctor. The center of the world was immediate: a town hall built with terra-cotta tiles in Spanish mission style and flanked by a library, police department, fire station, courthouse, and stumpy palm trees.

But the towns were separated by all sorts of differences. Each had its own climate which grew warmer the farther away a town was from the San Francisco fog. At the southern end of the Peninsula the summer climate was positively Mediterranean and a little seminary that overlooked Cupertino could easily have been set on a quiet hillside in Tuscany. The towns had their own councils and taxes, their own ordinances and quirks, their newspapers and habits. There were mayoral elections brimming with the rumors and innuendo stirred by a community where people, if they did not know the mayor, at least knew someone who did. And the towns were, of course, separated by jealousy and snobbery.

The lawyers and doctors who built homes in the hills of Los Gatos said to themselves—with not a touch of jest—that the brains of San Jose slept in Los Gatos. The people who lived in Los Altos Hills looked down on the Los Altos folk who lived in the flatlands. Palo Alto with its gracious trees and Stanford University had an airy feel and a few electronic businesses started by former students. Towns like Woodside and Burlingame, set above the plain, had the tony touch of horses, polo games, and rigidly exclusive golf clubs. Burlingame had been home to the first country club on the West Coast. But the people who lived in nearby Hillsborough often gave their addresses as Burlingame for fear of being mistaken as parvenus. And beyond San Carlos, San Bruno, and Redwood City there was windy South San Francisco—an industrial footnote to the city itself—sited below the approach and takeoff paths to the San Francisco airport. Here was a clump of steel mills, foundries, smelters, refineries, machine shops, and lumberyards where the City Fathers had advertised their muscular temperament when they had authorized bulldozers to scrape in giant letters on the hill behind the town the slogan SOUTH SAN FRANCISCO, THE INDUSTRIAL CITY.

But now, right across the valley and especially around Sunnyvale, there were gaps in the orchards and signs of a new world moving in. Most of the trucks from the Kaiser Cement quarry were making for Sunnyvale. Draglines, cranes, and road scrapers were waiting for the concrete and steel that was being used to build the quarters for Lockheed Corporation's new Missile Systems Division. By 1957 Sunnyvale was six times larger than it had been at the end of World War II and was beginning to qualify for inclusion in national almanacs. The municipal chatter had an energetic ring of tax bases, assessed valuation, building permits, zoning requirements, sewer lines, and water power. There were rumors of new businesses, speculation that one of the major automobile companies would decide to build a factory in Sunnyvale. As the fifties drew to a close, Sunnyvale's Chamber of Commerce gleefully reported that the town's statistics were hourly becoming obsolete and that a new worker was arriving in Sunnyvale every sixteen minutes of the working day. The publicity pamphlets said it was "The City with the built-in future" and "Boomtown by the Bay."

The newcomers to the city that was "reaching high" and "pacing the future" were part and parcel of America's push toward a suburban way of life. The homes were insulated from the bustle of a community and a store was a car-drive away. The houses themselves had an unmistakable Bay Area look. They were low-slung, single-story homes with roofs that were either flat or tilted slightly like those of a garden shed. (The real-estate salesmen said that young boys found it easy to recover their model airplanes from the roofs.) But from the outside it was the garages that dominated the facades, making the rooms look as if they were tacked on as after-thoughts. The large metal garage doors seemed like the obvious entrance.

Brochures told of radiant heat, "the modern and healthy way to heat a house," of wood-paneled walls, cork and asphalt tiles, hardwood kitchen cabinets, and large closets with glide-in doors that "swing with the greatest of ease." What the pamphlets didn't say was that the local fire departments joked that these combinations of posts and beams would burn to the ground within seven minutes—and that the black community was isolated on the wrong side of the Southern Pacific railroad tracks and the wrong side of the freeway.

Most of the families who moved to Sunnyvale were lured by the prospect of jobs at Lockheed. Many were careful and studious. They asked the real-estate agents where the rumored freeway—Interstate 280—might run and checked the projected route on maps at the Sunnyvale City Hall. They asked friends for recommendations on schools and were told that Palo Alto and Cupertino had the best reputations along the entire peninsula. There was talk of enterprising teachers, federal grants, experiments with new math, and open classrooms.

They visited the school district and found a map that pinpointed the existing schools and revealed where future schools might be built. Then they discovered the eccentric nature of the boundaries of the Cupertino School District: They didn't have to live in Cupertino for their children to attend the Cupertino city schools. The school district included parts of San Jose, Los Altos, and Sunnyvale, and the fortunate houses sold at a premium. In a few places the boundary even divided houses.

Jerry Wozniak, an engineer in his mid-thirties, was one of thousands to be recruited by Lockheed at the end of the fifties. He, his wife, Margaret, and their three young children, Stephen, Leslie and Mark, settled in a home in a quiet Sunnyvale subdivision that lay in the catchment area of the Cupertino School District.

At the other end of the Peninsula, in the Sunset District of San Francisco, Paul and Clara Jobs adopted their first child, Steven. Often during the first five months of his life they wheeled their baby under the imitation nineteenth-century streetlamps, over the tram tracks, and across the beach in the shadow of the damp sea wall, the fog, the pewter skies, and the gray gulls.

SUPER SECRET SKY SPIES

Hush-hush, super-super, top-secret Lockheed became synonymous with Sunnyvale. As the missile division grew during the late fifties it changed the scale of business in the Santa Clara Valley, more or less turned Sunnyvale into a company town, and helped propel the community toward the fringes of mystery. Lockheed came to be talked about as a place where the subjects of science fiction had been reduced to everyday occupations. Lockheed was woven into the weft of the national space program and, in Sunnyvale, aspects of Discoverer, Explorer, Mercury, and Gemini came to be as familiar as the names of some of the astronauts. It would have been easy to believe that H.G. Wells worked in Lockheed's public-relations department, batting out bulletins on a never-ending source of marvels.

There were rumors of a laboratory that would simulate conditions in space, of a tape recorder small enough to be held in the palm of the hand, and of "Hotshot," the strongest wind tunnel in private industry. Teams of Lockheed engineers were investigating a special fuel cell to power spacecraft, and were drawing up plans for a prefabricated, four-hundred-ton manned space platform shaped like the wheel of fortune. There were also more sinister rumors. Some Lockheed engineers were known to be working on an intermediate-range ballistic missile known as the "super-secret Polaris" and a "sky spy," a "super-super" secret earth satellite armed with a television camera that could peep at the Russians. The company proudly disclosed that its space-communications laboratory picked up seven minutes of the first journey of an Explorer satellite and also boasted that its dish-shaped radio telescope could monitor twenty satellites simultaneously. There were other reports of an astonishing electronic computer installed at Lockheed that was supposed to have the intelligence of a human but could also play a sly game of tic-tac-toe.

So when in 1958 Jerry Wozniak began working at Lockheed, he was joining a company that, at least so it seemed to the outside world, had large ideas. A meaty man with a thick neck and large forearms, Wozniak had been strong enough to play offensive tailback on the football team at the California Institute of Technology in Pasadena where he studied electrical engineering. After about a year working as a junior engineer at a small company in San Francisco he had quit and together with a partner spent twelve months designing a stacking, packing, and counting machine for raw materials like asbestos sheeting. But the pair had run out of money before completing a prototype, leading Wozniak to conclude: "It was probably a good technical idea but we didn't understand what it took to put a business together."

After graduating from Cal Tech, Wozniak had married. His wife, Margaret, had grown up on a small farm in Washington State and had spent a college vacation working as a journeyman electrician during World War II at the Kaiser shipyards in Vancouver, Washington, installing wiring on baby flattops as they rose on the ways. Eventually her parents had sold their spread and moved to the warmth of Los Angeles. "California," Margaret Wozniak had thought. "That was the greatest place in the world." But with the failure of Jerry's business fling and the arrival of their first son, Stephen, in August 1950, the Wozniaks were drawn back into the grip of corporations. For several years they traveled around the Southern California aerospace industry, which had been grafted onto the tumbling tricks of the early aviators. And like thousands of other families, the Wozniaks soon associated towns like Burbank, Culver City, and San Diego with companies like

Lockheed, Hughes Aircraft, Northrop, and McDonnell Douglas. For a time Jerry Wozniak worked as a weapons designer in San Diego, later helped build autopilots for Lear in Santa Monica, and bought his first house in the San Fernando Valley before the guiding lights at Lockheed decided to form a division in Sunnyvale.

While his children spent months playing in cardboard houses made out of Bekins moving cartons, Jerry Wozniak grew accustomed to the rhythm of the short commute that took him to Lockheed. "I never intended to stay at Lockheed very long. I intended to move to the area first and settle down later." The company kept its distance from family affairs. Lockheed was hidden behind shields of security clearances, special passes, uniformed guards, and barbed-wire fences. About the only time children glided through the company gates was when the general public was invited to watch the aerobatic stunts of the Blue Angels over the Independence Day weekend. When Jerry Wozniak had to collect work from his office on Saturday mornings, his children stayed in the car surrounded by the vast parking lots painted in flat, herringbone patterns. Lockheed was like an elderly aunt who wanted children to appear only for dinner.

When Jerry Wozniak brought his work home in the evenings and over the weekends and settled down in the family room with sheets of blue-lined grid paper and drafting pencils, he was usually concerned with designs that took full advantage of the miniaturization of electronic components. Inside the Missile Systems Division Wozniak worked on the attitude-control system of Polaris and slightly later on a proposed scheme for using computers to design integrated circuits. Later still he worked in an area known as Special Projects which, he told his children, had something to do with satellites. So Jerry Wozniak was in a position where it became part and parcel of his job to read trade journals, plow through conference proceedings, flip through monographs, and generally keep abreast of developments in the world of electronics.

While the satellites designed at Lockheed were engineered to travel millions of miles, the orbits of Lockheed families were more circumscribed. The Wozniaks never took long vacations. A holiday was usually a Christmas or Easter trip to visit grandparents in Southern California. There was the occasional dinner out, a trip for brunch to Sausalito, an outing to a San Francisco Giants baseball game, but for the most part the center of their world was Sunnyvale.

Jerry Wozniak was as keen about war games and sports as he was about electronics. He spent hours in the backyard tossing baseballs with his sons and became a coach for The Braves, a Sunnyvale Little League team. But most of all he looked forward to the Saturday morning golf foursome he played with neighbors at the nearby Cherry Chase Country Club—a grand name for a club where, to play eighteen holes, golfers circled the same course twice. Here, too, Wozniak senior and Wozniak junior won a father-and-son golf tournament. Sunday afternoons were devoted to televised football games.

And for the Wozniaks, as for thousands of other California families who raised their children in the sixties, swimming was the sport of primary interest. The nearby Santa Clara swim team earned a national reputation and swimming quickly turned into something more than a pastime. It was a sport, the elder Wozniaks thought, that could be used to instill a sense of team spirit, of competitiveness, and individual achievement. They enrolled their children in the Mountain View Dolphins.

Margaret Wozniak was a woman with very definite ideas who didn't hesitate to let her children know what was on her mind. When she lectured them about austerity they sometimes harked back to her wartime occupation and called her Rosie the Riveter, but Margaret Wozniak was something of a feminist before the term became fashionable. ("When I realized I wasn't a person anymore I started to branch out.") She became president of the Republican women in Sunnyvale—"I liked having friends on the city council"—and occasionally enlisted the help of her children for humdrum precinct work.

The Wozniaks played classical records in the background, hoping that their children would be attracted to the subliminal levels of the music. But Leslie preferred teen pop magazines and the San Francisco radio shows she could hear on her transistor radio while her brothers preferred television programs with an element of intrigue like *The Man from U.N.C.L.E.* and *I Spy* and horror shows like *Creature Features, The Twilight Zone,* and *The Outer Limits*. The sci-fi rubbed off, along perhaps with traces of Lockheed's secrecy and the staunch podium-pounding speeches of local worthies worried about the Communist threat.

Stephen Wozniak wanted to start a top-secret spy agency at junior high school. "We were going to be so secret that we couldn't even feel anybody else." The Wozniak children kept an eye on a suspicious neighbor they were convinced was employed by the Russians.

In Sunnyvale in the mid-sixties electronics was like hay fever: It was in the air and the allergic caught it. In the Wozniak household the older son had a weak immune system. When Stephen was in fifth grade he was given a kit for a voltmeter. He followed the instructions, used a soldering iron to fasten the wires, and successfully assembled the device. Stephen showed more interest in electronics than either his sister or his younger brother, Mark, who observed, "My father started him very early. I didn't get any of that kind of support."

Most of the neighbors on the Wozniak block were engineers. One neighbor who bought a home on the tract the same year as the Wozniaks never bothered to have his yard landscaped, but some of the local children discovered that he had run a surplus electronics store and would trade odd jobs for electronic parts. They weeded or scraped down some paintwork, kept note of the hours, and swapped their labor for parts. A couple of houses in the other direction was someone who specialized in radios, transceivers, and direction finders left over from World War II and the Korean conflict. One of Stephen Wozniak's neighborhood friends, Bill Fernandez, said, "There was always somebody around who could answer questions about electronics." The children learned to discriminate between the men's specialties. Some were good on theory, some favored explaining things in math, while others had a practical bent and relied on rules of thumb.

One man offered lessons to people who wanted to obtain ham-radio licenses. When Stephen Wozniak was in sixth grade he took the operator's exam, built a 100-watt ham radio, and began tapping out his code letters. At one point electronics and politics merged. For when Richard Nixon was engaged in his 1962 California gubernatorial race Margaret Wozniak arranged for her son to offer Nixon the support of all the ham-radio operators at Cupertino's Serra School. Even though Stephen was the school's only bona fide operator, the ploy worked. Nixon and a stubby, crewcut.

Wozniak appeared together in a photograph on the front page of the *San Jose Mercury*.

Wozniak found ham radios more entertaining when they were modified and connected to friends' houses. He rigged up wires attached to speakers to send Morse code from one house to another and discovered with his friends that if they talked into the speakers they could hear each other: "We didn't know why but from that day we were into house-to-house intercoms."

At about the same time, Stephen entered a tic-tac-toe game in Cupertino Junior High School's science fair. He and his father calculated an electronic simulation of the paper game and worked out combinations in which man battled machine. Stephen figured out designs for the electric circuits that would duplicate the moves while his father secured a supply of resistors, capacitors, transistors, and diodes from a friend. To his mother's irritation Stephen assembled the game on the kitchen table. He hammered nails into a sheet of plywood to form electrical connections and laid out all the smaller parts. On the flip side of the board he installed a collection of red and white light bulbs and at the bottom he arranged a row of switches that would allow a player to select a move.

A couple of years after completing the tic-tac-toe game Wozniak spotted an intriguing diagram in a book about computers. This was a machine called a One Bit Adder-Subtracter which would do what its name suggested: add or subtract numbers. Wozniak could follow some of the technical discussion from the lessons he had learned while messing around with kits and designing the tic-tac-toe board. But there were other aspects that he found entirely foreign. For the first time he came up against the idea that electronic calculating machines could provide solutions to problems of logic. He began to explore the algebra of logic and learned that switches—which could be only on or off—could be used to represent statements—which could be only true or false. He became familiar with the binary numbering system—a series of 1s and 0s—that had been developed to represent electronically two voltage levels in a circuit.

The diagram for a One Bit Adder-Subtracter was very limited. It could cope with only one bit, one binary digit, at a time. Wozniak wanted something more powerful that would be able to add and subtract far larger numbers so he expanded the idea to a more complicated device that he called The Ten Bit Parallel Adder-Subtracter. This was capable of simultaneously dealing with ten bits at a time. He designed the necessary circuits by himself and laid out dozens of transistors and diodes and capacitors on a "bread board"—a laminated sheet drilled with a regular pattern of holes. The board was about the size of a picture book and was attached to a wooden frame. Two rows of switches lined the bottom of the board. One entered numbers into the adder, the other into the subtracter, and the result was displayed—again in binary form—in a row of small lights. Wozniak had, to all intents and purposes, built a simple version of what engineers called an arithmetic logic unit, a machine that was capable of coping with arithmetic problems. The machine could operate on the instructions, or program, that were entered by hand through the switches. It could add or subtract numbers but couldn't do anything else.

When the machine was complete, he carted it off to the Cupertino School District Science Fair where it took the first prize. Later it took third place in the Bay Area Science Fair even though Wozniak was competing against older challengers. To compensate for the disappointment of finishing third, he was rewarded with his first trip in an airplane—a whirl over California's Alameda Naval Air Station.

"It'll make the greatest flight simulator in the world," *Schweer said.*

Half a dozen managers from the Crocker Bank sat around a large L-shaped table, sipped coffee from bone-china cups, and watched a white screen unroll from the ceiling. They might have been in an interior designer's idea of a Hollywood dressing room for a movie star who happened to be a computer. The table rested on aluminum cylinders, and potted ferns dappled the purple rug with triangular shadows. Framed sketches hung on the wall and mirrors ran like a modern brocade around the top of the walls. Dan'l Lewin, an Apple marketing manager with a smooth, square jaw, neatly knotted tie, and freshly pressed blue suit, let the screen unroll. He pressed a concealed button and a pair of maroon slats, which ran along two walls of the hexagonal room, hummed sideways. Spotlights shone over the backs of some chairs onto two smooth counters that held six Lisa computers.

Lewin had been playing corporate guide for several months and had shepherded similar groups from dozens of large companies into the same room and through the same script and tour. Though Apple mimicked the movie industry and called these daylong sessions "sneak previews," they were plotted as carefully as story-boards. They were aimed at persuading visitors from *Fortune* 500 companies to order scores of Lisa computers and at quelling suspicions that Apple was a flimsy company unable to support what it hoped to sell. Most of the visiting groups had been a mixture of longtime computer-operations managers with a professional distrust of desk-top computers, and amateurs whose passion for computers had been kindled by the smaller machines. All the visitors to the sneak room signed forms binding them to secrecy, but Lewin readily admitted, "By the time we announce Lisa, everybody who is important will already have seen it."

Lewin crisply spat out a ream of numbers that sounded like the authoritative opening paragraphs of an annual report. He told the group that Apple produced an Apple II every thirty seconds and a disk drive every eighteen seconds. He steered them through a management chart and observed, "We are growing into a more traditional organization." He acknowledged that some details about Lisa had seeped into the press but said this was part of a corporate strategy. "Apple," Lewin noted, "is controlling the press very well. But until you see what we've done I doubt whether you can understand it. No other company would be prepared to take the risk. Most companies are interested in making big computers." Lewin explained that the conceptual foundation for the Lisa had been laid, not at Apple, but at Xerox Corporation during the mid-to late seventies. "We took those ideas," Lewin said, with the pride of a muffler-franchise holder, "and we internalized them. We Apple-ized them."

After he finished with the opening remarks, Lewin introduced Burt Cummings, a round-faced, curly-haired engineer. Cummings sat beside one Lisa whose screen was enlarged on two television monitors fitted to the wall. He immediately plunged into technical details. "Why do you call it Lisa?" interrupted one of the men from Crocker Bank.

"I don't know," Cummings shrugged. "There really isn't much of a reason for anything." He continued with the demonstration and suddenly the screen became a distorted jumble of letters. Cummings wriggled uncomfortably, surveyed the mess, and added hastily, "It tends to bomb. It's six-month-old software."

Cummings typed some commands into the computer, which proved to be the right medicine, and proceeded with his demonstration, flashing a string of different pictures onto the screen. "Is this all canned?" asked Kurt Schweer, another of the Crocker visitors.

"You've seen the Xerox Star," Lewin said. "That's what makes you think this is canned. This is incredibly fast. That's what our engineers are proud of."

Every fifteen or thirty minutes Lewin introduced another manager from the Lisa group. John Couch, the head of the Lisa division, who looked worn and weary, gave an antiseptic history of the computer's development and of the importance Apple placed on the control of software. Lisa, he explained, was part of a concerted effort to shield the user from the crust of the machine with snowfalls of software. He explained that the Apple III had been introduced with about ten times as much software as the Apple II, while Lisa was going to come with about ten times as much software as the Apple III. He stressed that Apple had moved from supplying programming languages like BASIC with the Apple II to programs for things like financial analysis with the Apple III, while on Lisa the user could do a variety of tasks with a minimum of fuss. "Lisa," Couch emphasized, "originally stood for 'large integrated software architecture.' Now it stands for 'local integrated software architecture.'" He took a quiet jab at the competition: "Quite a bit of the problem with Xerox was that they weren't building a personal computer. They weren't giving it to the individual."

The bankers were ushered, with much flashing of security badges, into an adjoining building which served as the center of assembly for Lisa. Wasu Chaudhari, a genial manufacturing man, gave them a tour of the test production racks where dozens of computers were running through proving cycles. Chaudhari demonstrated that Lisa was easy to take apart. He removed the back panel and slipped out different parts. "One person builds one product," he smiled. "It's a modified Volvo concept."

"Rolls-Royce would be better. Aston Martin better still," countered Tor Folkedal, a burly Crocker manager.

After lunch in a cluttered conference room which had been hurriedly converted into dining quarters, the bankers were steered back to the computers. They were allowed to play with the machines, nudged and prompted by Lisaguide, the computer's private Baedeker, which appeared on the screen. After spending a couple of minutes working his way through the pictures and explanations, Tor Folkedal exhaled: "We'll have managers at the bank playing with this all day. It's a video game."

"You've got to get some games on this," Schweer agreed. "Goddamn! It'll make the greatest flight simulator in the world."

Ellen Nold, a thin woman from Apple's training department, tried to assuage any fears about Apple's commitment to its customers. "We assume when Crocker buys hundreds of Lisas you'll want a training program." She told them that training sessions would be specially tailored for the bank and that drill exercises would be based on the workaday subjects familiar to bankers. Wayne Rosing, Lisa's chief engineer, fielded questions. The bankers wondered when Apple would be able to connect several Lisas together and swap information between machines. They worried about the difficulty of connecting a Lisa to IBM computers, to "the terminal world," "the Bell world," and "the DEC world." One of the technical types wanted to know the speed at which data would travel between computers and whether software written for other computers would run on Lisa. Rosing leaned back in his chair and answered all the questions in a leisurely way. He explained, in answer to one question, why Lisa had no calendar. "We're so far along that I had to say, 'Darn it! We're going to stop here even if this feature only takes a week because otherwise we'll never get it out the door.'" As the afternoon wore down the bankers were asked for their impressions.

"I'm not sure you're clear about who would actually use this," said Betty Risk, a dark-haired woman who had listened and watched for most of the day. "Is it for the executive, or the professional, or the manager?"

"Your security's tight," Schweer remarked. "It could have been an abacus sitting there." The flinty edge that hardened his early remarks had softened: "You guys have come a long way. This is the first time I've heard any company ask the right questions. Most companies say 'We can do anything for you if you stand on your head and punch the keyboard with your toes.'"

Despite the compliments the group from Crocker was reluctant to make any promises about ordering large quantities of the Lisa. Apple was just one of several computer companies they would visit before deciding which machines to order. Nobody mentioned numbers and nobody mentioned dollars.

"Trying to speak for a bank the size of Crocker is difficult." Schweer sighed. "You always bet your job when you propose a standard. It's easier to pick several different makes." He paused: "Of course, you could just put your hands over your eyes and pick, or get several and spread the blame."

"And then get half your butt fired," Lewin chuckled.

CARBURETORS AND MICROPHONES

When Steven Jobs was five months old his parents moved from the dank fringes of San Francisco to the iron cuddle of South San Francisco. There, Paul Jobs continued to work for a finance company as a jack-of-all trades. He collected bad debts, checked the terms of automobile dealers' loans, and used a knack for picking locks to help repossess cars that were scattered about Northern California.

Paul Jobs looked like a responsible James Dean. He was lean, had closely cropped brown hair and tightly drawn skin. He was a practical, sensible man with a Calvinist streak who was self-conscious about his lack of formal education and would conceal his shyness behind chuckles and a tough sense of humor. Jobs had been raised on a small farm in Germantown, Wisconsin, but when it failed to provide enough for the two families it was supposed to support, he and his parents moved to West Bend, Indiana. He left high school in his early teens, roamed around the Midwest looking for work, and at the end of the thirties, wound up enlisting in "The Hooligan Navy," the U.S. Coast Guard.

At the end of World War II, while his ship was being decommissioned in San Francisco, Jobs bet a shipmate that he would find a bride in the shadow of the Golden Gate. Nipping ashore, when port and starboard liberty allowed, Paul Jobs won the wager. He met Clara, the woman who became his wife, on a blind date. She had spent her childhood and high-school years in San Francisco's Mission District.

After several years in the Midwest where Jobs worked as a machinist at International Harvester and a used-car salesman, he and his wife returned to San Francisco in 1952. It was there that they started to raise their family and experience the perils of parenthood. They began to endure all the perils that children could find. When their young son Steven jammed a bobby pin into an electric outlet and burned his hand, they rushed him to the hospital. Some months later they had his stomach pumped after he and a young accomplice built a miniature chemical lab from bottles of ant poison. In the Jobses' South San Francisco home there was enough room for another child and Steven was joined by a sister, Patty. Confronted with the responsibility of filling four mouths, Paul Jobs characteristically took out two thousand-dollar-insurance policies to cover his funeral expenses.

Commuting occupied a prominent place among Paul Jobs's pet dislikes, so after the finance company transferred him to an office in Palo Alto the entire family was tugged farther down the Peninsula. Jobs bought a home in Mountain View, a stone's throw from the area's first covered shopping mall, where the neighbors were a mixture of blue-collar and lower-middle-class families.

At the Jobs home Steven took to waking up so early that his parents bought him a rocking horse, a gramophone, and some Little Richard records so that he could amuse himself without disturbing the entire household. Some children across the street made super-8-mm movies and Jobs junior, dolled up in his father's raincoat and hat, played detective. The family television set that normally was tuned to a steady diet of *Dobie Gillis, I Love Lucy, Groucho Marx,* and Johnny Quest cartoons.

Like Sunnyvale and Palo Alto, Mountain View had its share of electrical engineers. They brought scrap parts home from work, tinkered about in the garage, and when they built something interesting or novel, usually displayed it in the driveway. One engineer who worked for Hewlett-Packard and lived a few doors away from the Jobses brought a carbon microphone home from his laboratory, hooked it to a battery and speaker, and immediately turned into an electronic Pied Piper. Steven Jobs, who had picked up some elementary electronics from his father, was baffled by something that seemed to violate the rules that he had learned: The carbon microphone had no amplifier and yet sound emerged from the speaker. He reported this to his father who couldn't provide a satisfactory explanation so he returned and badgered the expert from Hewlett-Packard. He was soon presented with the object under inspection and was frequently invited to dinner at the engineer's house where he learned some more rudiments of electronics.

Jobs senior found automobiles altogether more interesting than electronics. As a teenager he had scraped together enough money to buy a car and had turned into a perpetual moonlighter— buying, trading, and swapping automobiles. He took pride in the fact that he stopped buying new cars in 1957 and thereafter relied on instincts and the wit in his hands to rescue and restore old models. Jobs concentrated fiercely on fixing examples of a particular model until something else caught his fancy. He mounted snapshots of his favorite automobiles either in a scrapbook or in a picture frame, and would point out subtleties that only a collector would appreciate: a seat decorated with a rare trim or a peculiar set of air vents.

After work he would clamber into a set of overalls, trundle out his clinically clean toolbox, and disappear under the car of the week. He came to know most of the clerks at the local department of motor vehicles by their first names and on Saturday mornings he trailed around the junkyards on the Bayshore frontage road in Palo Alto, sorting through the pickings. He frequently took his son along and let him watch the negotiations and bargaining at the front counter: "I figured I could get him nailed down with a little mechanical ability but he really wasn't interested in getting his hands dirty. He never really cared too much about mechanical things." Steven said he was more interested in wondering about the people who had once owned the cars.

One of the Mountain View neighbors convinced Paul Jobs he should try his hand at real estate. He earned his Realtor's license, did well for a year or so, but disliked the hustle, the sycophancy, and the uncertainty. During his second year he didn't make much money. Circumstances were so grim that he had to refinance his home to tide the family over. To help make ends meet, Clara Jobs found part-time work in the payroll department at Varian Associates, a firm that made radar devices. Finally Paul Jobs became so disenchanted with the vagaries of real estate that he decided to return to his trade as a machinist. When he was finally hired by a machine shop in San Carlos he had to work his way up from the bottom again.

The setback wasn't something that escaped Steven Jobs. There were no family vacations, the furniture was reconditioned, and there was no color television. Paul Jobs built most of the home comforts. In fourth grade when his teacher asked her pupils, "What is it in this universe that you don't understand?" Steven Jobs answered, "I don't understand why all of a sudden we're so broke." That same teacher, Imogene "Teddy" Hill, saved her nine-year-old charge from going astray after he had been expelled from another class for misbehaving. Her pupil recalled, "She figured out the situation real fast. She bribed me into learning. She would say, 'I really want you to finish this workbook. I'll give you five bucks if you finish it.'" As a consequence Jobs skipped fifth grade and though his teachers suggested he attend junior high school and start to learn a foreign language, he refused. His sixth grade report noted, "Steven is an excellent reader. However he wastes much time during reading period. . . . He has great difficulty motivating himself or seeing the purpose of studying reading. . . . He can be a discipline problem at times."

For the Jobses, as for the Wozniaks, swimming was important. They first ferried Steven to swimming lessons when he was five and later enrolled him in a swim club called the Mountain View Dolphins. To pay for swimming lessons Clara Jobs spent her evenings babysitting for friends. Some years later, when he was old enough to become a member of the club swim team, Jobs met Mark Wozniak. Jobs, Wozniak recalled, was taunted and roughhoused by some of the other swimmers who liked to snap wet towels at him. "He was pretty much a crybaby. He'd lose a race and go off and cry. He didn't quite fit in with everyone else. He wasn't one of the guys."

*   *   *

Steven Jobs did, however, change schools and started attending Mountain View's Crittenden Elementary School. The school drew children from the lower-income eastern fringes of Mountain View and had a reputation for attracting ruffians and fostering hooliganism. Local police were frequently summoned to break up fights and discipline children who jumped out of windows or threatened teachers. After a year, Steven Jobs, who found himself miserable and lonely, issued an ultimatum: He would refuse to return to school if it meant another year at Crittenden. Paul Jobs detected the firmness. "He said he just wouldn't go. So we moved." Once more the Jobses hopped another step down the Peninsula, attracted by the lure of the Palo Alto and Cupertino school districts. In Los Altos they bought a house with a gently raked roof, a large garage, and three bedrooms, all of which happened to sit within the curious embrace of the Cupertino School District.

THE CREAM SODA
COMPUTER

When John McCollum arrived to teach electronics at Cupertino's Homestead High School the day it opened in 1963, Classroom F-3 was almost empty. There was a cold concrete floor, cinder-block walls, some gray metal chairs, and on a swivel stand a television which carried the school's closed-circuit announcements. The classroom and the rest of Homestead High School looked like a minimum-security prison and its boundaries were certainly well defined. The houses that McCollum could see through his classroom window were in Sunnyvale, but his blackboard hung in Cupertino. When Homestead opened, Classroom F-3 was so barren that even the most enterprising student would have had difficulty electrocuting himself. McCollum immediately made some changes.

He hoisted a long, yellow slide rule above the blackboard, pinned the stars and stripes high on a wall, unrolled a bright poster that said SAFETY IS NO ACCIDENT and a bumper sticker that carried the exhortation FLY NAVY. A couple of long wooden laboratory benches were bolted to the floor and gradually covered with equipment. Rather than scrimp and save for a few new devices, McCollum used his wits. The shelves above the benches started to fill as Classroom F-3 became a well-stuffed wastepaper basket for nearby companies like Fairchild, Raytheon, and Hewlett-Packard. McCollum turned into a decorous alley cat prowling up and down the Santa Clara Valley looking for parts. He found his students sooner or later managed to destroy about one third of everything he brought into the classroom. "Onezees," as electronic distributors disparagingly called on order for any quantity under fifty, would not do. McCollum, or rather his students, dealt in bulk.

Fortunately, the electronics companies were selling to customers who were so finicky that they sometimes seemed to reject more parts than they bought. They would refuse to buy a transistor that had a blurred part number, or a resistor whose pins weren't straight, or a capacitor with a small bubble baked in the paint. McCollum's greatest coup came when Raytheon gave him nine thousand transistors (then going for sixteen dollars a piece), which a components-evaluation engineer at NASA considered too flimsy to packet to the moon. There were other substantial trophies and some came from a warehouse that Hewlett-Packard maintained in Palo Alto. It was Hewlett-Packard's version of a Salvation Army store packed with used and surplus test equipment which high-school teachers were free to rummage through. McCollum paid regular visits and on a few occasions returned with expensive dual-trace oscilloscopes and frequency counters. Within a few years, and by the time Stephen Wozniak—and later Steven Jobs—enrolled in Electronics 1, Classroom F-3 had become a miniature parts warehouse. McCollum had accumulated as much test equipment as they had at nearby De Anza Community College, and compared to the hoard at Homestead, some of the electronics labs in neighboring high schools might as well have been in the Upper Volta.

For some of the brighter students and for those who had been tutored at home, many of the projects assigned by McCollum were old hat. The formal theory was not. Electronics 1, 2, and 3 became Stephen Wozniak's most important high-school class, fifty minutes a day, every day of the week. McCollum's class also brought a definite divide between matters electrical and matters electronic. For the students this wasn't a semantic difference;

it was something that separated the men from the boys. Electrical devices were the stuff of play kits composed of batteries and switches and light bulbs. Electronics was an altogether higher calling that journeyed into the world of technology, the ethereal realms of physics, and was devoted to the peculiar behavior of the mighty and entirely invisible electron.

Standing in front of the class, wearing a woolen cardigan, McCollum drummed home electronic theory. Stories and set speeches from the twenty years he had spent in the navy, before he retired in pique at a rule requiring infrequent pilots to fly with a backup, spilled out with such regularity that some students took to giving the old favorites code numbers. McCollum would fidget with his spectacles, placing them on his nose, removing them and tucking them into his shirt pocket behind the pens in the streaked plastic pouch. He started with theory and followed up with applications. The students were paraded through Ohm's law, Watt's law, basic circuitry, magnetism, and inductance. They found that if they paid attention the lessons stuck and that their teacher planted seeds that kept sprouting. They solved elementary equations, linked resistors in series and parallel, and watched capacitors charge up. They built power supplies and amplifiers and learned how to manipulate alternating and direct currents.

McCollum was also the quality-assurance center. When students finished building radios, he disappeared into his stockroom, inserted some faulty parts and urged them to troubleshoot with their minds rather than their eyes. "You have got to be able to think it through," he repeated. Keen students brought the devices they built in their bedrooms and garages for McCollum to scrutinize. He would jab loose parts with a screwdriver and wiggle the solder joints much like a rough dentist. On one occasion he criticized a knob on a power supply that Bill Fernandez had built because it behaved in the opposite manner to most knobs. Fernandez later said, "It was the first time I started to think about standards and human design."

To reveal the power of electricity McCollum became a showman. He chilled his students with tales of acid burning the faces of people who carelessly jump-started automobile engines. With a flourish he produced props from a locked desk drawer and demonstrated well-tried tricks. He indulged in the mundane and would rub a balloon against his sweater and hang it from the underside of the television. Or he would dim the lights and throw the switch on a Tesla coil that generated high-frequency currents. The class would be left watching one hundred thousand volts leap from the end of the coil and illuminate a fluorescent tube held close by. And on other days the students in Classroom F-3 would see flames crackling up the rods of a Jacob's ladder. McCollum made his mission plain. "I try to dispel the mystery of electrons. You cannot see them, but you can see the effect of them."

Electronics was not, however, a purely intellectual quest. It was also a practical matter that with very little skill produced all manner of shrieks, sirens, ticks, and other noises calculated to amuse, irritate, and terrify. The same parts that built sturdy voltmeters and ohmeters could be turned to far more diverting purposes. From an early age Stephen Wozniak had a penchant for practical jokes and he usually managed to add a twist of his own. Throwing eggs in the dark at passing cars didn't strike him as either entertaining or ingenious. But painting an egg black, attaching it to string hooked to lampposts on either side of the road, and suspending it at a height calculated to smack a radiator grill was more his style. Electronics opened up a new realm for pranks.

For instance, during his senior year at Homestead High School Wozniak salvaged some cylinders from an old battery that looked deceptively like sticks of dynamite. He fastened an oscillator to the cylinders and placed the combination in a friend's locker with some telltale wires trailing from the door. Before long the tick-tick-tick of the oscillator attracted attention and not much later the school principal, Warren Bryld, was risking his life as he clutched the device and dashed for the empty air of the football field. "I just pulled the wires out and phoned the police. I was promptly chewed out for being a jackass." The perpetrator was tracked down quickly enough, though Wozniak, on his way to the principal's office, thought he was about to be congratulated for winning a math contest. Instead he found himself in the hands of the local constabulary and heading for a night's stay in San Jose's Juvenile Hall. The following morning Margaret Wozniak wasn't appeased by the sight of her son and yelled at the wardens: "Why haven't you tattooed a number across his chest?" Wozniak's sister, Leslie, an editor of the school newspaper, told him that space was being held for an exposé of conditions at the Juvenile Hall. When Wozniak returned to Homestead—chastened, embarrassed, but with no charges filed against him—he was given a standing ovation by his classmates.

On occasion students sought John McCollum's help with a temperamental oscillator and he usually gave practical advice. But McCollum taught his pupils about electronics, not computers. The Homestead students who were interested in computers in the late 1960s were not just the smallest minority in the school but could be counted on the fingers of one hand. Electronics and computers were masculine pursuits, though most boys considered it a rather odd pastime. So the peculiar interests bridged differences of age and grade and drew the loners together. They shuttled their private diversions—what really amounted to obsessions—between their homes and the schoolroom.

At Homestead, Wozniak began to spend his homeroom classes staring through thick spectacles and scribbling circuit diagrams in pencil on yellow writing tablets. His sister said, "I felt sorry for him at high school. He was lonely. He suffered because of his nature and because he didn't fit in. He was always made fun of. I always felt that I wanted to protect him." But Wozniak, unlike his sister, did not feel trapped by the provincial attitudes of Sunnyvale or restricted by the dress code at Homestead. He was immensely suspicious of marijuana and other drugs, had no difficulty accepting warnings about their perils, and told his parents when he spotted some telltale seeds in his sister's bedroom. His mother recognized her son's inclinations: "He was very square at high school. . . . He wasn't too much with the girls." Wozniak was Mister Straight.

Left to his own devices he collected the electronics awards in his last two years of high school and was president of the electronics and math clubs. Wozniak began to design circuits for a machine that could perform additions and subtractions, and gradually he began to add features to the machine. He managed to figure out how to cope with the more complicated problems posed by multiplications, divisions, and even square roots. Allen Baum, two years younger than Wozniak, was puzzled by the squiggles and lines. "I asked him what he was doing and he said, 'Designing computers.' I was impressed as hell."

Baum, a lean boy with dark hair and soft brown eyes, had lived in suburban New Jersey until he was thirteen. Then his family moved to California where his father, Elmer, started to work at the Stanford Research Institute. He later realized: "I would have been totally stunted in New Jersey. I always assumed I'd be an engineer and I always assumed the time would come when I'd learn about electronics." He trailed around the cool SRI computer room viewing the machines with a skeptical eye until his father showed him how to operate the terminal: "Within an hour, Allen was doing things I couldn't do."

Unlike Wozniak, Baum had not competed in science fairs, but he shared his interest in the theory and design of computers. When Wozniak persuaded McCollum to find a place where he could learn something more about computers, Baum was included in all the plans. Through a friend McCollum arranged for his two students to spend every Wednesday afternoon in the computer room at GTE Sylvania, a company that made electronic devices for the military. For an entire school year, the two teenagers made weekly trips to the reception desk at Sylvania's Mountain View headquarters.

They signed the visitors' book, clipped plastic badges to their shirts, waited for an escort, and padded off down the corridor, through the tight, metal door into the computer room where the drum and the hum of the IBM 1130 slowed conversations to full-bellied shouts. The white, tiled floor vibrated under the weight of the computer which occupied a cabinet the size of an eighteenth-century French wardrobe. There was a stern-looking keyboard that could be used to enter commands. Programs to produce items like the corporate payroll were punched on sheaves of thin, khaki cards that were fed into a card reader. Information needed by the computer was stored in rows of magnetic tapes, which lined the walls and resembled large tape recorders, while a noisy printer, like the ones used by telegraph companies, clattered out type.

This was the first large computer—the first mainframe—that Wozniak had ever seen. Over the course of the year Wozniak and Baum were provided with tips and hints and fragments of an education. The men at Sylvania introduced Wozniak to a compiler, the software that turns commands entered in a computer language formed of ordinary letters and numbers into a binary machine code that the computer can digest. Wozniak was surprised. "I didn't know the compiler was a program. I figured a compiler was a piece of hardware and I kept pointing at boxes asking, 'Is that the compiler?'" The Sylvania programmers also solved the difficulty he had experienced in designing a calculator capable of multiplying large numbers. But the two teenagers preferred programming to instruction.

They wrote programs in the computer language FORTRAN, punched them onto thin cards and fed them into the card reader. They used the computer to raise numbers to many powers and watched the printer laboriously type out the results. They searched for prime numbers and calculated square roots to dozens of places. They also collaborated on a program to make a knight hop around a chessboard, landing on a different square with every move. The first time they ran the program, nothing happened. The computer sat bone idle while the air conditioner hummed and whirred. They rewrote the program, instructing the computer to report progress after the knight completed every move. It reported the first couple of dozen quite quickly and then started to slow and finally stopped.

One of the Sylvania programmers told the pair about a mathematical shortcut to estimate how long the program would take before it offered an answer for the knight's pilgrimage. Wozniak tried the procedure and found the answer disconcerting: "I calculated it would take ten to the twenty-fifth years to find a single solution. I wasn't going to wait." After Wozniak had spent a few months at Sylvania, McCollum allowed him to give a talk on computers to one of the Homestead electronics classes: "It was a fine lecture. There was only one thing wrong. He should have given it to a sophomore class at college."

The visits to Sylvania, the privilege of being allowed to use a computer, and the tidbits dropped by the programmers not only formed the highlight of Wozniak's week but also spawned other activities. Along with Baum, he started to drift toward the Stanford Linear Accelerator Center whose purpose was far more rigorous than its unfortunate acronym, SLAC, might have suggested. The pair's interest didn't lie in the electrons fired down a two-mile-long concrete streak that ran like a skewer below Interstate 280 and toward the fields around Woodside. They headed instead for the SLAC administration buildings that sat on a hillside overlooking Palo Alto and Stanford University's

Hoover Tower. There they wandered around the computer room and inspected SLAC's IBM 360, a mainframe computer that formed the keystone of the IBM line in the late sixties. They were allowed to use one of SLAC's card punchers to prepare programs they later ran on the smaller IBM computer at Sylvania.

But the library was the main lure. The pair spent Saturday and Sunday afternoons browsing through the stacks, reading magazines and scouring computer manuals. Few places around the Peninsula had richer pickings. The SLAC librarians subscribed to magazines that were broadsheets for programmers and engineers: *Datamation, Computerworld, EDM,* and *Computer Design.* Most of the magazines contained survey cards inviting readers to check boxes alongside the names of companies they wanted to receive information from. Pretty soon the Wozniak mailbox started to bulge with heavy envelopes that contained brochures, product descriptions, and manuals of some of the newer computers. The envelopes bore names like Digital Equipment Corporation, Data General, Scientific Data Systems, Data Mate, Honeywell, and Varian. Almost all these companies made mini-computers, scaled down versions of the room-sized mainframe machines.

Named after the short, narrow skirts made popular by London's Carnaby Street, the minicomputers were usually no larger than a combination refrigerator-freezer for a family of six. The minicomputer makers, just like the companies that designed satellites and rockets, capitalized on the great shrinking world of electronics. As the semiconductor companies developed their manufacturing techniques, they squeezed more and more transistors onto single pieces of silicon. This made it possible for companies like Digital Equipment to produce computers that, even if they didn't match the performance of a contemporary mainframe, were more powerful than some of the mainframes that had been made five years earlier. Every graph that appeared in the trade magazines and plotted price against performance showed the machines would become still cheaper and even more powerful.

But even though minicomputers were far smaller than mainframes, they still needed bulky attachments. Programs were entered on paper tape; the memory was formed out of dozens of small doughnut-shaped pieces of iron linked by wires and built into blocks that were the size of cigar boxes. Results of programs appeared on a Teletype printer. The handbooks and manuals revealed something of the complexity of trying to control the flow of millions of bits moving in all sorts of directions. Digital Electronics Corporation's *Small Computer Handbook,* which the Sylvania analysts gave to Wozniak, became something of an industry classic because it revealed so much about the computer. It included detailed descriptions of the quirks of the central processing unit, provided directions about how the memory should be managed, presented ways of making connections with the Teletype machine, and provided flow charts to help with the writing and testing of programs.

The computer trade magazines were accompanied by a more specialized literature: the component magazines. At the end of the sixties these focused on the integrated circuits, the chips made by semiconductor companies like Fairchild, Signetics, Synertek, Intel, and Motorola. For Wozniak and Baum these magazines became almost as important as the computer magazines and computer manuals. Though no semiconductor company was making a single chip that performed like a computer, some did make chips that, with sufficient ingenuity, could be combined to act as a computer. The companies themselves released details of the features and performance of their new chips on what were called data sheets which were chockablock with technical information. These too became sought-after items. Designing a decent computer, a computer that approached that distant world, the state of the art, required intimate familiarity with the diagrams and details of the data sheets.

Though he pored over DEC's *Small Computer Handbook,* the Varian 620i was the first minicomputer Wozniak subjected to close inspection. It was packed into a brown cabinet with rows of black and white switches on the front panel. For the first time, Wozniak tried to design his own version of a minicomputer with chips he selected: "I didn't know how to make a complete computer but I understood what a computer was." He began to understand the layers between the program that a user would type into a computer and the very heart of the machine. He focused on the heart and understood the idea of a set of precise instructions that formed a code to control the machine.

But if he had not mastered all the links of computer design, Wozniak had fastened onto the idea of using as few parts as possible.

He was delighted when he discovered a way of combining or eliminating gates, the circuits that form the basis of digital logic. When chips contained circuits that would replace several gates they became the cause of jubilation. Wozniak began to concentrate on making parts perform as many functions as possible. "I started moving toward higher levels of integration." Both Wozniak's and Baum's parents were startled by their sons' progress. Like many other teenagers they were free from life's dreary distractions and had the luxury of enough time to pursue their obsessions.

Wozniak and Baum soon sorted out their favorite minicomputers and their bedroom bookshelves began to bulge with computer pamphlets. They started to differentiate among computers, between clever and clumsy designs. They appreciated abstruse features like the way in which some machines handled floating decimal points. Occasionally a name, or cosmetic appeal, tickled their fancy like the Skinny Mini which was named for its thin cabinet. Elmer Baum said, "After about three months I gave up. They were designing computers and I couldn't understand what they were talking about."

When Wozniak left high school for college he took his interests with him. He was rejected by his father's alma mater, Cal Tech, and after a miserable day at De Anza Community College in Cupertino, he enrolled at the University of Colorado in Boulder. Jerry Wozniak viewed his son's attempts to abandon California and join some high-school friends with suspicion. "Stephen wasn't ready to leave home and go off to college at the same time." One of the items packed into his suitcase was an oscillator that had been specially tuned to jam television reception. Wozniak started to interfere with closed-circuit lectures, provoking the professors to try to adjust the television set. He kept twiddling his oscillator until the teachers were in contortions, convinced that if they kept an arm or leg in the air the interference would disappear. He also managed to infuriate some classmates by jamming a transmission of the Kentucky Derby just as the horses were about to cross the line.

Wozniak's life at Colorado revolved around the University's Control Data computer, CDC 6400. He read the computer's manuals, learned some more techniques in FORTRAN programming and also became familiar with another computer language, ALGOL.

For the college administrators Wozniak was a nuisance who spent too much time hanging around the computer room and far too much time using the computer. He ran a couple of programs that spat out reams of paper saying: FUCK NIXON and GOOD SCRAP PAPER. "I was spending ten hours on computers for every hour of class." Late-night bridge sessions and hundred-mile jaunts for hamburgers didn't help his academic performance either. He was badgered by one of the deans and threatened with expulsion. Wozniak retaliated by hiring a lawyer to write a threatening letter but that hardly improved matters. At the end of his first year he left Colorado with a suitcase full of more-refined computer designs and a bundle of Fs, and returned to his parents' home in Sunnyvale where he enrolled once more at De Anza Community College.

Home again, Wozniak was pulled back into the same small circle and the milieu of cosmetic rejects, data sheets and science fairs. He and Allen Baum took some of the same classes at De Anza while Elmer Baum also enrolled in a course that taught the programming language FORTRAN. After a few weeks he dropped out and his admiration for the skills of the younger pair increased. Wozniak ran afoul of more teachers as he toyed with computer designs during linear algebra lessons.

At the end of the year he and Baum accidentally found summer work. They were out looking for the local office of a minicomputer company when they strolled into the headquarters of Tenet, a small company that was trying to make computers for customers like the California Department of Motor Vehicles. The pair talked themselves into jobs as programmers and though Baum soon left to start his studies at MIT, Wozniak stuck it out and learned how to program a computer system that could serve many users simultaneously. He made the occasional jaunt to Los Angeles— "I wanted to marry my young cousin down there but she never liked me"—stayed at Tenet until it fell victim to the 1972 recession, and then registered for unemployment benefits.

Meanwhile, he was learning, in a haphazard manner, much more about computer design. He read the Xerox copies of computer textbooks that Baum mailed from MIT and he still visited school science fairs. During one visit he spotted an enlightening entry. The item that grabbed his attention was a mechanical machine that stepped, in sequence, through several instructions. At each step it was wired to fire off particular signals. Wozniak made a copy of the writeup that accompanied the machine and took it home to read. He translated the concept into electronics and grasped the idea of a circuit that would step through many small operations in an ordained sequence before performing an instruction: "All of a sudden I understood sequencing steps. I knew immediately that I knew how to design computers and I hadn't the day before. You just know it. As soon as a good concept clicks you just know that it got you there."

The self-taught lesson was of considerable help when Wozniak delved into the innards of Data General's Nova mini-computer. Designed by a team of refugees from Digital Equipment Corporation, the Nova gained a reputation for clever and aggressive design. A fancy poster that the company mailed out was a sought-after item in the small world of camp followers. Wozniak and Baum both hung the poster among the parade of idols that decorated their bedroom walls and the former explained the attraction. "There was no other computer around that looked as if it could sit on a desk."

The Data General Supernova was a sixteen-bit machine—it handled sixteen binary digits at a time—and everything apart from the memory was mounted on a single laminated board. Over one hundred semiconductor chips were slotted into holes in the green board and linked by squiggly solder traces. The lines of solder were etched on what was called a printed circuit board that formed one of the basic building blocks of computers. The chips mounted on the "mother board" controlled the most important functions of the machine. Almost every aspect of the Data General computer provided some commentary on the progress of electronics. Though the computer's arithmetic logic was far more sophisticated, it was still akin to the adder-subtracter Wozniak had designed when he was thirteen. But what had, in 1963, required a large board and hundreds of parts was contained on a sliver of silicon in 1970.

Along with Baum, who spent his summer vacations in California, Wozniak started to design his own version of the Nova. He wrote to Data General asking for more information and received several hundred pages of internal company documents. The pair gathered data sheets on new chips made by Fairchild Semiconductor and Signetics, pored over the technical specifications, and selected the chips that suited their needs. They drew schematics—diagrams that illustrated how the chips would be linked—for a couple of different versions of the computer. One used chips made by Fairchild; the other used chips made by Signetics.

Though Wozniak was the driving force, Baum was more than a cheerleader. He was familiar with every aspect of the design and would suggest how the maximum amount of power could be extracted from the chips. They concentrated on the digital electronics and shrugged off more humdrum concerns. Baum recalled: "We didn't worry about things like the power supply." At one stage the pair even considered building their own version of the computer, filled a folder with schematics, and wrote to companies asking for parts. Wozniak recalled: "Every computer I designed I intended to build. Getting the parts was the problem."

The rigor of designing several different versions of the Nova provided Wozniak with some illuminating lessons. To help his son understand some subleties, Jerry Wozniak arranged for him to meet the designer of a Fairchild semiconductor chip. The Fairchild engineer explained that the number of chips used in a design formed only one aspect of the final goal. He told Wozniak that the space occupied by the chips on a printed circuit board mattered just as much as the number of chips. Henceforth Wozniak focused on the twin objectives of combining as few chips as possible in the smallest amount of space.

The experience with the Data General Nova prodded Wozniak toward a grander diversion. He decided to try to build his own computer. He managed to spur the interest of one of his neighborhood chums, Bill Fernandez, to help with the effort. They had known each other for several years and their fathers played golf together. Though several years younger than Wozniak, Fernandez with his tense, thin, ivory features had a broader range of interests. He became a member of the Bahai faith, studied aikido, and seemed like the sort of person who might have been at home in sixteenth-century Japan as the student of a samurai warrior. He too was lured by science fairs and one year had entered an electric lock that had flat switches nailed to a piece of plywood. He built sirens from oscillators and was, as he readily admitted, thorough and competent but not given to whim or impulse. He was fastidious, good with his hands, and had a knack for installing items like car radios.

In his final year at McCollum's electronics class, Fernandez had worked as a technician in NASA's spacecraft-systems laboratory. There he built, tested, and modified circuits, learned about special soldering techniques, was taught how to dress leads properly, and was lectured on the perils of nicking wires. Fernandez carved out a corner of his parents' garage to work on his hobby. He squeezed his own shelves and workbench between the family water heater and clothes dryer. "Space in the garage was a constant battle. They were saying I had a quarter of the garage when I only had a sixteenth." But the Fernandez garage offered a sturdy place to build Wozniak's machine.

Wozniak knew what he wanted from his computer. "I wanted to design a machine that did something. On a TV you turn a knob and it does something. On a computer you push a button and some lights come on." To build a machine that would blink, Wozniak and Fernandez started scavenging for parts from a bundle of semiconductor companies. Intel furnished them with eight memory chips each of which could store 256 bits. Intersil gave a couple of expensive chips that contained arithmetic logic units. They rounded up some switches from a batch of samples belonging to a salesman for a switch company, light-emitting diodes from a Monsanto engineer, and a metal frame from one of Hewlett-Packard's scrap piles. The largest batch of parts came from a couple of applications engineers at Signetics. Wozniak and Fernandez spread their trophies out on the latter's living-room floor and sorted out all the adders, multiplexers, and registers. They checked the part numbers against the data sheets and stuffed them into rows of small, carefully labeled manila envelopes.

Once they set to work there was a division of labor. Wozniak designed the computer on a couple of sheets of notepad paper and concentrated on the logic design. Fernandez designed the timing circuits and the circuits that hooked the computer to the lights. Wozniak watched his younger pal, who was still at high school, play technician and assemble the computer. "He didn't really have any engineering background but he knew how to build it with straight wires and a soldering iron. He was slow but very careful and very neat." For several weeks the pair used their evenings and weekends to build the computer and managed to swig down a considerable number of bottles of Cragmont cream soda in the process. Fernandez bicycled down to the local Safeway with the empty quarts and used the deposits to help buy the few parts they still needed.

The Cream Soda Computer was a small version of the minicomputers that had caught Wozniak's fancy—"It was the absolute minimum hardware"—and the design was dictated by the off-the-shelf parts in the manila envelopes. The center of the machine was formed by two four-bit arithmetic-logic units which Wozniak rigged in tandem to give an eight-bit-wide computer. The completed computer was mounted on a metal frame. One board carried the chips and a smaller one contained the timing circuits—a crystal oscillator and frequency-divider circuit adapted from a Signetics manual. Fernandez fastened eight switches into holes he had drilled in a piece of Bakelite.

After the Cream Soda Computer was completed, Wozniak started to exercise his control over it by writing a few programs. The programs were based on the semiconductor data sheets that revealed which instructions were needed to make the chips perform functions like addition and subtraction. He listed the bits, figured out the operating code, and wrote it down. All the instructions were executed within five steps and followed an intimate sequence that Wozniak muttered to himself: "Load; load the next byte of the instruction into the memory address register; put that through the alu into the alu output register; dump the alu output register into the next memory location."

The timing circuit, which Fernandez designed, ensured that five signals were generated in the right order of every instruction. The programs performed actions like multiplying the values entered into four switches by the values entered into the other four switches and displayed the answer in the lights. Wozniak reflected on the importance of the results. "I cannot explain why that means so much to me. Multiplying two four-bit numbers by each other doesn't sound like a lot. But being able to do something which you couldn't have done without a computer is worth something."

When the computer was almost complete, Fernandez invited his friend Steven Jobs to drop by the garage, take a look at the computer, and meet its designer. Jobs was, in his own way, impressed by the machine and by Wozniak: "He was the first person I met who knew more electronics than I did."

Wozniak decided to reveal his computer to the world and called a *San Jose Mercury* reporter that his mother knew. The reporter, accompanied by a photographer, appeared in Wozniak's bedroom for a demonstration. As Wozniak explained some of the subtleties of the ugly contraption that lay on the floor, smoke started to emerge from the power supply Fernandez had built. The computer expired as a stream of high voltage from the power supply blew out every integrated circuit on the board. Fernandez examined the power supply and found the fault lay in an unmarked chip he had earned by doing a gardening chore for one of the neighbors. He was miffed: "We didn't get our pictures in the paper and we didn't become boy heroes."

"He sells goldfish," Goldman said.

Inside a nineteenth-century red-brick building set among the antique stores, restaurants, and law offices of San Francisco's Barbary Coast, a group of four men gathered to plan Apple's advertising for the coming year. It was an afternoon of Indian summer and the conference room, which didn't have any windows, was stuffy. The room belonged to Chiat-Day, a medium-sized advertising agency that was perpetually rumored to be on the verge of losing its largest client, Apple Computer. A couple of long-leaved potted plants sagged from the heat, a movie projector was concealed behind a sheet of smoked glass, and alongside a wet bar a refrigerator heaved like an iron lung. The four men were seated in plush chairs around a laminated conference table.

Henry Whitfield, Apple's advertising manager, was in the greatest discomfort. Although he was only in his thirties, he already looked as if he had run through too many airports and the ghost of an older man appeared around his temples. The other three worked for Chiat-Day: Fred Goldberg, who had just moved from the East Coast and had taken charge of the Apple account fifteen days before; Maurice Goldman, an account executive who was balding and in his thirties; and Clyde Folley, another executive who was neatly turned out from his carefully trimmed beard to a pair of soft, tasseled shoes. The four were meeting to discuss Apple's general image and to start work on a plan that would help buyers sort out the differences between the Apple II, Apple III, Lisa, and Mac.

Whitfield, dragging hard on a cigarette, attacked his first worry with excited determination. A marketing campaign for the Apple II had lowered the price of the computer to $1,995 and had been so successful that the introduction of an enhanced version of the computer had been delayed for several months. But Whitfield was worried that Apple was emphasizing the price of its best-selling computer.

"There are these guys at Apple," Whitfield said, "who are saying, 'Let's make a lot of hay out of price.' Then the left hand says, 'Don't advertise price.' And the right hand says, 'Promote the hell out of price.' We look like idiots if the right hand doesn't know what the left hand is doing. I don't think price is an advantage for Apple. The price of the Apple Two isn't all that low compared to other machines. People don't know what price means."

"It's almost deceptive advertising," Goldman agreed as he stretched out his legs. "Everybody and his brother has to buy a box, drives, monitor, and printer. It's plain misleading. The preconception is that they can get into an Apple for thirteen hundred dollars. Then they go into a dealer's, find they have to spend three thousand dollars, and come out without a computer." He paused. "And pissed off."

"It makes it easy for people to price-shop," Whitfield said, shaking his head in dismay.

"The nineteen ninety-five suggested retail price," Folley elaborated, "meant a loss of eight percent for the dealers. The dealers are taking it in the shorts."

"We've got fifteen suits against us from mail-order people for price fixing," said Whitfield as he thumped the table with his fist. "You can see them now trying to convince a judge, moaning about this poor little retailer and this big company. It's conceivable that a judge could say there was a pattern of price-fixing. We want an image like Sony or IBM. You don't see those guys running an ad for price."

"Our whole strategic position," said Goldman, "is to enhance position for Apple. We have to add brand preference. We've got a lot of people who don't know about PCs. People don't even know they need these damn things, and we're trying to sell them something they don't think they need on the preference of price."

Whitfield started to complain about Paul Dali, director of marketing for the Apple II, who was keen to advertise the price of computers. "How do you convince him otherwise? He sold thirty-three thousand computers or whatever the hell the number was in July. I've racked my brain and we just don't have enough research to convince him that it isn't price."

"It's cost benefit," said Goldman.

"He's got to step back and look at himself as part of an organization," suggested Goldberg who had his feet propped against the edge of the table.

"How do you say that diplomatically?" asked Whitfield.

"Wake up, schmuck!" Goldberg said as he smoothed his fawn tie. He rephrased the suggestion: "Take a global perspective!"

After the chuckles subsided, Goldberg turned to the greater issue. "Apple has to be careful not to get down and dirty. An Apple means more than just a computer. Apple means plugging yourself into an energy source."

"We can't fight it out with the unwashed masses," Goldman agreed. "We've got to show Apple is the brand of choice. Stick in the price and you become the cheapo."

"Start cutting price," Goldberg warned, "and you erode position. You can get thrown out at some point. If IBM steps in above you. You get thrown out."

"How the hell are the unwashed masses out there going to figure out what to do?" Goldman wondered. "Everybody is trying to beat themselves over the head for the current market which is only three percent of what it will be."

"It's the whole corporate image," Whitfield said. "Crocker Bank doesn't want to buy a computer from a company for eleven ninety-five."

Whitfield, who looked as if the cares and the future of the company were resting on his shoulders, pointed out, "Apple isn't like General Foods. At General Foods the Sanka guy doesn't have to worry about hurting the Jell-O guy. They're separate. At Apple every brand manager affects the other brand managers."

"Every brand manager wants to sell product," said Goldberg.

"Yeah," Whitfield agreed, as he replaced his cigarette with a strip of bubble gum and continued to enlighten Goldberg about the ways of Apple. "At Apple there's a fundamental disagreement. Dali's job is to sell product but others want to sell image and the idea that a computer is more than just a computer. Going to nineteen ninety-five we were overpriced. We were selling an overpriced machine. Suddenly there was IBM, and suddenly there was Osborne who was saying, 'We're going to give you more than Apple for seventeen ninety-five.' Then we featured price and said, 'Hi, Mr. Dealer! We love you so much we're going to take eight percent out of your hide.'"

"What are the corporate objectives?" asked Goldberg.

"To reestablish Apple as not being behind in technology," answered Whitfield. "We're hung up in our own underwear. The perception is we're out here peddling old machinery. We've got to show Apple is back on the track. People don't know where we're going and we don't have enough advertising dollars to beat them over the head with it. They've heard all the rumors: 'Gosh, they're out of date. They're late with new products.' We've got to reinforce the impression that Apple's out there with a full line of products."

"By announcing and making hoopla out of the interface, you run a major risk of hurting the Two and the Three," Goldberg said.

"We've got to show that Apple is *the* computer company," Maurice Goldman added. "The unwashed masses don't know the difference between eight and sixteen bits, much less between a mouse and a green screen."

"Price isn't the news," Whitfield repeated. "The customer doesn't know whether price is a good price."

"Technology is the news," Folley suggested tentatively.

Whitfield embarked on a sudden diversion. "I've been looking at the dealer numbers," he said. "IBM is getting so friggin' smart. They've got four hundred ninety-five outlets now. They've been adding them like crazy. We've only got four hundred ninety good dealers. IBM only went to the guys who didn't have a history of discounting. The Computerland dealers wouldn't think of selling an Apple. What we should do is buy a dealer, buy fifty truckloads of IBMs, load 'em up and sell 'em for five hundred dollars and bust their price level. We need two lawyers sniffing down their throats to catch 'em price fixing." He caught his breath. "IBM has no high risk in this marketplace."

Goldberg returned doggedly to the issue of price. "We've got hundreds of millions tied up in the image. If we sell on price we're selling equity. We're selling the franchise."

"Apple makes money on the boxes," Whitefield emphasized. "Our strategy is for accessories, peripherals, and software to take lower margins."

"Then there are dealers who discount the box," objected Folley.

"Like Billy Ladin," said Goldman.

"Who is he?" asked Goldberg.

"Billy Ladin's this dealer in Texas," explained Goldman. "He's got something like four stores and he sells goldfish."

"Goldfish?" asked Goldberg who was baffled.

"Yeah," said Goldman. "Goldfish. He says, 'I'll give the goldfish away for nothing. The little boy runs home and in an hour he's back with five bucks from his mom and then I'll sell him the bowl, the gravel, and the food.'"

Returning to the problems posed by the introduction of the new computers, Whitfield remarked, "We have an image that we're a one-shot company. We want to be your personal computer company. We're not just selling Lisa. If it was my company, I'd be saying this interface is the greatest thing since sliced bananas and all the others are obsolete. I'd be hitting every city in the country with seminars. We were going to announce Lisa and ship. But now we cannot. We've been burned so many times at Apple that I know that's what's going to happen. It's going to slip. Then rumors will get out that Mac's a cheap version of Lisa and people will be saying why should we buy a Two or a Three when we can wait a few months and buy a Mac."

"We want to be your personal computer company," Folley echoed. "We're not selling Lisa."

"You just said it," Goldberg noted.

"The question is not Apple but which Apple," Goldman amplified.

"This way," Goldberg said, "you're not running any downside risk. There's no downside here."

"We've got the line," Whitfield said. He pointed toward Goldman. "He gave me the line. It was so memorable I've already forgotten it."

"Evolution. Revolution," Goldman said.

Goldman explained that Regis McKenna, the head of the public-relations agency retained by Apple, was trying to arrange stories that would coincide with the company's stockholders' meeting and the announcement of Lisa. "McKenna is talking about a front page on *The Wall Street Journal* and they're also talking about a cover on *Business Week*. That should enhance the editorial launch of these products."

"The stockholders' meeting should reestablish your personal computer company," said Goldberg. "It should reestablish everybody's personal computer company."

"They should say, 'Buy stock, buy computers, buy everything,'" said Goldman.

The four also had to grapple with the fact that there would be a four-to-five-month gap between the announcement of Lisa and the day when it would be available at dealers.

"When Lisa is in the store we drop a business insert into the world," said Whitfield. "It'll say 'See this wonderful, mouse-activated computer.' Then when Mac's available we start with ads saying that mouse-activated computers are taking over the friggin' world."

"Are you concerned," asked Goldberg, "that another competitor could preempt all this?"

Goldman calmed his fears. "We've got pretty good G-Two. Unless there's the tightest security in the world on this."

"The day of the stockholders' meeting someone is going to stand up on a podium and they're going to announce the bloody thing," said Whitfield.

"What happens if editorial press ever pumps McKenna about a low-cost Lisa?" asked Goldman.

"If they do that, we're friggin' dead," said Whitfield. "We'd be in real deep trouble. It'll kill the sales. People can ask it and we'll have some line like we'll be coming out with a low-cost computer in a couple of years."

THE CONDUCTOR

Stephen Wozniak, Bill Fernandez, and Steven Jobs came to view each other's peculiarities through the telling eyes of friends. They were introspective and wrapped up in the privacy of their own worlds. When they stopped to look, each thought the others were shy and withdrawn. They were loners. Fernandez first encountered Jobs after he arrived at Cupertino Junior High School: "For some reason the kids in eighth grade didn't like him because they thought he was odd. I was one of his few friends." Neither Jobs nor Fernandez was as obsessed with electronics as Wozniak. They didn't pore over computer manuals, or linger around computer rooms or spend hours messing with instruction sets on sheets of paper but they still found electronics an engaging and diverting pastime.

Fernandez and Jobs meddled together in the quiet of their garages. They struggled in their combined ignorance to build a box with a photocell that, when a light was flashed, would switch another light on or off. They didn't know enough mathematics to form a model but they drew diagrams and tried to build the device with relays and transistors and diodes. When Paul Jobs started to work as a machinist at Spectra Physics, a company that specialized in lasers, Fernandez and Jobs fiddled with the laser parts that, in due course, dribbled back to Los Altos. They played rock music, balanced mirrors on stereo speakers, pointed lasers at the mirrors, and watched images play against a wall.

Like Wozniak and Fernandez, Jobs found the forum provided by science fairs irresistible. While he was still at Cupertino Junior High School he entered a science fair for which he built a silicon-controlled rectifier, a device that can be used to control alternating current. So when he began to attend Homestead High School it was natural for him to enroll in John McCollum's electronics class. Unlike Wozniak he didn't become a teacher's pet, wasn't given access to the closely guarded stockroom, and dropped the course after a year. McCollum drew his own conclusions. "He had a different way of looking at things. I'd put him down as something of a loner. He would tend to be over by himself thinking." On one occasion when McCollum couldn't supply him with a part he needed, Jobs called the public-relations department of the supplier, Burroughs, in Detroit. McCollum objected. "I said, 'You cannot call them collect.' Steve said, 'I don't have the money for the phone call. They've got plenty of money.'"

But the whirl of electronics was certainly strong enough to intrigue Jobs. He made some trips to NASA's flight simulator which had been built at Sunnyvale's Moffett Field. He attended meetings of the school's electronics club. Along with a few others he went to meetings of the Hewlett-Packard Explorer Group where company scientists gave lectures. There were talks on some of the features included in Hewlett-Packard's latest calculators, developments in light-emitting diodes and laser inframetry. After one lecture Jobs buttonholed a scientist, wangled a tour of Hewlett-Packard's holographic lab, and was given an old hologram. On another occasion he called the home of Bill Hewlett, one of the co-founders of Hewlett-Packard, and asked for some parts. Hewlett provided the parts and also gave Jobs the name of a person to contact for a summer job. So at the end of his high-school freshman year Jobs spent the summer working on an assembly line, helping to build Hewlett-Packard frequency counters. Spurred by the devices passing in front of his eyes at the factory, Jobs set about trying to design his own frequency counter but never completed the project.

The resistors, capacitors, and transistors that were used by Jobs and Wozniak came from the local electronics stores and mail-order firms. Jobs was at least as familiar as Wozniak with the quality and reputations of these outlets. As they both grew older, and as they graduated from bicycles to automobiles, their shopping choices expanded. Sunnyvale Electronics was one of the most convenient spots. Just off El Camino Real, it was sheeted with fake rock but its contents were more substantial. It stocked new parts, dozens of magazines and manuals, and also the eighteen-dollar walkie-talkies for which Wozniak saved his thirty-five-cent lunch money while at junior high school. They learned to avoid the Radio Shack outlets because they thought the parts were inferior. Radio Shack, with its garish neon signs, was a last resort, a place to be visited late at night when every other place was closed.

Sunnyvale Electronics, Radio Shack, and other stores like Solid State Music were dwarfed by Haltek, which occupied a block long, light-chocolate building in Mountain View across the freeway from three brobdingnagian hangars the navy had built in the 1930s to house airships. From the outside it looked like an army mess hall. Inside it was an electronic junkyard which, like all junkyards, was a cross between a graveyard and a maternity ward. The haggling at the front counter and the thick parts catalogs mounted in folders with steel spines gave some sense of supply and demand in the world of electronics. Some items, usually small and cheap parts, were brand new, but it usually took a few months for the latest parts to filter down to Haltek. However, the store also carried the electronic equivalent of dinosaur teeth: vacuum tubes. A customer certainly had to know what he was after and even the experienced rifler couldn't always know whether a part was made in the United States or the Far East. It was the sort of place where electrical engineers stopping by after work would bump into youngsters perched on the top of metal steps rummaging for the perfect switch among a selection of cherry switches, push switches, alternating-action push switches, lighted-lever switches, push-pull switches, and slide switches.

Narrow aisles were shaded by wooden shelves mounted on metal frames that reached from a concrete floor to a ceiling carrying grimy pipes and dusty neon lights. Hundreds of thousands of parts filled bins fashioned out of old cardboard cartons. Some of the cartons sprouted spasticated leads. Resistors lay packed in rolls while there were entire shelves devoted solely to capacitors.

The more expensive pieces of equipment were housed in glass cases or along more hallowed aisles. Some had exotic names like the Leeds and Northrup Speedomax and the Honeywell Digitest. Even generators, which convert mechanical energy into electrical energy, had as many varieties as the rose: signal and sweep, multisweep, ligna sweep, and (a hybrid) varisweep. According to one frequent visitor, wandering around a surplus store like Haltek "was like walking around an immense tool kit. It gave you an idea of what was possible." It was also a place where the engineers came to hear about the reputations of machines that needed piano movers and others that were lighter than a leaf.

Jobs spent some weekends working behind the counter at Halted Specialties located in Sunnyvale. He became familiar with the value and going rate for parts ranging from the latest semiconductor chips to measurement instruments. At one point he astonished Wozniak when the pair spent a Saturday morning sorting through the pickings at the San Jose Flea Market, a vast combination of garage sale and country fair which seemed to attract every scavenger south of San Francisco. Jobs bought some transistors which he later resold—at a profit—to his boss at Halted. Wozniak recalled: "I thought it was a flaky idea but he knew what he was doing."

But there was a lot more to Jobs's life than electronics. He was curious and adventurous and open to the sensations of life. He spent as much time dabbling with artistic and literary pursuits as he did with frequency counters and laser beams. He was attracted by literature and classic movies, studied some Shakespeare, idolized his English teacher, and was enchanted with movies like *The Red Balloon*. When swimming practice started to devour too much of his time, he quit and took up water polo but abandoned that when the coach encouraged him to knee opponents in the groin. "I wasn't a jock. I was a loner for the most part." Some high-school contemporaries, like Stephen Wozniak's younger brother, Mark, thought Jobs was "really strange." For a time he played the trumpet in the school marching band.

With a few friends he formed an offbeat group called the Buck Fry Club whose name could be unraveled into an obscene message. They painted a toilet seat gold and cemented it on a planter and they hoisted a Volkswagen Beetle onto the roof of the school cafeteria.

At the end of Jobs's junior year he, Wozniak, and Baum engineered a stunt for the graduating class: a king-sized sheet, tie-dyed in the school's green and white colors, which unfurled down the side of a building to reveal a giant hand giving a time-honored gesture. Baum's mother painted the hand, having been told that it was a Brazilian good-luck sign. At the bottom of the sheet the three combined their initials! SWABJOB PRODUCTIONS. It wasn't long after Jobs was summoned to the principal's office to do some explaining that Paul Jobs arrived to act a counsel for the defense.

Steven Jobs also ventured farther afield in both body and spirit. The arrival of his first car, a red Fiat coupe that Paul Jobs considered small, cramped and unreliable, made it easier to leave Los Altos. Jobs found that his car let him visit friends. Unlike many high-school students—when a difference of a year seems like a decade—Jobs was friendly with people several years his senior. A couple were students at Berkeley while one or two others attended Stanford. Jobs took to driving his temperamental car across San Francisco Bay to Berkeley and he also liked lingering around the Stanford University coffee shop. The forays into a larger world broadened his general interest. He started to experiment with sleep deprivation and several times stayed up for a couple of consecutive nights. He started smoking marijuana and hashish, took to puffing on a pipe, and left the drugs in the car where his father happened on them.

"What is this I found in your car?" Paul Jobs asked his son. "That's marijuana, Father."

As a high-school senior Jobs met his first serious girl friend. The object of his attentions, Nancy Rogers, trailed him by a year because she had spent two years in second grade. With long fawn hair, green eyes, and high cheekbones, she had a bohemian edge and a compelling fragility. Rogers lived two blocks from Homestead in a house where her mother and father, an engineer in GTE Sylvania's Electronics Systems Division, were engaged in bitter squabbles. "I was going through turmoil because my family was splitting up. Steve was kind of crazy. That's why I was attracted to him." Her father thought, "Nancy needed

someone she could latch onto and Steve was kind to her."
The pair met while Rogers was working on an animated movie
which the school authorities did not look kindly on. To escape
surveillance, much of the movie work was done after midnight in
the shuttered school buildings. A few students, like Jobs, dropped
by with lights and stereos. Wozniak, who observed some of these
activities from a distance, harbored wild (and unfounded) specu-
lations that his younger friend was engaged in the production of
pornographic epics.

Jobs and Rogers became high-school sweethearts. In Jobs's
final year of high school they played hooky, spent afternoons
drinking wine, and talking. It was as bucolic an existence as suburban Santa Clara would allow. Jobs dropped his first LSD with
Nancy in a wheat field. "It was great. I had been listening to a lot
of Bach. All of a sudden the wheat field was playing Bach. It was
the most wonderful experience of my life up to that point. I felt
like the conductor of this symphony with Bach coming through
the wheat field."

When he graduated from high school Jobs was thin and lean.
The combination of long dark hair and a sparse beard convinced
his mother not to buy more than one graduation photograph.
After leaving Homestead, Jobs decided to spend the summer living
with Nancy. The pair rented a room in a small cabin in the hills
overlooking Cupertino and Los Altos. Nancy recalled, "It wasn't a
great statement. We just did it. Steve was headstrong so we could
do it and my parents were falling apart so I could do it. We were
really in love." Jobs announced the move to his parents.

"I just said one day, 'I'm going to live with Nancy.'
"My father said, 'What?'
"'Yeah. We rented this cabin. We're going to live together.'
"He said: 'No, you're not.'
"And I said: 'Yes, I am.'
"And he said: 'No, you're not.'
"And I said: 'Well, bye!'"

Jobs and Rogers shared a romantic teenage summer. There
were strolls to peer through the gates of the Maryknoll Seminary
and long walks on Baldi Hill where Rogers painted a picture of
a black woman on a wooden post. Jobs tried his hand at poetry,

picked at a guitar, and along with Wozniak, was attracted by the music of Bob Dylan. They found a store in Santa Cruz that specialized in Dylan esoterica and sold reprints of songbooks, magazine profiles, and bootleg tapes of recording sessions and European concerts. They took some of the Dylan songbooks to SLAC where they copied them on a Xerox machine. There was also the occasional disaster where family ties came in handy. When Jobs's Fiat short-circuited and caught fire on Skyline Drive, his father, towed it home. To help pay for the damage to the car and keep ends together Jobs, Wozniak, and Rogers found jobs at San Jose's Westgate Shopping Center, where they donned heavy costumes and, for three dollars an hour, paraded around a children's fairyland in a concrete *Alice in Wonderland*. Though Wozniak reveled in the activity, Jobs took a more jaundiced view: "The costumes weighed a ton. After about four hours you'd want to wipe out some kids." Nancy played Alice. Wozniak and Jobs took turns masquerading as the White Rabbit and the Mad Hatter.

THE LITTLE BLUE BOX

In a litigious, Victorian English, American Telephone and Telegraph made its policy absolutely clear: "No equipment, apparatus, circuit or device not furnished by the Telephone Company shall be attached to or connected with the facilities furnished by the Telephone Company." Dr. No, Cheshire Cat, The Snark, Cap'n Crunch, Alefnull, The Red King, and Peter Perpendicular Pimple disagreed. They were phone phreaks who spent their lives perfecting blue boxes—electronic gadgets the size of cigarette packets— which they used to make free long-distance telephone calls and tease, outwit, and infuriate the biggest company on earth.

At the time, and especially in later years, the excuses for playing around with blue boxes and the mighty telephone system were as diverse and imaginative as the nicknames. The blue box offered an opportunity to explore the largest collection of computers devised by man. It provided a worldwide introduction to the marriage of hardware and software. It was an intellectual exercise. It was a challenge. It brought satisfaction. It grabbed people's attention. It appealed to a passion for power. It was a privilege to converse with some of the legendary phone phreaks. Some even liked to explain, with straight faces, that there were practical advantages. Blue boxes, they said, provided quieter, more direct circuits than the phone company could furnish. And though they knew it was illegal very few admitted that they were stealing from AT&T, GTE, or any of the hundreds of small, independent telephone companies. "We thought it was absolutely incredible," Steve Jobs explained, "that you could build this little box and make phone calls around the world."

Jobs and Wozniak were inadvertently turned into blue-box builders when Margaret Wozniak glanced at an article in *Esquire* that she thought would appeal to her older son. She was right. About a fifth the length of a respectable-sized book, the piece was called "Secrets of the Little Blue Box" and was subtitled "A story so incredible it may even make you feel sorry for the phone company." The story, published in October 1971, was guaranteed to stir anybody's sense of the fantastic but especially teenagers who had made dummy bombs out of oscillators and played laser beams on bedroom windows.

It told of an underground society composed of phreaks scattered all across America in pools of emotional loneliness whose best companions were voices at the other end of telephone lines. Among the notable characters were Joe Engressia, a blind man in his early twenties who could fool telephone switching equipment by the clarity of his whistle, and Captain Crunch who assumed his name after discovering that the sound from plastic whistles given away in a Cap'n Crunch cereal promotion could be used to help make free toll calls. The 2,600-hertz tone produced by the whistle happened to coincide with the basic signal used by the phone company to direct long-distance calls.

Wozniak tore through the story, intrigued by the authentic ring of the technical detail and the way it dripped with references to frequencies and cycles. Before he had even finished he called Jobs, who was still a sophomore at Homestead High School, and started reading chunks from the magazine. Telephones and the telephone system weren't anything that the pair had given any serious thought to but blue boxes were clearly electronic and they promised to perform a more than useful function. The *Esquire* story started the pair on a paper chase and a four-month quest to build a reliable blue box. They peeled up to Palo Alto and rummaged among the stacks in the Stanford Linear Accelerator

Center library looking for books that might offer more clues. The telephone company, alarmed by the detail revealed in the story, had asked libraries to remove technical telephone manuals from their shelves. Many of the manuals like *The Bell System Telephone Journal* and *The Bell Laboratories Record* where proud scientists had revealed the most intimate details of their work had disappeared. Most of the shelves at SLAC had been picked clean, but the purgers had missed a few vital works and Wozniak and Jobs found the CCITT Masterdata book which had survived the purge. They scoured the index for references to multifrequency tones and descriptions of how to build the circuits that emitted the tones, checked the details, and found that they matched the descriptions given in the *Esquire* story.

Building a reliable blue box was quite another matter. To start, the pair decided to build an oscillator to generate tones that they planned to record on cassette tape. They designed an oscillator from some circuits described in *Popular Electronics* but soon discovered that it was incredibly difficult to get stable tones. Oscillators were temperamental and susceptible to changes in temperature and the telephone company's equipment wasn't tolerant of shoddy work. They spent hours tuning the oscillator by hand, trying to hit the right notes and Jobs measured the results with his frequency counter. Finally, they recorded the tones they needed to make telephone calls but still couldn't get the cassette recorder to fool the phone company.

Unable to tame the vagaries of the wave forms and analog circuitry of oscillators, Wozniak turned his attention to a digital design. Though a digital blue box was far trickier to build than an oscillator, it provided more precise tones. Wozniak was spurred by the informal competition that had developed among phone phreaks to build compact blue boxes. He had to design circuits that would convert pressure on the push buttons into clear, consistent tones. To help with some of the arithmetic he wrote a program to run on one of the Berkeley computers.

After some weeks, he had wired his first digital blue box. Thanks to a clever trick, the box, which contained a small speaker that ran off a 9-volt battery, didn't have a special power switch. Any of the push buttons turned on the power. Jobs and Wozniak tried to place their first call to Wozniak's grandmother in Los Angeles but managed to dial the wrong number, presumably leaving some disconcerted Angeleno wondering why anyone should shriek, "It actually works. It actually works. We called you for free."

For Wozniak and Jobs, cornering Captain Crunch, tracking down the uncrowned King of the Phreaks, became as obsessive as the quest to build a reliable box. They called the author of the *Esquire* story who politely refused to reveal Crunch's real name. Jobs then heard that Crunch had given an interview on a Los Gatos FM radio station. So the pair trooped off to the station and again were told that the name couldn't be disclosed. Finally, the world of phreaking being small and intimate, another Berkeley phreak told Wozniak that he had worked with Captain Crunch at KKUP, an FM radio station in Cupertino, and that his real name was John Draper. Jobs called KKUP, asked for Draper, and was told by the receptionist that he could leave a message. A few minutes later the phone rang: Captain Crunch speaking. They made a date to meet in Wozniak's dormitory room at Berkeley, where he had enrolled in 1971, a few nights later.

What virtually amounted to a papal visit was treated as such. When Jobs arrived from Los Altos, Wozniak was sitting on the edge of his bed scarcely able to conceal his excitement, and several others were waiting for the knock on the door. When they heard the sound Wozniak opened the door to find a ragged figure standing in the corridor. He wore jeans and sneakers, had hair that ran amok, an unshaven face, eyes that squinted, and several missing teeth. Wozniak recalled: "He looked absolutely horrid and I said, 'Are you Captain Crunch?'" Draper replied: "I am he." Despite his quirky mannerisms and his scabrous looks Draper provided a full evening's education. He started playing tricks on the dorm phone, made some international telephone calls, checked out a few dial-a-joke services and recorded weather forecasts in foreign cities.

He also showed his listeners how to "stack tandems" by bouncing a call from one tandem to another in different cities across America, finishing with a call to a telephone across the hallway. Once the telephonic chain reaction was created, Draper hung up the one phone while Jobs and Wozniak listened at the phone that rang across the dorm hallway. They heard the tandems hanging up along the echoing line as the call cascaded to a close: k-chig-a-chig-a-chig; k-chig-a-chig-a-chig.

The lessons continued after they adjourned to Kips, a Berkeley Pizza Parlor. Draper was impressed by Wozniak's blue box: "It never drifted and never needed tuning but it sounded a bit tinny." Draper gave Jobs and Wozniak numbers of other phone phreaks, special telephone numbers, country codes, undersea-cable codes, satellite codes, access codes. He barraged them with details of toll switching trunks, conference bridges, routing indicators, supervisory signals, and traffic service position stations. Draper warned Wozniak and Jobs never to carry a blue box around and to make blue-box calls only from pay phones. Wozniak thought: "It was the most astounding meeting we'd ever had."

The same evening on their way back to Los Altos (where Wozniak had left his car) Jobs's red Fiat broke down. For the first time they used their blue box from a pay phone near a freeway ramp and tried to reach Draper who was heading in the same direction. They dialed an operator to get an 800 number and started to get the jitters when she called back to check whether they were still on the line. Jobs tucked the blue box away and was dialing a legal call when a police car pulled up alongside. The policemen ordered them out of the booth and started inspecting the bushes and shrubs. Just before they were ordered against a wall with their legs astride to be patted down, Jobs slipped Wozniak the blue box, which was soon uncovered.

"What's this?" asked one of the policemen.
"A music synthesizer," Wozniak replied.
"What's this orange button for?"
"Oh, that's for calibration," Jobs interrupted.
"It's a computer-controlled synthesizer," Wozniak elaborated.
"Where's the computer then?"
"That plugs inside," Jobs said.

Finally, satisfied that the long-haired pair weren't carrying any drugs, the policemen gave Jobs and Wozniak a ride back along the freeway. One of the policemen pivoted in his seat, returned the blue box, and said: "Too bad. A guy named Moog beat you to it."

"Oh, yeah," Jobs said, "he sent us the schematics."

To cap off the night, Wozniak picked up his Ford Pinto from the Jobs house and was headed back up the Nimitz Freeway toward

Berkeley when he dozed off and destroyed the car after ramming it into the crash barriers.

Wozniak and Jobs plumped on suitable names for their new pursuit. The first chose the safe sounding Berkeley Blue while the latter decided to call himself Oaf Tobark. By the end of his first quarter at Berkeley Wozniak was fully occupied with blue boxes. He began to collect magazine articles and newspaper stories, pasted the better clips to the wall, and found the printed matter most illuminating. He subscribed to a newsletter published by TAP, the Technological American Party, and was aware of other underground journals like *TEL*, the *Telephone Electronics Line*, and of cells like "Phone Phreaks International" and "Phone Phreaks of America." But for the most part he and Jobs floated on the periphery of a circle that attracted the sort of people who studied computers at MIT, hung around the Artificial Intelligence Laboratory at Stanford, and knew about computer files that provided the latest phreaking tricks.

Wozniak and Jobs were much more interested in practical matters and in expanding their collection of gadgets than in lingering around a university. Following instructions printed in Abbie Hoffman's *Steal This Book* and the left-wing magazine *Ramparts*, Wozniak equipped himself with a black box that allowed free incoming calls and a red box that simulated the sound of coins dropping into a pay phone.

But the most lucrative and amusing part of the arms collection was the blue box. Wozniak soon showed its virtues to his friends. He displayed its power to Allen Baum at two phone booths near Homestead High School. Wozniak phoned one booth from the other which allowed Baum to say hello into one receiver and scamper around to hear his greeting echo through the other. Wozniak made some calls to his sister who was working on a kibbutz in Israel. On Jobs's urging the pair turned a pastime into a small business and began selling the devices. "He wanted money," Wozniak said of his partner.

The pair employed their own marketing techniques for uncovering customers and boosting sales. They crept along the corridors of male dormitories at Berkeley (convinced that few women would be interested in their little device), knocking on doors and measuring the response to their rehearsed patter. "Is George here?" one of them would ask cagily. "George?" came the surprised response. "Yeah, George. You know the blue-box guy. The guy who does the phone tricks. The guy who has the blue box to make free long-distance phone calls." Jobs and Wozniak watched the expression of their potential customer. If they were greeted with puzzled, timid looks they apologized for knocking on the wrong door and padded off down the hallway. If their ploy provoked a curious response, the potential customer was invited to attend a blue-box demonstration.

After a few weeks the dormitory sales pitches assumed a pattern. Wozniak hooked a tape recorder to the telephone with some alligator clips and he and Jobs explained the basic principles of the blue box. Then they followed up with a display of its power. Wozniak, in particular, relished being the center of attention. "It was a big show-off thing." They called the home numbers of friends and relatives of some of their audience in the United States. Then they started phoning overseas and finally they tried to build a global link—starting in Berkeley and bouncing through operators in several countries—and finishing at another nearby Berkeley telephone. On one occasion Jobs used the box to make room reservations for a large party at the Ritz Hotel in London and, unable to suppress his giggles, handed the receiver to Wozniak. Another time Wozniak said that he pretended to be Secretary of State Henry Kissinger and phoned the Vatican asking to be connected to the Pontiff. A Vatican functionary explained that the Pope was still asleep but that somebody would be dispatched to wake him. Another official came on the line and tumbled to the ruse.

The demonstrations provoked curiosity and Jobs and Wozniak made cassette tapes of tones that friends would need to call their favorite long-distance numbers. The evening shows also produced orders. The pair came to an informal agreement about the manufacture of the blue boxes. Jobs arranged a supply of about $40 worth of parts and Wozniak took about four hours to wire a box which was then sold for about $150. To cut down on the time it took to build boxes the pair decided to stop wiring the boxes by hand and to have a printed circuit board made. Instead of spending four hours wiring a box, Wozniak could now finish a box within an hour. He also added another feature that turned one button into an automatic dialer. A small speaker and battery were attached to the printed circuit board, a keypad glued to the lid, and when all was finished, a card bearing a message written in purple felt pen was taped to the bottom. It read "He's got the whole world in his hand" and it was linked to an informal guarantee. Wozniak promised that if a faulty box was returned and still contained the card he would repair it free of charge.

After about a year Jobs, through a combination of boredom and fear of the possible consequences, bowed out of the business. There were, after all, only so many relatives, friends, weather recordings, automatic clocks, and dial-a-jokes to call. There was also good reason to be anxious: The telephone companies were cracking down hard on the phreaks and employed security agents to snap photographs at phone-phreak conventions, placed houses under surveillance, installed tracing equipment at switching stations, rewarded informants, paid double agents and launched occasional raids. Sinister aspects and disquieting rumors accompanied the pastime. Some phone phreaks even placed tarantulas in the mail boxes of security agents and there was talk of organized crime taking an unseemly interest in the lucrative nature of the business.

Jobs was also suspicious of Captain Crunch. Draper's frantic tone, his habit of interrupting phone conversations with emergency calls, his hysterical behavior when cigarettes were lit, and his invitations to physical exercise sessions made Jobs wary. "He was spaced out and weird." Jobs thought that the legend, portrayed in the *Esquire* article, ran ahead of the facts. Even the bootleg 65-watt FM radio station San Jose Free Radio that Draper broadcast most weekends from the back of a van parked in the hills near the Lick Observatory didn't compensate for his quirks. Jobs's judgment was borne out. Though Jobs didn't know it at the time, General Telephone had placed a trace on Draper's telephone to tape his outgoing calls. Among the names and telephone numbers eventually handed over to the FBI was that of the Jobs household. In 1972 Draper was convicted of a wire-fraud charge but escaped with a $1,000 fine and five years of probation. The hobby also proved dangerous in another way. Preparing to sell a box one evening in a parking lot outside a Sunnyvale pizza parlor, Jobs suddenly found himself staring at a customer with a gun. "There were eighteen hundred things I could do but every one had some probability that he would shoot me in the stomach." Jobs handed over the blue box.

For a while Wozniak ran the business by himself. He discovered other tricks, such as how to make free calls from the telephones that hotels and car-rental firms leave at airports. On occasion he also tapped the housemother's phone at Berkeley and listened in on conversations at the FBI office in San Francisco. For about a year before their interest petered out and the phone company started to refine its switching equipment, Jobs and Wozniak switched roles. The former kept his distance while Wozniak took orders at his parents' house and casually minded the operation. Nevertheless he split with Jobs the $6,000 or so that he earned from the sale of about two hundred blue boxes: "It was my business and Steve got half of it."

A couple of Wozniak's friends distributed the boxes around Berkeley while a high-school student who masqueraded under the name Johnny Bagel helped arrange sales in Beverly Hills. Some of Wozniak's blue boxes wound up in the hands of international swindler Bernie Cornfeld and rock singer Ike Turner. At times the distributors harassed Wozniak who became bored with the repetitive assembly work. He took to ordering parts from electronics distributors under an assumed name and sometimes flew to Los Angeles to deliver blue boxes, checking his small suitcase as baggage to avoid the airport X-ray detector. On one occasion his attempts at subterfuge ended in confused embarrassment. He booked a plane ticket to Los Angeles under the name Pete Rose, oblivious to the fact that it belonged to one of the best-known major-league baseball players. Wozniak arrived at the airport, told the ticketing agent he was picking up a ticket for Pete Rose, and then discovered that he didn't have enough cash for the ticket but also didn't want to pay with a check that carried his real name.

Wozniak had proved himself a master of the hardware terminal, the blue box. It was built from an original design and was capable of competing with the smartest around. He gave further evidence of his prowess by concealing a blue box inside the case of a Hewlett-Packard calculator. His command of software was more questionable. He didn't devote the time needed to master the telephone system as thoroughly as some of the other phreaks, and though he eluded capture, many of his customers weren't so lucky. In the informal hierarchy of phreaks, Wozniak fell more into the realm of hacker than phreak.

He didn't even experiment with placing calls on AUTOVON, a telephone system used for military communications that was a playground for the hardened phreaks. One AUTOVON habitué, Burrell Smith, felt Wozniak "didn't understand the network which takes devotion and a full-time passion." There was another penalty: his college work. Though Wozniak had arranged a dream timetable of two courses that were taught one after another in the same lecture room on four afternoons a week, he found telephones more entertaining. By the summer of 1972, he had again fallen foul of a college dean and was receiving letters scolding him for his poor academic performance.

"We've yet to see diddly squat," Carter said.

Bottles of apple juice, packets of potato chips, and plates of turkey, chicken, and salami sandwiches lay at one end of a long conference table. At the other end Steve Jobs, rigged out in shirt, tie, and corduroys, was tapping his feet on the rug and drumming his fingers against the tabletop. He was waiting to start a weekly lunch meeting with the managers of different departments in the Mac division. Bob Belleville, the head of engineering, Matt Carter, the head of manufacturing, Mike Murray, the marketing manager, Debi Coleman, the financial controller, Pat Sharp, Jobs's personal assistant, and Vicki Milledge from the human resources department strolled into the room.

"C'mon! We've got a lot of shit to get through today," Jobs said to the six managers as they chatted and sauntered around the table. He began to quiz Bob Belleville, the bespectacled engineer, about a dispute between two of his staff.

"What are you going to do about George eventually?" Jobs asked.

"Eventually," Belleville replied in a mild tone, "I'll be dead."

"The only way we'll keep George," said Jobs ignoring the quip, "is to give him all the analog electronics. Unless he feels responsible for all analog electronics he'll go somewhere else. He'll get a great job offer to run engineering in some start-up."

Belleville predicted that any such promotion would upset Hap Horn, another engineer who was working on a troublesome disk drive.

"If Hap blackmails you and says he'll quit," Jobs said, "you go by him. Once Hap gets off the critical path you ought to do it."

"We need to finish this discussion off line," Belleville said demurely.

Turning his attention to the long agenda, Jobs fretted about the production of instruction manuals. Activity in the publications department served as a rough barometer of progress since it monitored conditions between two fronts. One was formed by the gusty tinkering of the lab bench while the other loomed in the shape of the implacable introduction date.

"I see this stuff slipping and slipping out of pubs," Jobs said turning to Michael Murray, the marketing manager. "They're doing a great job but they're not getting anything done. Get on top of it." Murray nodded.

Jobs worked his way farther around the table and addressed Matt Carter, who was responsible for manufacturing the computer and monitoring progress at Apple's factory near Dallas. "Can I suggest something?" Jobs said. He didn't wait for a reply and his supplicatory tone evaporated. "Your group doesn't interact with marketing or engineering. They're not back in the lab. They've got to get into the spirit of Mac. Introduce them to everyone. You've got to push 'em into interaction."

"I'm taking a party to Dallas," Carter grinned. "So that they can interact the shit out of each other."

Jobs abruptly changed the discussion to the growth of the division. Recruiting new people was a perennial feature of life at Mac and gobbled up much of the time of its senior managers. Jobs glanced at a sheet of paper and said: "We had forty-six people last month."

"We've got sixty today," corrected Vicki Milledge, the woman from human resources.

"God! Wow! We're really cracking," said Jobs.

"There's been a whole trail of people through here," Michael Murray observed and mentioned a candidate from Xerox. "She's in the process of resigning from Xerox which takes much longer than interviewing at Apple."

"When's Rizzo going to let you know?" asked Jobs, referring to a candidate for the same position.

"He's procrastinating," said Murray.

"I'd pick Rizzo," said Jobs. "He'll get into the trenches faster. Get clear in your mind who you want."

Murray dropped the name of a woman who was working for a venture-capital firm but had indicated she would take a $40,000 drop in salary to work at Apple.

"Is she beautiful and single?" Jobs inquired.

"She's not single," Murray chuckled.

"Are we interviewing for the Barbizon School of modeling?" Debi Coleman asked.

Jobs latched onto another name.

"He's doing planning," said Murray.

"He's a venture capitalist," retorted Jobs. "Sounds like a bullshit job to me."

"What about Steve Capps?" asked Jobs.

"He works at Lisa," Belleville remarked as though he wasn't about to embark on a raiding mission at another division of the company.

"I heard through the grapevine he wants to work over here," Jobs replied.

Matt Carter asked what his colleagues thought about a possible recruit for the manufacturing team, provoking Debi Coleman to venture, "He talked a good line. He asked the right questions."

"His batteries are too low. I didn't trust the guy," Jobs said and immediately suggested an alternative. "They'll like Duke a lot more. He's awake. He's more conservative, drives a two-eighty-Z and wears glasses."

Vicki Milledge chipped in that she wasn't allowed to have a secretary, or what at Apple was known as an "area associate."

"Why not?" Jobs demanded.

"Because of the budget," Milledge said.

"Screw 'em," Jobs retorted.

Pat Sharp, a woman with curly hair and spectacles, broached the subject of moving the division lock, stock, and barrel to a larger building. The Mac group was squeezed into one half of a single-story, red-tiled building, and some of its members worked in an annex. It was poised to move into another building on the opposite side of Cupertino's Bandley Drive, a road Apple had turned into a corporate alley. Apple's presence along the road was so pronounced that the buildings were known by the order in which the company had occupied them rather than by street numbers. "I was wondering about the layout," Sharp ventured.

"I'm willing to spend a million bucks to fix up Bandley Three," Jobs announced. "We'll fix it up real nice and that's it. That's our final resting place. Put your energy into it. It's going to be laid out for one hundred people. I don't have any interest in running a division of more than a hundred and you're not interested in working with more than a hundred. There will be no trailers, no outhouses, no nothing. If Bob wants a new software guy, someone else will have to go."

"Can we put a weight room in or an exercise clinic?" asked Murray.

"No," Jobs said. "We'll have a few showers and that'll be it. Think about what you want," Jobs urged. "If the software or pubs people want private offices, now's the time to think about it."

He turned to a more immediate concern, a pilot build of two hundred Mac printed circuit boards that would be used for testing. Matt Carter reported the progress. "The kits are almost in. We're going to stuff 'em next week."

"Why don't we order another twenty-five boards?" Jobs asked.

Debi Coleman agreed. "Is there any logic behind the two hundred? Last time we built fifty and then we wanted seventy-five."

That reminder prompted Jobs to worry aloud that some of the existing printed circuit boards would fall into the hands of a competitor or one of the offshore firms that specialized in churning out low-priced, copycat computers. "I want to pull the first fifty and I want to trash them and have them compressed into a giant garbage compactor.

"When do we start building?"

He heard the date for the pilot-build start and was struck by another thought.

"What about beer busts?" he asked, referring to a recent party. "Do you want any more like that?" He paused briefly: "When's our next party?"

"Christmas," said Murray.

"That's in January because everybody's so busy," said Jobs. "What about early November? What about a rock 'n' roll party? We've just had a square dance. Rock 'n' roll. Square dance. That's the universe. We'll have a Halloween rock 'n' roll dance."

Carter told his colleagues that he was about to depart on a trip to the Far East to inspect possible parts suppliers and had already begun to place orders. Jobs exhaled at the news.

"This is like a train starting up that takes a quarter of a mile to stop and we haven't even got the track laid." He paused and turned to Carter and Belleville. "We've got to really test the main logic board. We've got to test hot and cold." He slapped the table. "Details. Details. Details. There's a lot more money in the digital board than the analog board. If we're going to have a fuck-up let's have it in the digital board."

"We're really in trouble with the analog board," Carter countered. "Right now we're being told it'll be ready in forty-five days but we've yet to see diddly squat. We kicked 'em in the butt and they said they want ninety days. They're going to have to bust ass even more than they think." Carter returned to the need to place orders for parts and Jobs mentioned two suppliers: "I like Samsung better than Aztec. Can we negotiate with them?"

"We cannot take the risk," said Carter. "We've got to give them both big incentives."

The group moved on to consider the possible pricing of the computer. For some months the general aim had been to sell the computer for $1,995. Jobs wanted to be assured by the financial controller, that it would still meet Apple's profit targets if it was priced at $1,495. Coleman, who had been considering what effect changes in price might have on sales volume, started to draw a graph and curves on a blackboard. Jobs watched for a moment, listened to Coleman as she explained her diagram, and said, "We could pull numbers out of our ass and do anything. Any curve is total crap. If you believe it you're being fooled."

"We could print it out on a blotter in color and it doesn't mean a thing," Murray echoed.

Jobs had a mischievous idea about how to test the effect of a $500 difference in price. "We should do some test marketing. We should drop the price in L.A. and raise the price in Seattle and hope the dealers don't talk to each other." He started to explain the conclusions of a task force Apple had established to set guidelines for building prices from profit targets: "There were eighteen million marketing and finance people who didn't know what the fuck they were doing. We're always going to make judgments and a lot of it is unknowable. So we just ended up with a rule of thumb for the rate of return we want." He turned to Coleman and his voice rose half an octave. "Don't drive us into the land of assholes with graphs. The last thing we want is people trying to out-Visicalc one another."

Murray began to complain that whatever the price, Apple was not allocating anywhere near enough money to launch Mac. "If we were Kodak or Polaroid we'd have a giant pot of money to launch products." Jobs played devil's advocate and pretended he was in charge of the division selling Apple IIs and IIIs. "Let me put on another hat and play PCS manager. The only way I'm going to sell more Apple IIs is to merchandise the hell out of it. I don't have a hot product. I don't get free editorial. I don't get the cover of *Byte*."

"I'm trading futures," Murray said.

"I'm paying the light bills," Jobs said.

There was some talk of a sales meeting in Acapulco for Apple's dealers and of a quarterly gathering of four hundred Apple managers at which Jobs was to give a report on progress with Mac. They sorted out which members of the Mac division should attend the two-day meeting. Then Vicki Milledge laughed nervously. She surveyed her boss and reported that all the managers, apart from Jobs, had given her performance reviews on their staffs.

"I hate doing reviews. I like salary increases," Jobs explained.

"Into every good life some rain must fall," Matt Carter said consolingly.

HONEY AND NUTS

When Steven Jobs started to sift through university brochures he showed that he was capable of both originality and obstinacy. He approached the task with all the stubbornness he had previously used to persuade his parents to move to Los Altos. Jobs had spent enough time hanging around the colleges that his older friends attended to conclude they were unsuitable. He thought that Berkeley, with its enormous lecture theaters, was a degree mill and he considered Stanford too staid. Eventually, after visiting a friend who was attending Reed College, a small, liberal, and expensive university in Portland, Oregon, Jobs decided he wanted to try life in the Pacific Northwest.

He returned from a tour of inspection and broke the news at home. Paul Jobs, horrified by the prospect of enormous tuition bills, remembered the gist of the discussion: "We tried to talk him out of it." Clara Jobs had a blunter recollection: "Steve said that was the only college he wanted to go to and if he couldn't go there he didn't want to go anywhere." So the senior Jobses buckled to some emotional blackmail, tucked their son into the back of their car, drove him to Reed, and said their farewells on a deserted campus a few days before the start of the 1972 school year. The parting was etched on Steven Jobs's memory. "It wasn't real cordial. I sort of said 'Well, thanks, 'bye.' I didn't even want the buildings to see that my parents were there. I didn't even want parents at that time. I just wanted to be like an orphan from Kentucky who had bummed around the country hopping freight trains for years. I just wanted to find out what life was all about."

Portland's natural setting provided enough distractions to give some sense of life's sensations. The weather was more melancholy than along the southern reaches of the San Francisco Peninsula but there were other consolations. There was the remote splendor of Mount Hood for backpacking, the thunderous vigor of the Columbia River Gorge for hitchhiking, and desolate beaches along the Oregon coastline where redwoods perched on the edge of cliffs. For students contemplating their new surroundings Reed College presented a deceptive face. Its Victorian Gothic buildings—complete with slate roofs, ivy, copper gutters, and window boxes—had bay windows that overlooked spacious gardens. It seemed like a drizzly home for Portland's cafe society, a movable stage for poets, filmmakers, artists, and free spirits.

Some former Reed students had started The Rainbow Farm, which became one of the regional keystones of the hippie movement, and ripples from the psychedelic tone of the late sixties flowed through the campus. Reed was a regular stopping point for a caravan of lecturers like author Ken Kesey, poet Allen Ginsberg and the very guru of "Turn on, tune in, drop out," Timothy Leary. But behind the graceful air and dreamy throwback to Parisian life in the twenties was an ironclad curriculum with long, compulsory reading lists. The three hundred or so students who enrolled in each class found the large flock of professors kept a close watch on their progress and the college tolerated their quirks only if they coped with strenuous academic standards. During the early seventies about a third of each class failed to return for their junior or senior years after discovering that, at Reed, liberal was spelled with a capital L.

Jobs found an eclectic collection of students and, for the first time in his life, started to bump into people from other parts of the country. Since Reed gave scholarships to a goodly sprinkling of minorities, Jobs had his first taste of cosmopolitan flavors. One of his classmates, Elizabeth Holmes, commented, "In the early seventies Reed was a campus of loners and freaks." Even against that colorful backdrop Jobs managed to stand out and his picture was missing from the booklet of freshman profiles distributed to the new arrivals. Among the other members of the freshman class was Daniel Kottke. A bony, bearded teenager with a gentle way of speaking and soft brown hair, Kottke had grown up in an affluent New York suburb, won a National Merit Scholarship and turned to Reed after being rejected by Harvard. He was quiet, slightly lethargic, had a disdain for material possessions, and liked to play the piano. Within a few months he began to consider Jobs his closest male companion. "It didn't seem like he had too many other friends."

Another of Jobs's friends was one of the most visible students on campus. Robert Friedland, who was several years older than Jobs, paraded about the campus dressed in Indian robes while campaigning for the student presidency. His campaign theme was blunt. He was running for the post to help erase the stigma of a two-year jail sentence for what was, at the time, the largest LSD bust east of the Mississippi. Friedland, a slight smooth talker, had rubbed up against the Nixon administration's determination to clean LSD off the tongue of America and made the mistake of informing the judge at his trial that he shouldn't pass sentence without trying the drug. The judge decided he didn't need to enhance his mind to settle on a punishment and gave Friedland a two-year sentence for manufacturing and distributing thirty thousand tablets of LSD. Eventually Friedland was paroled and enrolled at Reed.

Jobs, who was trying to raise some money by selling his IBM electric typewriter, first met Friedland in potentially embarrassing circumstances. He arrived with his typewriter in Friedland's room to discover that the chief occupant was busy making love to his girl friend. Friedland wasn't flustered and invited Jobs to sit down and wait. Jobs sat and watched. "He wasn't intimidated at all. I thought, 'This is kind of far out. My mother and father would never do this.'"

For Jobs, Friedland quickly became an important figure, a mentor and surrogate elder brother. "Robert was the first person I met who was really very firmly convinced that the phenomenon of enlightenment existed. I was very impressed by that and very curious about it." For his part Friedland recalled that Jobs was one of the youngest students at Reed. "He was always walking about barefoot. He was one of the freaks on the campus. The thing that struck me was his intensity. Whatever he was interested in he would generally carry to an irrational extreme. He wasn't a rapper. One of his numbers was to stare at the person he was talking to. He would stare into their fucking eyeballs, ask some question, and would want a response without the other person averting their eyes."

Jobs's sense of the romantic prompted him to enroll in a dance class where he hoped, like so many college students, that he would find true love. Instead, he began to discover that despite the attractions of ballet, his ideas about education certainly didn't coincide with a curriculum that for the first semester prescribed heavy doses of *The Iliad* and *The Peloponnesian Wars*. By the end of 1972, Jobs had discovered plenty of other diversions. There were the emotional calls of college life such as the time he rushed a pal who tried to commit suicide to the local hospital, the startling, unpredictable tastes of women, and pressure from his parents who were upset at the idea they were underwriting a bohemian life. Jobs's academic work suffered and at the end of his first semester he dropped out in spirit if not in body. For the following six months he stayed in the dormitory, shuffling among the rooms deserted by other malcontents.

At Reed the interest in political activism that was typical of the late sixties had been softened into a spiritual activism slightly reminiscent of movements that had flourished around Aldous Huxley in the 1920s. Some of the students were interested in pure philosophy and the disconcerting questions that are unanswerable—about the meaning of life and the truth of existence: What are we? Why are we here? What are we doing? What are the real values of human life? The appeals to a higher consciousness, to "working on yourself," struck a chord. There was talk of karma and trips and the intellectual excursions fueled experiments with diets and drugs. Jack Dudman, Reed's dean of students, spent hours talking with Jobs. "He had a very inquiring mind that was enormously attractive. You wouldn't get away with bland statements. He refused to accept automatically received truths and he wanted to examine everything himself."

Jobs and Kottke suggested books to one another and gradually read their way through the standard works of the time: *Autobiography of a Yogi, Cosmic Consciousness, Cutting Through*

Spiritual Materialism, Meditation in Action. The most influential, however, was *Zen Mind, Beginner's Mind.* Jobs took to spending time in the college library reading Buddhist literature and became attracted by Zen Buddhism. "It placed value on experience versus intellectual understanding. I saw a lot of people contemplating things but it didn't seem to lead too many places. I got very interested in people who had discovered something more significant than an intellectual, abstract understanding." He also started to believe that intuition formed a higher state of intellect and meditated in a crawl space above Kottke's bedroom, which was furnished with incense and a dhurrie rug.

The pair also hitchhiked to the Hare Krishna temple in Portland for free Sunday night vegetable-curry dinners. On one occasion Kottke and Jobs decided to stay overnight at the Krishna house and were awakened in the early morning and sent out into a suburban Portland neighborhood to pick flowers from private gardens to decorate the shrine of Lord Krishna.

After moving out of the dorms at the end of his first year, Jobs rented an upgraded coachhouse for twenty-five dollars a month in a well-upholstered Portland suburb that rubbed up against Reed. He was secretive about aspects of his life, and even his closest college friends had no idea that Wozniak, who made occasional visits, sold blue boxes to a couple of Reed students who were caught using the device in a telephone booth.

Strapped for cash, Jobs borrowed some money from a fund the college kept for just such contingencies and found a job maintaining electronic equipment used by the psychology department for animal-behavior experiments. Ron Fial, an assistant professor who looked after the lab and tinkered with electronics, was impressed by Jobs and the knowledge he brought from California. "He was very good. He often didn't want to just fix something. He often ended up bringing in something that was completely redesigned."

Though he fixed fish tanks and helped design better mouse-traps, Jobs was still pressed for money. His rented room was unheated and when he sat there throwing I Ching he was always dressed in a thick down jacket. For several weeks he lived on a thrice-daily diet of a porridge made from Roman Meal cereal and milk that he lifted from the college cafeteria. Jobs reckoned that one box of the cereal would sustain him for a week. "After three months of Roman Meal I was just going out of my gourd."

To keep some flesh on his friend, Kottke and his girl friend provided Jobs with his only substantial meals. The trio jointly labeled cafeteria food Meat by Monsanto and became vegetarians. They paraded through the infinite varieties of brown rice, banana bread, and oatmeal bread suggested by vegetarian and macrobiotic cookbooks. Through a combination of circumstance and curiosity, Jobs and his friends linked their intellectual wandering and interests in mysticism with physical experiments. They were interested in stimulating fresh areas of the mind and rejuvenating the body and experimented with different drugs and diets. Drugs were used more for metaphysical reasons than for recreational purposes and they linked diets with other aspects of life.

Jobs became interested in the writings of Arnold Ehret, a nineteenth-century Prussian who attached his name to such books as *The Mucusless Diet Healing System* and *Rational Fasting*. Jobs was intrigued by Ehret's assertion that diet was the cornerstone of physical, mental, and spiritual rejuvenation and that an accumulation of mucus and other body wastes were sure to be ruinous. Ehret asserted, with all the confidence of an Archimedes, that $V = P - O$, which in layman's language meant *vitality* equals *power minus obstruction*. He taught that mental illness was caused by "gas pressure on the brain," which could be cured by fasting, and that meat, alcohol, fat, bread, potatoes, rice, and milk were to be avoided at all costs. He even prescribed special "mucus eliminators" like combinations of figs, nuts and green onions, or grated horseradish and honey.

Jobs started to examine the diets of the higher primates and even investigated their bone structure. Years afterward he still clung to his convictions. "I believe that man is a fruitarian. I got into it in my typically nutso way." For a time Jobs lectured his friends on the dangers of bagels, insisting they were filled with mucus, and started to lunch on carrot salads. Friedland recalled, "The whole world revolved around the elimination of mucus." Like Ehret, who boasted that he once lived off a fruit diet for two years, Jobs experimented with fasts. He carefully worked his way from fasts that lasted a couple of days to ones that stretched for a couple of weeks. He watched his skin turn different colors as a result of the fasting, learned how to break fasts with plenty of roughage and water, became convinced that man was a fruitarian and was enthusiastic about the results of these experiments: "After a few days you start to feel great. After a week you start to feel fantastic. You get a ton of vitality from not having to digest all this food. I was in great shape. I felt I could get up and walk to San Francisco anytime I wanted." His friend Elizabeth Holmes noticed the extent of Jobs's devotion. "When he started crusading about something he could be overbearing."

Others led their own crusades, and Robert Friedland became the disciple of one that tied diet, drugs, and philosophy together. When he and Jobs meditated they were accompanied by the customary sitar music, surrounded by incense, and overlooked by a photograph of a tubby man with jug ears and gray bristles who was wrapped in a plaid blanket. The pudgy figure was Neem Karolie Baba, an Indian guru, celebrated in *Be Here Now,* Richard Alpert's popular account of the changes he encountered while he journeyed from an American academic life to quiet contemplation in a remote part of India. Friedland found the lure irresistible and spent the summer of 1973 in India listening to Neem Karolie Baba, and returned with a chattering knapsack of tales for his younger friends. He regaled them with tales of meditation sessions inside rings of fires and baths in ice-cold rivers, and described "an electric charged atmosphere of love."

At the beginning of 1974 Jobs decided that an electronics company might supply the means to reach the electric-charged atmosphere of love. He broke away from the fringes of Reed College, returned to his parents' home in Los Altos, and began to look for a job. He wasn't seeking anything grand or permanent but just something that would allow him to stash away enough money for a trip to India. One morning, browsing through the classified advertisements in the *San Jose Mercury,* he spotted an opening for a video-game designer at Atari. He knew nothing about the young company but had spent many quarters on Pong, the monotonic simulation of table tennis that Atari was operating in pool halls, bars, pinball arcades, and bowling alleys.

Jobs's arrival in Atari's Sunnyvale lobby was monitored by an observant receptionist. According to Al Alcorn, the chief engineer,

"The receptionist said, 'We've got this kid in the lobby. He's either a crackpot or he's got something.' He looked pretty grubby. He was talking a mile a minute and claimed to be working on the HP thirty-five calculator. He said he could turn the HP forty-five into a stopwatch. He implied he was working for HP. I was impressed, said 'Hey, fine,' and didn't bother to check." Alcorn, a jovial, rotund man, offered Jobs a position as a technician for five dollars an hour. Jobs, for whom stock options and some of the other benefits offered by Silicon Valley companies were mysteries, accepted. Some of his friends were surprised that he managed to get on the payroll. Bill Fernandez, for one, thought Jobs lacked the qualifications. "He must have been a good salesman. I didn't really think that Jobs was that hot."

Jobs became one of Atari's first fifty employees and had his first prolonged taste of corporate life in a company where a succession of novel ideas managed to withstand any number of managerial torpedoes. The company was started and dominated by Nolan Bushnell, son of a Utah cement contractor whose first business coup took place at the University of Utah where he sold ink blotters framed by advertisements. In 1972, at age twenty-nine, Bushnell introduced his first video game. Computer Space appealed to engineers but was too complicated for the general public.

As the game failed Bushnell decided to start his own business to make video games and operate pinball machines. He called the company, which he based in a rented garage space, Syzygy, for no better reason than it was the last word in the dictionary that began with the letter *S*. Within weeks Bushnell discovered that Syzygy had been used by another firm and so he changed the name to Atari (taken from the Japanese game Go and roughly equivalent in meaning to *check*) but early advertisements read FROM ATARI INC., SYZYGY ENGINEERED.

Bushnell viewed business as "a type of war" and employed pinches of diplomacy and charm, cunning and force to cajole his employees and bamboozle the competition. Dressed in sharp suits, flowery shirts, and polka-dot ties, he became Atari's six-foot-four-inch juju man. "It was life in the fast lane with Nolan," one of the founders recalled. "He always wanted everything at once." To persuade Chief Engineer Alcorn to design Pong, Bushnell pretended it had been ordered by General Electric. "I'd never even had any negotiations with General Electric," Bushnell recalled, "but I wanted to test out Al's skills." Nobody, let alone Bushnell, placed any great hopes in Pong. "I didn't perceive it as a big marketable item."

The first game, with a coin box bolted to the outside, was placed in Andy Capp's Cavern, a popular Sunnyvale pool parlor. Almost immediately it became clear that the electronic game was making more than the bar's pinball machines. A few days after it was installed, the rush of quarters backed up and jammed the coin box and within weeks people wanting to play Pong lined up outside the bar.

While Pong came to enjoy popular success, the people who mattered treated the company with suspicion. Some bankers thought it was an offshoot of the Mafia. Suppliers were leery about extending credit to a firm that looked as if it might take to the air any day. To quell complaints, Bushnell started an offshoot, Kee Games, which he furnished with designers, managers, and plans from Atari. According to Bushnell, the new company was formed to produce a parallel line of games and to sop up the money that might have flowed to potential competitors. A series of contrived press releases charted the formation of Kee Games, and Bushnell later chortled, with something bordering on contempt, "There are just so many ways you can use the press for strategic advantage." When Kee Games began to prosper and there were rumors that it wanted to shrug off ties with Atari, Bushnell issued a bland statement that read "We are happy that the people at Kee and Atari have been able to resolve the problems that led to the original split."

Bushnell's control of the press was more refined than his control of the company. Many of his early employees were eager to dispense with routine corporate drudgery like memos and staff meetings. Attracted by the unconventional, Bushnell fueled brainstorming sessions with marijuana and made no secret of his belief that drugs and alcohol helped spark ideas. Recruitment was equally unpredictable. One candidate was startled when Bushnell strolled into the room, posed one question—"Are you a spy for Bally?"—and then disappeared, satisfied he wasn't about to hire a quisling. Easily bored by daily chores, Bushnell hired his brother-in-law, a psychiatrist, to manage the company. Financial controls were so lax that a three-month supply of one game, Trak Ten, was virtually given away before an accountant discovered that it was being sold for $100 less than it cost to build. Bushnell admitted that "we wrote contracts guys were able to weasel out of." He also was reluctant to cede control to a strong board of directors and made sure he always owned more than half the outstanding shares.

Nevertheless, during its first three years Atari managed to sell $13 million worth of video games and capitalized on the popularity of Pong by selling variants that included Dr. Pong, a wood-grained version aimed at physicians, dentists, and hospitals, and Puppy Pong, which was clad in a Formica doghouse. On the rush of its early success Atari built a large factory only to find there weren't enough orders to keep it busy. More money disappeared when Bushnell attempted to start a manufacturing offshoot in Japan. Life wasn't made any easier by seasonal swings, the nationwide recession, a shortage of venture capital or the popular perception that a leisure business was a frivolous enterprise.

On several occasions, especially between the spring and fall of 1974, when Atari's future rested on the success of Gran Trak, a driving game, the company came within seven days of bankruptcy. At lunch during one savage week Bushnell broke down in tears thinking all was lost. Suppliers refused to deliver parts and creditors camped out in the hallway. The tempestuous backdrop didn't escape Atari's employees. Ron Wayne, a one-time employee, said, "Working at Atari was like driving with a rubber steering wheel." Steve Jobs formed his own impressions of a company that was hardly a model for the business textbooks. "It was always chaos. It was not a well-run company."

But for all the thrills and spills, most of the Atari employees were conservative and Jobs was considered peculiar. He poked his nose into other engineers' business and made no secret of his disdain. Bushnell recalled that Jobs "regularly told a lot of the other guys they were dumb shits," and Jobs himself said, "Some of their engineers were not very good and I was better than most of them. The only reason I shone was that everyone else was so bad. I wasn't really an engineer at all." Yet Jobs's appearance, his lunches of yogurt, his strict adherence to the mucusless diet, and his belief that a fruit diet meant that he could go without showers, were considered nonconformist. By his own admission Jobs was oblivious to the animosity he stirred up. Finally, to keep peace in the lab, Alcorn arranged for Jobs to work after hours and late at night. "The engineers didn't like him. He smelled funny."

Despite his lack of formal electronic training, Jobs quickly bridged the gap between being a technician and being an engineer. One of his early tasks was to add refinements to a game called Touch Me, which sported bulbous rubber suckers. Working within the discipline of specified boundaries Jobs tailored the performance of the chips to what was wanted on the screen. He understood the chips' subtleties, plotted out a new design, and made substantial improvements to the game. Wozniak admired Jobs's work. "He did the creative stuff. He realized how he could build the same thing a lot simpler and better. It was engineering."

When Jobs decided to accompany his college friend Dan Kottke to India and see the topography and intellectual scenery for some of Robert Friedland's elaborate tales, he asked Alcorn to supply the air fare. Alcorn gave the request a blunt reception. "Bullshit, I'm not giving you any money to go see the guru." The pair arrived at a convenient compromise. Some games Atari had shipped to West Germany were causing interference on television sets, and the German engineers were unable to solve the problem. Alcorn gave Jobs a crash course in ground loops and agreed to pay his air fare to Europe, ordering him to "say hi to the guru for me."

Jobs's arrival in Europe caused some consternation among the Germans, who cabled Alcorn wondering what he had dispatched. For his part Jobs (distressed that he couldn't find the German word for *vegetarian*) adroitly applied the curative to Atari's troublesome machines.

In the telling, Jobs and Kottke's trip to India seems crammed with the snapshots of young innocents abroad, faintly credulous Westerners caught in the blank light of ashrams, swamis, and sadhus. Kottke felt "the trip was a kind of ascetic pilgrimage except we didn't know where we were going." Before Kottke arrived, Jobs spent a few weeks by himself, and in succeeding

years, they were cloaked in surrealistic images. He attended the
Kumbhmela, a large religious festival that takes place every twelfth
year in Hardwar in north central India. "Seven million people,"
Jobs observed, "in a town the size of Los Gatos." He saw priests
emerge from the river, watched the flames of funeral pyres and
dead bodies floating down the Ganges. He met a Parisian fashion
designer at an ashram, and a guru who, impressed by the smoothness of his skin, dragged him up a hillside and shaved his head.
He also spent a nervous night in an abandoned temple sitting near
a fire which flickered around a trident. His only companion was a
Shivite, with matted hair and a body covered in ashes, who puffed
on a chillum until dawn.

Dressed in light, white cotton pants and vests, Kottke and
Jobs used New Delhi as their base. Nightly walks took them
through shantytowns of corrugated iron and cracked packing
cases, past cows eating garbage and people sleeping on cots on
the sidewalks. Their sorties from Delhi were made on buses with
worn shock absorbers and small metal seats, and they spent
several days trekking to see a number of yogis. They hiked along
dried riverbeds, carrying water bottles, their feet rubbed raw
by sandals. Enticed by the promise of Tibet they journeyed into
the foothills of the Himalayas but wound up at the old spa
town of Menali, where they both contracted scabies from greasy
bedsheets.

Though Neem Kardie Baba and his plaid blanket had
been consumed by a spectacular funeral pyre, Jobs and Kottke
dutifully trooped to Kainchi. They strolled among the gaudy
icons and plastic Krishnas and found the ashram perverted by
musicians who were being paid to perform devotional chants.
Despite the changes, the pair stayed in Kainchi for about a
month and rented a one-room cement hut from a family who
ran a potato farm. It was convenient enough, allowed them
to read in peace and quiet, and had one other advantage:
It was close to a field of marijuana plants which they dried and
smoked. They also had rudimentary room service supplied by
the wife of the potato farmer who sold them water-buffalo
milk which she heated and stirred with sugar. On one occasion Jobs took issue with the way she watered down the milk.
Gestures bridged the language barrier and the woman wound
up denouncing Jobs as a criminal. At the Kainchi market where

merchants sold vegetables from donkey carts, Jobs also drove a hard bargain, Kottke recalled. "He looked at prices elsewhere, found out the real price, and haggled. He didn't want to get ripped off."

The hot, uncomfortable summer made Jobs question many of the illusions he had nursed about India. He found India far poorer than he had imagined and was struck by the incongruity between the country's condition and its airs of holiness. He spotted a crucial lesson wrapped up in the blur of yogis and yellow health cards, darshan and pranas, sadhus and puja tables. "We weren't going to find a place where we could go for a month to be enlightened. It was one of the first times I started thinking that maybe Thomas Edison did a lot more to improve the world than Karl Marx and Neem Karolie Baba put together."

By the time Jobs returned to California he was thinner, thanks to a bout of dysentery, had closely cropped hair, and was dressed in an Indian attire that was a millennium away from Pong and oscilloscopes. Nancy Rogers remembered: "He was so weird when he got back. He was trying to live more detached and spiritually. He would look at me with his eyes wide apart and stare and wouldn't blink. He would invite me over to eat and then play guru. He would come over and look at all the little gifts he had given me and ask, 'Where did you get this?' It was as if he was breaking all ties."

Jobs's return from India in the fall of 1974 also marked the start of an eighteen-month period during which he played hopscotch. He flitted between Atari and the crumbling edges of consumer electronics and a three-hundred acre Oregon farm that Robert Friedland was managing for a wealthy relative. But first he headed north to an old hotel in Eugene, Oregon, that a student of the California psychiatrist Arthur Janov had converted into the Oregon Feeling Center. Jobs, who had read Janov's best seller *Primal Scream,* paid a thousand dollars and enrolled in a twelve-week course of therapy that was supposed to provide solutions to deeply rooted problems. Janov and his students at the Oregon Feeling Center seemed to be offering an emotional spring cleaning. "Feeling is what this therapy is all about. . . . We are after the feelings which say 'Daddy, be nice. Mama, I need you.'"

Jobs's curiosity was piqued. "It seemed like such an interesting thing. You could gain some insight into your life and experience some new realm of feeling. This was not something to think about. This was something to actually go do: to close your eyes, hold your breath, jump in and come out the other end more insightful."

For Jobs Janov's writings appeared to hold the key for an immensely personal quest. As he turned twenty, the question of his adoption and the whereabouts of his natural parents came to assume more prominence. Nancy Rogers recalled: "He was sometimes in tears to see his mother." Robert Friedland had his own interpretation: "Steve had a very profound desire to know his physical parents so he could better know himself." Questions about his natural parents spawned hours of private speculation. His friends gently teased him that he was probably Armenian or Syrian. Jobs began an extensive search for his natural parents and learned a little about them. "Both were teaching at a university. My father was a visiting maths professor." Jobs reckoned that his adoption had at least one effect: "It made me feel a little bit more independent." After about three months in Eugene, Jobs's infatuation with Janov's work and methods dulled. "He offered a ready-made, button-down answer which turned out to be far too oversimplistic. It became obvious that it wasn't going to yield any great insight."

Disappointed by the ministrations of the Oregon Feeling Center, Jobs drifted back to California, rented a room in a house in Los Gatos, took to meditating for an hour at dawn, and started to work again at Atari. There he continued to ruffle feathers. Bushnell noticed the tensions Jobs created in the engineering laboratory and wound up appointing him to a casual position as a consultant. "It was a rescue of a would-be fire. I said, 'Hey, if you guys don't want him, I want him.'" Bushnell appreciated Jobs's sense of urgency. "When he wanted to do something, he'd give a schedule in terms of days and weeks, not months and years." Jobs again worked in the small hours and spent his time on a variety of different projects. Wozniak, meantime, had discovered video games and was a frequent visitor at Atari where he spent hours playing the video games that stood on the assembly line. He even spent several weeks designing and building his own version of

Pong and for the first time drew up a design that displayed images on a television screen.

Wozniak also helped Jobs after Bushnell decided he wanted a game that would let players destroy a wall of bricks with a bouncing ball. Bushnell offered Jobs a bonus plan, tying payment to the number of chips that were used in the design. With fewer chips, games were not only cheaper to manufacture but also usually more reliable. Jobs recruited help from Wozniak who thought "Steve was not quite capable of designing something that complex." The pair spent four consecutive nights working on the game with Wozniak designing and Jobs wiring the prototype.

Bushnell was impressed by the finished game and offered Wozniak a job at Atari anytime he wanted. However, Al Alcorn, who didn't discover that Wozniak had been involved with the game until years later, thought, "It was a brilliant design but it wasn't produceable because the technicians couldn't figure out how to make it work." The game was entirely redesigned before it was eventually released as Breakout.

Meanwhile, Jobs, who was anxious to flee to Oregon, discovered that it would take two weeks before he and Wozniak would receive the seven hundred dollars they had been promised. Jobs persisted and was given the cash on the same day and disappeared to Friedland's farm leaving the straitlaced Wozniak to nurse furtive thoughts. "I had no idea what they were doing." There was one other result of the press to complete Breakout: Both Wozniak and Jobs came down with mononucleosis.

Jobs first started to feel the symptoms when he arrived at the farm. Friedland had applied dollops of mysticism and evoked the notions of universal oneness and the highest concept of being when he named his spread All One Farm. He also gave his newborn son a Hindu name and took one for himself. ("He was calling himself Sita Ram Das but we called him Robert," Kottke said.) The farm's location was published in "The Spritual Community Guide" and it attracted a variety of drifters, psychedelic beggars, members of nearby Hare Krishna temples, and on one occasion, some patients from a mental hospital. For the caravan of a dozen or so regular visitors that included Jobs, the farm became the setting for daily dramas and crises. They converted chicken coops into crude flophouses and funneled well water toward a wood-burning sauna. When Jobs installed electricity in a barn so that it could be used as a wood-stove dealership, Friedland was surprised by his alacrity with conduits and wiring diagrams.

For the visitors to All One Farm the lure of the East gripped tight. They held meditation classes, had protracted debates about banning marijuana and other drugs and about the possibility of adopting the purest form of life. Insecticides and herbicides were banished from the pastures and vegetable patches where they built beehives, planted winter wheat, and touted the virtues of organic farming. They also used chain saws to trim and prune an apple orchard that was full of badly neglected Gravensteins. "Steve," said Friedland, "became one of the apple people." The fruit was pressed into cider and left out overnight on the stone porch where it turned into applejack.

Jobs was so deeply wound up with his dietary experiments that, on occasion, he ate dinners that he forced himself to throw up. Years later he considered that the farm provided "a real lesson in communal living. I spent one night sleeping under a table in the kitchen and in the middle of the night everybody came in an ripped off each other's food from the fridge." Jobs felt that he was becoming a cog in a rural conglomerate and was a trifle disillusioned with his friend. "Robert walks a very fine line between being a charismatic leader and a con man." Jobs was also upset with the general drift of life on All One Farm. "It started to get very materialistic. Everybody got the idea they were working very hard for Robert's farm and one by one started to leave. I got pretty sick of it and left."

BUCKETS OF NOISE

The end of the Menlo Park cul-de-sac looked like a sad used-car lot. Dented Volkswagen Beetles, sun-bleached vans and sagging Ford Pintos straddled the shoulders of the rough gravel road. The cars were parked at angles, squeezed up against a wall of ivy, drawn alongside a driveway where a couple of engines squatted on blocks, or left in front of an unpainted picket fence. Most of the drivers and passengers had either heard about or spotted an inconspicuous handbill pinned to notice boards at the Stanford University Computer Center, the Berkeley Computer Science Department, and the Whole Earth Truck Store in Menlo Park. The poster, which carried two headings: AMATEUR COMPUTER USERS GROUP AND HOMEBREW COMPUTER CLUB, fought for attention among appeals for roommates and lost cats. But the questions printed below provided some clues: "Are you building your own computer? Terminal? TV Typewriter? I/O device? Or some other digital black-magic box? Or are you buying time on a time-sharing service?"

Stephen Wozniak, Allen Baum, and thirty other hardware engineers, computer programmers, technicians, and parts suppliers were sufficiently intrigued by the notice to drive from Palo Alto, Los Altos, Cupertino, Sunnyvale, and San Jose up Interstates 280 and 101, or from Oakland and Berkeley across the Bay Bridge and through San Francisco, toward the shingled ranchhouse that belonged to Gordon French.

In the mouse-gray twilight of March 5, 1975, French and his friend Fred Moore were bustling about the garage. A computer programmer in his late thirties with a speckled beard and strong spectacles, French spent his days devising a record-keeping system for the Social Security department in Sunnyvale. Moore had a look of monkish austerity, with strands of thin brown hair tied into a ponytail, a pinched nose, and plastic front teeth. The two carted some chairs from the house and arranged them in a semicircle, covered the oil drips on the concrete floor with newspapers, and set a tape recorder, a couple of plates of cookies, and jugs of lemonade on a picnic table beside a door that led to a utility room.

French and Moore were casualties of disappointment. Both had belonged to the People's Computer Company, which was in the mid-seventies one of the more prominent outposts for computer hobbyists along the San Francisco Peninsula. It had been started by Robert Albrecht, an early apostle of the power of small computers, who wanted to help people, especially children, learn about computers and how to program in BASIC. The author of books such as *My Computer Likes Me* and *What to Do After You Hit Return,* Albrecht's main reason for starting the People's Computer Company (PCC) was to publish a tabloid newspaper. The paper was covered in doodles and drawings, poked fun at computers, and tried to remove the veils of mystery that surrounded the subject.

During the early seventies a small group of staff writers gathered at the PCC offices for weekly potluck dinners where they chatted about technology and computers. When, toward the end of 1974, Albrecht decided to stop the dinners and concentrate on his newspaper, Moore and French were left without the company of soulmates. To top things off, Moore felt he had been cheated out of the editor's job at PCC; he complained that "Bob Albrecht wanted to be the Chief Dragon of all alternative computer users" and suggested to his friend that they call a meeting for anybody interested in small computers.

For Moore the Homebrew Club was another alternative to add to the list of alternatives that he had been advocating for most of his adult life. A Berkeley student at the end of the fifties, he had helped abolish compulsory membership of the ROTC. In the mid-sixties he had gone on speaking tours for the Committee for Nonviolent Action, visiting college campuses and criss-crossing America in a car loaded with placards and brochures. He had served a two-year prison sentence for violating the selective service law and had been a single parent at a time when the term was an oddity. After Vietnam he started delving into alternative economics. He thought of work as a gift and preached against conventional economics, the value of money, the ownership of land, and toying with nature. He tried to build an Information Network centered around Menlo Park's Whole Earth Truck Store and stretching into the Peninsula towns. His byword was "Put your trust in people, not money," and he insisted on using slogans like "Wealth is the synergy of multi-interdependent relationships."

He maintained card catalogs listing people with an unusual reach of common interests. Along with conventional pastimes like auto repair, camping, theater, swimming, photography, and fishing, Moore also listed beads, biofeedback, burial, domes, garbage, hardware conspiracies, plumbing, massage, looms, venereal disease, and yurts. His index system listed phone numbers of people interested in electronics and computers and Moore himself had become familiar with the IBM 360 at the Stanford Medical Center where some terminals were made available to students and outsiders. For Moore the makers of large computers—most notably IBM—were as worthy of suspicion as New York banks, government agencies, monetarists, and oil drillers. So the idea for a Homebrew Club was one expression of broader interests: "There was no reason for computers to be as expensive as IBM's machines. I was just trying to promote the exchange of information on microcomputers."

Moore's kindly and woolly outlook was shared by others who strolled into Gordon French's garage. One was Lee Felsenstein who had grown up in Philadelphia and dropped out of Berkeley during the sixties to work as a reporter on fringe broadsheets like the *Berkeley Barb* and the *Berkeley Tribe*. Armed with a silvery tongue and quick mind Felsenstein had worked as an engineer at Ampex, had been rejected by Al Alcorn at Atari, and lived at

Resource One, a commune squatting in a resolute building in San Francisco's warehouse district. There, surrounded by loaves of banana bread and blocked sinks, he nursed an SDS 940, one of the more admired mainframe computers of the sixties. Felsenstein and others hoped that the obsolete computer, which had been inherited from the Stanford Research Institute, would come to form the keystone of what was called the Community Memory Project. He had written articles in periodicals like *Coevolution Quarterly* explaining how computers were "convivial tools" that could furnish "secondary information" and link people with common interests. By hooking terminals onto one large computer, Felsenstein and his cohorts hoped they could start an electronic bulletin board. Felsenstein had a fissiparous vision: "It could be a grass-roots network. It could be everywhere and nowhere."

Reality was far less grand and the electronic boundaries of Resource One extended only to Teletype machines installed at Leopold's Records and the Whole Earth Access Store in Berkeley. At the record store, musicians and others swapped information about concerts and trades. From time to time the Teletypes carried memorable questions like "Where could we find good bagels in the Bay Area?" which prompted the answer "An ex-bagel maker will teach you how to make bagels." At one time the list of items for sale even included a pair of Nubian goats. Amusement aside, democratic impulses were restrained by the limitations of the technology. It was easier to make a telephone call, scan a notice board or place a classified ad in a newspaper than it was to use the slow, clattering Teletypes. The Community Memory Project was one of those well-meaning ideas that foundered because it was ahead of its time. So for Felsenstein, as for Fred Moore, computers were a refinement for some aspects of the underground politics of the sixties.

Around the time of the first Homebrew Club meeting, Felsenstein was talking about capitalizing on some of the advances in electronics to help make life easier for the sort of people who wanted to find Nubian goats. He wanted to design a small machine that he called The Tom Swift Terminal to replace the cumbersome Teletype machines. It was that precise issue—the world being opened by enormous advances in electronics—that formed the main topic of conversation in Gordon French's garage.

The scale of change was made apparent when one member demonstrated a new computer called the Altair 8800. Hailed on the cover of the January 1975 issue of *Popular Electronics* ("The World's Largest Selling Electronics Magazine") as a "Project Breakthrough" and the "World's First Minicomputer Kit to Rival Commercial Models," the Altair kit sold for $375, was about the size of an orange crate, and had some switches and lights on a metal front panel. The computer was made by MITS, a small company headquartered in Albuquerque whose initials, which stood for Micro Instrumentation and Telemetry Systems, revealed something of its original purpose. It had been started in 1969 to make and sell guidance equipment for model rockets.

The remarkable feature of the Altair was not the metal case, or the rows of switches and lights on the front panel, or the enthusiasm of *Popular Electronics,* or that it came from Albuquerque. Rather, it was one electronic component that lay inside: a semiconductor chip mounted on a piece of inch-long black plastic and marked in tiny lettering INTEL 8080. The chip, which was no larger than the numbers 8080 as they appear on this page, contained the central processing unit of a computer and was the most notable example of what the semiconductor companies had taken to calling a microprocessor.

The conceptual framework for the microprocessor corresponded with the ideas that lay behind all digital electronic computers produced after World War II. The Electronic Numerical Integrator and Computer, IBM's 1130, Varian's 620i, Digital Equipment's PDP-8 and Data General's Nova all used the same principles as the Intel 8080. The only difference was size. The thirty-ton ENIAC with its eighteen thousand vacuum tubes was less powerful than the Intel 8080 which, with its five thousand transistors, could be swallowed. The central processing units of computers like the Data General Nova had been composed of dozens of chips, each of which was designed to perform a limited task. Chips like the 8080 approached the power of some of the early minicomputers but freed engineers from the tiresome task of ensuring solid connections along the hundreds of solder traces that ran between the chips.

The 8080 was the third microprocessor produced by Intel, a semiconductor company founded in Santa Clara in 1969, whose name was a contraction of Integrated Electronics. Intel's first microprocessor, the 4004, was part of a set of chips designed to control a desk-top calculator. Though the company had advertised the 4004 as introducing "a new era of integrated electronics," its portentous content had been difficult to appreciate. Under a microscope the patterns on the 4004 looked like a busy suburban road map. Yet the microprocessor, dozens of which were etched on a single wafer of silicon, were a more significant advance in the techniques of mass production than Henry Ford's moving assembly line.

The infinite flexibility of the microprocessor, which could be programmed to perform any number of tasks, had been accompanied by similarly prodigious advances in another area of semiconductor technology—memory chips. Computer programs, composed of millions of 1s and 0s that had, until the late sixties, been stored in bulky core memories could now be stored on chips. This made it cheaper and easier to write programs. Microprocessors could be connected to two sorts of memory chip. They could read programs stored on chips called ROMs and they could read and change programs written on a more complicated chip called a RAM. Because the microprocessor could be programmed to perform dozens of tasks, it reduced the cost of anything that required mechanical parts while simultaneously increasing its value.

The Homebrew Club members were, understandably, more interested in the practical applications of microprocessors than in the history of mass production. Most of them knew about a small computer kit, the Mark 8, that had been built around Intel's second microprocessor, the 8008. That microprocessor had prompted a Southern California schoolteacher to publish the "Micro-8 Newsletter" whose primary purpose was to keep hobbyists abreast of programs written for the 8008. But by the spring of 1975 the 8080 had become the center of interest. It was twenty times as powerful as the 4004 and could handle eight bits (rather than four bits) at a time. Unlike the 8008 which needed about twenty other chips to make it useful, the 8080 could manage with six peripheral chips. It could also be hooked to 65K bytes of memory compared to the 4K bytes of the 4004.

One of the Homebrew members revealed that he had driven all the way from California to New Mexico just to take delivery of his Altair. But the computer that was eyed with curiosity in French's garage didn't do much: It sat on the table with its lights flashing. Even for diehard tinkerers and hobbyists the Altair was a daunting proposition. The basic computer needed attachments like a Teletype machine or a television screen, extra boards of memory chips, and programs before it would do anything dimly amusing. Those attachments pushed the price toward $3,000. Meanwhile, the owner needed enough patience and skill to plow through pages of arcane instructions, sort components from plastic bags, test the chips, wield a soldering iron, and deal with problems like a chunky power supply that was prone to overheat.

At the first Homebrew meeting the members spent some time speculating on what microcomputers might be used for. They seemed to recognize—albeit by instinct rather than science—the implications of giving computing power to individuals. Some ventured that microcomputers would be used for text editing and by businesses. Others thought they could be used to control heating systems, automobile engines, burglar alarms and lawn sprinklers, play games, make music, control small robots and, of course, form neighborhood memory networks. Their cloudy crystal balls revealed more spirited visions than those of the semiconductor companies. There, most of the professional marketing men believed that microcomputers would be used to control machines like engines, elevators, and domestic appliances.

When he compiled the first Homebrew newsletter, Fred Moore had to resort to the implacable foe. Typed on an IBM composer during the middle of the night at the Whole Earth Truck Store, the two-page letter contained a summary of the first meeting which Moore believed revealed "a spontaneous spirit of sharing." Moore also included the addresses and interests of the club's first members. The newsletter disclosed that Stephen Wozniak liked "video games, pay movies for hotels, scientific calculator design, TV terminal design."

Whether because of Moore's newsletter, the arrival of the Altair, or the huge advances in semiconductor design, the Homebrew Club grew like a chain letter or a pyramid club. Within eight months the membership had risen to about three hundred, and for a time, the Homebrew members became a band of vagrants holding their fortnightly meetings in schoolrooms or at Stanford's Artificial Intelligence Laboratory.

As the club grew it attracted all sorts from all the towns up and down the Peninsula. Most were hobbyists and tinkerers like Wozniak or the phone phreak John Draper. Some, like Adam Osborne, a tall, dark-haired man with a British accent, had commercial reasons for attending: From a cardboard box, Osborne fished copies of his book about microcomputers and sold them to club members. Others came from the electronics companies, the Stanford Research Institute, the Stanford University Artificial Intelligence Laboratory, and the Free University of Palo Alto, an institution that offered courses in astrology, Zen, and nonviolence. However, many of the faculty from nearby universities and colleges and most of the engineers at the semiconductor and electronics companies viewed microcomputers as playthings. The Homebrew Club had an appeal for those with a shallow pocket and a practical rather than a theoretical bent, which left members like Allen Baum disappointed. "I got real bored pretty soon."

When it became clear that there was a swollen, permanent band of fellow travelers, the Homebrew Club's meetings were held in a large, steeply sloping auditorium at the Stanford Linear Accelerator Center. Though some members suggested the club be called Eight-Bit Byte Bangers, Midget Brains, or the Steam Beer Computer Group, the name Homebrew stuck. The tone of the meetings was heavily influenced by the first evening in Gordon French's garage. There were no quorums, formal dues, or wrangling over elections of officers. The Homebrew Club developed its own ritual and, like a bazaar, became a fulcrum for display, barter, and rumor. The meetings were divided into "random access periods" and "mapping periods" where people with common interests could get together. The fortnightly gatherings provided incentive, deadlines, criticism, village-pump gossip, and for Wozniak, "the Homebrew meetings were the most important thing in my life."

New parts selling at bargain prices also had a way of appearing at the Homebrew Club. Stanford University, anxious to preserve its reputation, banned any trading on the campus, but that only made members like Marty Spergel seek other spots. Spergel became the most notorious hub for sales and always drove an automobile whose trunk was crammed with electronic parts. He had a thick Brooklyn accent, wore three-piece suits, had a throaty laugh and sharp eyes, and lived in a Sunnyvale mobile-home park earning money by assembling kits for microcomputers built around the Intel 8008. He darted about in a gray realm where a busy telephone provided connections to distributors, sales representatives, and offshore manufacturers, and he took pride in what he called "global logistics." He told club members that he would be able to find, within five business days, any semiconductor, connector, cable, or whatever obscure electronic device they might need.

Some of the parts imported from the Orient ran beneath the eyes of curious Customs inspectors. One carton, described on the accompanying bill of lading as "joysticks," was held until Spergel could prove that they were game paddles and not sex devices. Spergel and others traded in the Stanford parking lots until the security guards got wind of what was happening. Eventually they retired to the shadows and safety of an empty parking lot at a nearby Shell gas station.

Between meetings the club's newsletter, which within a year had a circulation of six hundred, kept members abreast of affairs. It included a summary of the previous meeting, applauded the appearance of interesting devices, published a calendar of electronic trade shows, announced the publication of useful articles, and also provided a steady stream of practical advice. It explained, for example, how typewriter keyboards could be built from plastic switches which could then be sprayed with Krylon paint ("Enamel takes longer to dry") and decorated with lettering from a stationery store. It consistently published pleas for more software and its guides to the stock at local electronics stores was given in a shorthand that only the enthusiast could unravel: "Socket kit, IC kit, transistor kit, diode kit, baud rate generator, trim pots, 2.4576 crystal, tantalum capacitors."

The newsletter also contained hints of wider interest and almost from the start showed signs that Moore's lifelong dreams about grass-roots networks had at last come true. Just as that happened, Moore was forced to leave the club because of marital troubles. When similar clubs started in Boston or San Diego or even in British Columbia, word soon appeared in the fortnightly bulletin. The Homebrew letter even carried lonely pleas from overseas. Salvatore di Franco wrote from Biccari, Italy: "Since in Italy there are no magazines, no books, no data where I could get the information and the know-how I need, that is the main reason for joining your club." And F. J. Pretorious sent a letter from Sasolburg, South Africa, noting the local state of affairs: "It is quite discouraging that no circuits are available on 8008 or 8080 microprocessors."

But most of all the Homebrew Club provided an audience for a group of lonely hearts like Wozniak whose primary interest in life was something that most people couldn't understand. And though, in later years, the club was fondly remembered as a movable science fair where like-minded souls gathered to share their secrets, display their machines, and distribute schematics— rather like older versions of school science fairs—it was also a skeptical, critical forum where sloppy designs would be savaged as "a bucket of noise." Despite Fred Moore's milky intentions, the brightest members of the Homebrew Club liked to work by themselves and Lee Felsenstein recalled the dominant tone: "We were all watching to see if someone else was infringing on our specialty or our little twist. It was difficult to get people together to work on the same thing. We all just had great plans with no one else to listen to but other people with their own great plans."

"Johnny Carson wouldn't be bad," Jobs said.

In the Valley of Superlatives dreaming up a fresh slogan for a new computer was a tricky business. For months the marketing managers at Mac had been scratching their heads trying to come up with a memorable phrase or line that would capture their computer's virtues. At one time or another, depending on the shape, mood, and ingenuity of the speaker, Mac had been referred to as The Next Apple II, The Interface for the Eighties, The Crankless Computer, The Crankless Volkswagen, or The Crankless Mercedes. As a company, Apple had exhausted variations on the theme of the personal computer. It had annexed the definite article to describe the Apple II as The Personal Computer and shortly afterward announced (mustering a magnificently straight face) that it had actually invented the personal computer.

Competitors had countered with similar braggadocio. Digital Equipment Corporation's advertisements read "We change the way the world thinks," Radio Shack was calling itself "The biggest name in little computers" and the founder of Osborne Computer Corporation, before his company went bankrupt, compared himself to Henry Ford. As the slogan race escalated, Apple had launched multiple adjectives describing its best-selling machine as "the most personal computer," a slogan that had spawned a mordant joke that Mac would simply become "the most most personal computer."

Partly to avoid lame tag lines, Marcia Klein, head of the Apple account at the Regis McKenna Public Relations Agency, arrived at the Mac building one morning to have a chat with Mike Murray. She wanted to bat around some ideas for a slogan but also wanted to start preparing for encounters with the press. Dressed in an olive suit and firehouse-red lipstick, Klein brought a touch of plate-glass fashion to the Mac conference room where Murray waited in slacks, a blue sports shirt, and boating shoes.

After they had disposed of the amenities, Murray said, "Down the road we want people to think that when they're hired in a new job they find pencils, a wastepaper basket, and a Mac. But that's impossible to do off the bat. I'm trying to make a case that there's a giant need for an appliance in the office. I'm pretty adamant about the appliance notion."

Klein listened and asked how Mac would fit in among Apple's other computers. "When somebody asks us about the Apple II or the Apple III, what are we going to say?"

"We don't know what we're going to say about the Apple III," Murray admitted. "It's something that just hasn't been worked out. It's a cop-out. We've got to be crystal clear about the future of the products. We cannot be really milquetoasty. People are hoping that maybe the Apple III will just go away."

Klein summed up her aim: "We're trying to convey the impression that the company has a general marketing plan, that there's overall corporate positioning and that what we say when we introduce Lisa will be consistent with what we say when we introduce Mac."

Murray sighed. "A lot of people tend to ignore us because it's a real messy problem. Other people don't realize the gravity of the problem."

Klein began to explain to Murray how to cope with journalists. "The press prefer to have you talk to them. They prefer not to have a sales pitch with lights and mirrors. You don't need anything as polished as slides. You just don't need to be slick."

"It's hard to say Mac is warm and cuddly," Murray said. "They'll have to put their arms around it and say it's warm and cuddly."

"We'd like to come up with a phrase for all of society," Klein said.

"Like desk appliance," Murray said hopefully.

"We've got to come up with new language," Klein said. "An appliance is old language. An appliance is something you buy at K-Mart. An appliance is boring and functional. It loses personality."

"I don't want to call it a desk-tool," Murray said.

Klein fiddled with a pen. "You need something like that for ads but you have the luxury when you're dealing with the press of being able to talk in paragraphs. You don't have to use just two words. The press is increasingly sophisticated but the audience isn't necessarily so. The whole point of talking to the press is to educate them so they educate their readers. For each publication you change a little bit of what you've got to say. Each publication looks a bit different and will ask different things. *Business Week* will want something different from *Time*."'

The door opened and Steve Jobs, looking disheveled and grumpy, strolled in, flopped into a chair, and slung his feet onto the table. He was dressed in jeans, argyle socks, a navy shirt, and loafers. Somebody had just told him that an MIT professor had been describing the features of Lisa and Mac on a Cable News Network program. Jobs was annoyed and turned to Klein. "I bet it was Marvin Minsky. That's the only person it could be. Get a tape and if it was Minsky I want to string him up by his toenails."

Murray and Klein continued to debate various approaches for the press until Jobs cut them short. "We ought to decide what we want and then start to cultivate something because I've got a feeling we'll get what we want." He continued, "What we need is a cover of *Time* or *Newsweek*. I can see the cover as a shot of the whole Mac team. We've got a better shot at *Newsweek* than *Time,*" he predicted. "We had lunch with the president of *Newsweek* and a bunch of editors in some room at the top of the building and they stayed and talked for a couple of hours after lunch. It just went on and on. Technology. Reindustrialization. All that stuff." He nodded to himself. "They'll really go for that. 'New computers from hi-tech kids' and all that."

"I can see the story now," Murray said. "It will have a dozen pictures inside with little bios underneath."

"Then we could do with an hour long TV special with Cavett interviewing Burrell and Andy," Jobs said.

"We need something more popular than that," Klein objected.

"Johnny Carson or something like that," Murray suggested.

"Johnny Carson wouldn't be bad," Jobs said.

"What about that British guy who did the Nixon interviews?" Murray asked.

"Once it starts to happen, it snowballs," Jobs said. "I can see *People* magazine coming down and putting Andy Hertzfeld on the cover. We can create a mini-fame for each of these people. It'll be a gas. We'll have stories that say 'Here's the guy that designed it,' 'Here's the factory that built it.' People will just keep hearing all about it. We've got to get a lot of free editorial."

Jobs spotted a dummy advert lying on the table. "Ooooh, I like that," he said in a softer voice. "Ooooh, that would be hot." He read the slogan: "APPLE COMPUTER DOES IT AGAIN. I like that. That's really hot."

"It'd be a nice cover for *Newsweek*" Murray volunteered.

"It would be nice for *Byte*" Jobs countered as his mood improved. "It's look so different from IBM."

"Its too classy for *Byte*," Klein objected.

"It'd be great for *Newsweek*," Jobs agreed. "They'd sell millions of them."

The conversation returned to the problems of creating an image for a computer. Jobs sighed, "You know the closest thing has been Charlie Chaplin. IBM has really given their computer personality." He paused. "I've got this idea for an ad. We'll have a sort of spastic Charlie Chaplin but he's constructed so he's not real funny and we could do it because IBM cannot trademark Charlie Chaplin. Then Mac Man drifts in and scrunches Chaplin, or walks all over him, or comes out in front of him and shoots arrows at him from inside his coat." He paused for dramatic effect. "Then it says, 'Charlie Chaplin meets Mr. Mac.'"

Murray and Klein smiled and said nothing. Jobs continued, "We need ads that hit you in the face. They've got to have visually high bandwidth. We have an opportunity to do an ad that doesn't talk about product. It's like we're so good we don't have to show photographs of computers."

"In advertising," Murray said as Jobs finished, "we say it goes without saying and then we go ahead and say it."

"We don't stand a chance advertising with features and benefits and with RAMs and with charts and comparisons," Jobs said. "The only chance we have of communicating is with a feeling."

"It's got to be like a Sony Walkman or a Cuisinart. It's got to be a cult product," Murray said.

Jobs frowned. "Yeah, we say, 'It's a cult,' and then we say, 'Hey, drink this Kool-Aid.'" He strolled toward the door and said, "We want to create an image people will never forget. We've got to build it and we've got to build it early."

Murray was struck by a thought, looked at Jobs, and said hopefully, "The personal computer that gives you personality."

Jobs ignored the suggestion, stopped and examined some photographs hanging on the wall that showed children and students using Mac computers. "Maybe if we give these photographs to the press they'd print them." He turned to Klein. "Don't you think they'd run something like this?"

"The *San Jose Mercury* might," Klein said.

STANLEY
ZEBER ZENSKANITSKY

Alex Kamradt was one of life's eternal optimists. He was tall, broad but not stout, and had a round face and a head of thick, black, curly hair. He often looked beleaguered or earnestly confused and was the Pickwickian founder of Call Computer, a house-sized company, that he ran from a higgledly-piggedly office in Mountain View. The corporate epicenter was a wooden, rolltop desk piled with papers, magazines, computer printouts, calling cards, pens, and pencils. The desk was surrounded by Teletypes, grubby lime walls, a dining table, some stern, straight-backed chairs, and bookshelves stacked with hefty, looseleaf binders.

A one-time physicist at Lockheed, Kamradt had become interested in computers while trying to write programs to solve scientific calculations. He sold a home, bought a minicomputer with part of the proceeds, and planned to use it to keep tabs on local real-estate deals. Instead he found himself renting out time on the computer to small companies along the San Francisco Peninsula. Together with a few high-school students he started to write programs that helped small businesses manage their accounts payable, accounts receivable, and inventories. His clients hooked into the computer by Teletype in the same way that Berkeley's barterers linked up with Resource One's Community Memory Project.

But Kamradt sensed that the arrival of the microprocessor could change the scope of Call Computer. He wanted to rent or sell his customers a more convenient terminal with a typewriter keyboard that could be connected to a television. He began to attend meetings of the Homebrew Club with the specific intention of finding someone to design his terminal. "I started asking people who was the sharpest engineer and they said Wozniak."

In mid-1975 Kamradt and Wozniak formed a subsidiary of Call Computer that they named Computer Conversor. Kamradt provided around $12,000 in start-up money and took 70 percent of the company while Wozniak was given 30 percent and a free account on the minicomputer. Though the arrangement was casual, Wozniak promised to produce a design for a terminal that would, as the company's name implied, converse with another computer. Kamradt saw the terminal as part of a grander scheme. "I wanted to have a computer terminal to sell and to rent. I knew that the first stage was to make a terminal and then gradually add more memory and turn it into a computer. Wozniak and I had an agreement that we were going to build a terminal then a computer."

Wozniak had a practical reason for designing the terminal. He had enviously eyed a similar machine that phone phreak John Draper had installed in the basement of his Los Altos home. It added an extra dimension to phone phreaking. Hooked to a telephone, the terminal let Draper delve in and out of ARPANET, a computer network financed by the federal government to link universities and research establishments. Armed with a few telephone numbers and the proper access codes, outsiders like Draper could connect to computers all over the United States, and some of these provided gateways to computers at European universities. Students and computer hobbyists nosed about the ARPANET files, left electronic messages for one another on informal bulletin boards, and sometimes devised ways of erasing records on distant computers.

Wozniak used the machine he had built to play Pong as a basis for the Computer Conversor terminal. Both he and Kamradt felt that microprocessors were too expensive, and so from the outset the terminal was not supposed to be much more than a television-typewriter. The finished terminal allowed a user to type text on a television screen and ran slightly faster than an ordinary Teletype. It also had a couple of rubber muffs which slipped around a telephone receiver and allowed information to travel between the terminal and Kamradt's minicomputer.

Wozniak managed to tame the quirks in his prototype and found it reliable enough to use on ARPANET. "It was pretty easy to figure out how to jump around from computer to computer." Though the terminal was satisfactory for Wozniak, the prototype presented Kamradt with a problem. "It was useful to Wozniak so he considered it finished. He could fix what was wrong. Nobody else could. The genius is nothing unless you can get it out of him. I couldn't. He was hard to reach and didn't want to build a company."

Wozniak felt that his primary responsibility lay with his full-time work. After a year of phone phreaking at Berkeley, he had left the university and had spent six months working on the assembly line at Electroglass, a company that supplied equipment to semiconductor manufacturers. He never considered going to work for his father's employer, Lockheed, which had lost the righteous glow it had acquired during the late fifties. In part Lockheed was a victim of fashion, and at the end of the sixties much of its work was seen in a sinister light rather than in the patriotic glow that had shone around any company working to protect Americans against scores of Sputniks. Lockheed was closely linked to the imbroglio in Southeast Asia, was suffering from the winding down of the space program, was tangled in bribery scandals, was the target of congressional committees investigating cost overruns on government contracts, and had received a federal bailout.

Life at Lockheed had acquired an antique ring. The corporate vocabulary was studded with the lingo of the industrial crescent and there was much talk of "mandates," "mass meetings," and "thorny noneconomic issues." More important, the generation that had grown up in the curve of Lockheed's satellite dishes was now dubious about the technical competence of the people who left their cars in the herringbone parking lots. They thought Lockheed scientists were more like civil servants than electrical engineers. Al Alcorn at Atari formed his impressions. "Lockheed engineers were notorious for having no breadth. They could design an aileron on a missile but they couldn't change a light bulb." Stephen Wozniak accepted all the stereotypes and, like so many others, looked for work in the dozens of smaller electronic companies that had flourished while Lockheed aged. "I didn't want to drink a lot. The standard picture of the Lockheed engineer was that he drank or beat his wife."

One of the companies that had grown while Lockheed had been covered in odium was Hewlett-Packard, and its engineers had gained their own reputation. They were younger than the Lockheed men, many had doctorates, and they had the advantage of working for a company that had its roots in the area rather than in some distant city. Hewlett-Packard had been started by some Stanford students in the Palo Alto garage just before World War II, and though the founders had become wealthy (and one of them Deputy Secretary of Defense), their underlings still called them Bill and Dave. In the late sixties and early seventies Hewlett-Packard was a steady corporate pillar on the Peninsula and had gained a formidable reputation for producing reliable laboratory instruments, computers, and calculators. It was certainly as respectable as Lockheed had been a decade before but, because of its youth, stock options, and size, Hewlett-Packard had a sprightlier edge.

Allen Baum was one of the bright young university graduates snared by Hewlett-Packard recruiters, and he immediately suggested that the company interview an older friend who designed computers, Stephen Wozniak. So when, in 1973, Hewlett-Packard offered Wozniak a job as an associate engineer in its Advanced Products Division, he jumped at the chance. The division made pocket calculators, which for Hewlett-Packard—with its traditional affinity for high-quality, low-volume electronic equipment—was a bold departure. The success brought by the arrival in 1972 of the HP 35, the first desk-top calculator to pack the punch of a slide rule, brought a blush to the entire division. For a time it was a whizzy place to work, and as competitors slashed the prices of their calculators, Hewlett-Packard concentrated on adding features to the HP 35 and giving them model numbers like HP 45 and HP 60. Six months after joining the company Wozniak was given his epaulettes and became a full-blown engineer. He, in turn, managed to persuade HP to hire his neighborhood chum Bill Fernandez as a lab technician.

Wozniak found the world of calculators and the problems they presented far removed from his exploits with minicomputers. He was assigned to work on a project to make refinements to the HP 35 and suffered the fate of many engineers who work for large companies when, after eighteen months of effort, the project was canceled. Myron Tuttle, an engineer who worked with Wozniak on the project that was code-named Road Runner, recalled, "I don't think anyone in the lab was thought of as exceptional. Wozniak was one of the few people without degrees. He didn't stand out. He was nothing out of the ordinary. He was a competent engineer." Wozniak was intrigued by rumors of a hand-held terminal for the handicapped that was being designed in the company's research laboratories; he applied for a transfer but was turned down. "They decided I didn't have enough education."

Aside from the repeated comments about his thin formal training, Wozniak enjoyed the way Hewlett-Packard allowed his mind to wander. He liked the doughnuts and coffee trundled around on a cart every morning, the regular paychecks, the attention paid to engineers (which included leave to appeal to the president if faced with dismissal), the manner in which the company enforced across-the-board salary cuts rather than resorting to layoffs, and the stock rooms that were open territory for engineers working on their own projects. From stock-room parts, Wozniak built Allen Baum an HP 45, converted Elmer Baum's HP 35 into an HP 45 (and attached a company label that gave warranty information in Japanese), worked out a way of solving square roots on the less powerful HP 35, and also challenged Fernandez to see who was "the fastest square root in the West."

While he worked at Hewlett-Packard Wozniak took lunch-time jaunts in light aircraft that belonged to his workmates. He conducted an eccentric private life from an apartment in Cupertino that resembled a bachelor's version of the Bronx Zoo. Pet mice roamed around the calculator and computer manuals, and there were boxes filled with videotape players that a group of HP engineers had bought in bulk. The one substantial piece of furniture was a sofa that could be converted into a pool table, while the bedroom was furnished with a mattress and the sink was usually piled with dirty dishes. Apart from a fancy stereo system the center of Wozniak's existence was still the telephone. He appropriated a used phone number for what he boasted was the Bay Area's first dial-a-joke. Each day he recorded a new message on his answering machine selecting most of them from a book of two thousand Polish jokes along the lines of "When did the Polack die drinking milk? When the cow sat down." Sometimes, after returning from work, Wozniak answered the phone, introduced himself as Stanley Zeber Zenskanitsky, and read jokes. After receiving angry letters from the Polish American Congress, he switched countries and made Italians the butt of his humor, though he still used the same accent and continued to introduce himself as Stanley.

When Pacific Telephone's answering machine broke under the strain, Wozniak rigged up his own and asked callers to ring the phone company and complain about the tardy service. The phone company, monitoring the heavy traffic and pestered by a local store that had the misfortune of having a number similar to Wozniak's finally gave him one of the lines from "the radio station bank" that were reserved for heavy use. One of the callers was Alice Robertson, a plump San Jose high-school student with long hair, wide eyes and a hefty laugh. Wozniak answered her call, chatted for a couple of minutes, abruptly announced, "I can hang up faster than you can," and slammed down the receiver. That peculiar exchange marked the start of a nervous series of calls that eventually culminated in a date.

As he embarked on his first major amorous adventure, Wozniak also had to contend with nagging obligations to Alex Kamradt and Computer Conversor. Kamradt had engaged several other engineers who spent months trying to unravel Wozniak's design. To help turn a prototype and some schematics into a product, Kamradt looked to the person who had accompanied Wozniak on several of his trips to Computer Conversor, Steven Jobs.

According to Kamradt, Jobs promised to take charge of guiding production on the terminal in return for salary and stock. Kamradt recalled, "He resented me having money. He was somewhat unscrupulous and he wanted to get as much as he could, but I liked his assertiveness." Wozniak, who scarcely visited Call Computer's one-room headquarters, was unaware of the scope of Jobs's interest. "Steve listened to Alex. He was very attentive. He listened to what Alex said a terminal could do for his business."

For several months Jobs worked with Robert Way, the head of a small engineering company that provided design services for electronic companies. Jobs monitored the layout of the printed circuit board and the design of a vacu-form case. Together with Way he drew up a bill of materials and a parts numbering system and also acquired a license from Atari for a video circuit that would hook the terminal to a television. Way found Jobs a hard taskmaster. "Nothing was ever good enough for him. He was the rejector." Way also observed the division of responsibilities. "Every check I ever received was signed by Kamradt. The responsibility for seeing the design got done was Jobs's." After some months Way, bemused by Kamradt's perennial optimism, threw up his hands and ducked out of the project. "They were the weirdest group of people I ever met in my life."

While Kamradt worried whether he would ever get the terminal to work, Wozniak, stimulated by the Homebrew meetings, was working on his own computer. He subjected some of the new microprocessors to minute inspection and quickly found out that they hadn't changed the essence of a computer. "I was surprised that they were like the minicomputers I had been used to." Though microprocessors hadn't changed the nature of the enterprise, diehards still looked to the early mainframes, when computer design was attacked by large teams, and hailed them as the grand old days when men were men. Yet even in the forties and fifties the challenge facing engineers was one of minimal design—though they were trying to limit the size of a computer to a room.

For microcomputer designers like Wozniak, the challenge was still to squeeze the maximum performance out of the minimum number of parts. A compact machine not only kept the cost down but was also the source of substantial pride. The size of the new components, the fact that a computer could be squeezed into a case the size of a bread box rather than manhandled into an office building, also made it possible for one person to exercise control over an entire machine. "In microcomputer design," one of the Homebrew regulars remarked, "you could express yourself in a way that hadn't been possible in the entire history of electronic computing."

Microprocessors did, however, bring a change of focus. With a computer's central processing unit reduced to a chip, engineers like Wozniak and Baum felt that some of the broader issues of computer design had evaporated. Instead, they were forced to focus on the best ways of linking the computer on a chip to a board of memory chips, to a television screen or printer, and to a typewriter keyboard. The data sheets accompanying the microprocessors prescribed the rules that bounded the microcomputer designer and left some of the purists feeling hamstrung. Allen Baum complained, "You're stuck with what you have and you've got to make it work right. If something doesn't work right, you cannot redesign it. It's a lot less fun."

If the problems of size had been eliminated, cost was still an issue for threadbare engineers. In 1975 microprocessors like Intel's 8080 were selling for $179 and Wozniak couldn't afford them. Baum heard that Hewlett-Packard's Colorado division was experimenting with the Motorola 6800, a microprocessor introduced about a year after the Intel 8080, which along with a few accessory chips was being offered to employees at a steep discount. Wozniak placed his order while his workmate Myron Tuttle scampered out to buy a technical manual that explained the intricacies of the chip. The choice of microprocessor was the most important decision that a computer hobbyist could make. It became the cause of frustration and exasperation, the source of pleasure and satisfaction, and also shaped the slant of his entire machine. Wozniak's choice of microprocessor ran counter to fashion in the summer of 1975.

That summer at the Homebrew Club the Intel 8080 formed the center of the universe. The Altair was built around the 8080 and its early popularity spawned a cottage industry of small companies that either made machines that would run programs written for the Altair or made attachments that would plug into the computer. The private peculiarities of microprocessors meant that a program or device designed for one would not work on another. The junction of these peripheral devices for the Altair was known as the S-100 bus because it used one hundred signal lines. Disciples of the 8080 formed religious attachments to the 8080 and S-100 even though they readily admitted that the latter was poorly designed. The people who wrote programs or built peripherals for 8080 computers thought that later, competing microprocessors were doomed. The sheer weight of the programs and the choice of peripherals, so the argument went, would make it more useful to more users and more profitable for more companies. The 8080, they liked to say, had critical mass which was sufficient to consign anything else to oblivion. Lee Felsenstein had plenty of companions who shared his belief that "the 6800 was another world. It wasn't worth any attention."

Wozniak bucked the trend and chose the 6800. His interest in the Motorola chip was shaped almost entirely by price but he also thought that it was more like his favorite minicomputers than the 8080. The signals that emerged from the 6800, for example, were synchrononous (and so bore a conceptual resemblance to the architecture of the Data General Nova) while the signals on the 8080 were less predictable. Wozniak started spending his time at Hewlett-Packard delving into the properties of the 6800: finding out how much memory it could cope with, the voltage that it needed, the speed with which it executed instructions, and the pattern of its signals. On paper he plotted out a design of a computer built around the 6800. The design was an enhancement of the prototype he had built for Computer Conversor. "I designed it just for fun. I could do a whole bunch of things I'd wanted to do five years before and didn't have the money to do."

The economics of the semiconductor industry were also in Wozniak's favor. Chips seldom sold long at their introductory price. Competing devices from the dozen or so major semiconductor manufacturers usually ensured that prices would fall fast and dramatically. In the fall of 1975 the laws of the industry held true and played havoc with the pricing of eight-bit microprocessors. Wozniak first stumbled on the change when he and Baum traipsed to an electronics trade show in San Francisco and spotted a new microprocessor, the MOS Technology 6502, made by a Costa Mesa, California, company. The men at MOS Technology were aiming the 6502 at high-volume markets like copiers, printers, traffic signals, and pinball machines rather than the small computer-hobbyist market. The 6502 was almost identical to the Motorola 6800 and the MOS Technology salesmen pointedly stated that their company was trying to make a smaller, simpler version of the older chip. The similarities were so blatant that they eventually became the subject of a lawsuit between the two companies but for Wozniak and other hobbyists, legal squabbles were a distant blur. The critical issue was price. The Motorola 6800 cost $175.

The MOS Technology cost $25. Wozniak fished a 6502 out of a large glass bowl brimming with microprocessors and immediately modified his plans. He abandoned the 6800 and decided to write a version of the computer language BASIC that would run on the 6502.

His decision to write the language and then to build the machine was tacit recognition of the importance of software. He envisaged using the computer to play the sort of games he had run across on larger machines, which consisted of bursts of type-written commands and retorts that appeared on a teletype or television screen. One of the more popular games had the lovely name Hunt the Wumpus which let players journey through a maze filled with monsters. At all the club meetings BASIC had proved to be the most popular language on the Altair and the 8080 microprocessor. "At the club all we talked was BASIC. I had a chance to have the first BASIC for the 6502. I wanted to demo the machine quickly."

Wozniak made every technical decision to satisfy his own interests and made an art of the homily "Adequacy is sufficient." The deadlines, pressure, and spur were imposed by the fortnightly Homebrew meetings and also by the prospect of his wedding to Alice Robertson. After some weeks of dithering, Wozniak had finally decided to get engaged after tossing three dimes in the air and waiting until they all landed heads up. As he started on the software he also developed asthma and wheezed loud enough for the neighbors to hear through the flimsy plasterboard walls. Frightened that fluid would fill his lungs while he slept, Wozniak took to writing programming code until the small hours.

Wozniak found writing software a more arduous exercise than designing hardware. The shape and style of his first major piece of software were dictated by necessity. He spent several weeks studying the grammatical rules for BASIC and found they were similar to the rules for FORTRAN with which he was familiar. Faced with a choice between two versions of BASIC, Wozniak chose the simpler. He wrote the programs in pencil on paper and a colleague at Hewlett-Packard wrote a program that simulated the behavior of the 6502 and which ran on a Hewlett-Packard minicomputer. The Hewlett-Packard computer was used to test some of Wozniak's programs. Wozniak conceded, "Fortunately I'd spent a lot of time in my math classes not doing math but trying to write compilers in assembly language when I didn't have a machine. I had gone off in directions which I had no way of knowing whether they were good or bad."

After he completed the code, he set about designing a computer and reverted to the schematics he had drawn for Motorola's 6800 microprocessor. He compared the features of the 6800 with the MOS Technology 6502 and its slightly cheaper brother, the 6501. Wozniak found that with a couple of alterations to some of the electronic signals that affected the chips' timing, his previous design needed no alteration—"I didn't have to change a single wire or pin on my design."

He used some of the techniques he had used in designing the Computer Conversor terminal to make significant advances over earlier designs like the Cream Soda Computer. The most significant difference was, of course, the inclusion of the microprocessor. But there were other advances that also helped to make the computer easier to use. Instead of using switches to toggle instructions to the computer, Wozniak attached a typewriter keyboard. He also used some chips called PROMS (programmable read only memories), which stored instructions that previously had to be entered into the computer every time it was switched on.

He was precise about the way in which the chips for his computer should be laid out on the bread board. He spent hours working out where the chips should be placed before plugging the sockets, the cradles for the semiconductors, into the board. Wozniak was more meticulous than most engineers when it came to making the wire connections between the semiconductor pins. He disliked the popular "wire-wrapping," which tended to wreath boards in a spaghetti jungle of wires, and favored "point-to-point" wiring, which required laboriously snipping and soldering lengths of wire between pins. The fastidious approach paid off when it came to troubleshooting and made it far easier to find troublesome pins and spot faulty connections.

Wozniak's private interests consumed more and more of his time. He carted his prototype to work and spent much of his time at the lab bench making further refinements. Especially after Hewlett-Packard announced that the calculator division would be moved to Oregon, Tuttle said, "We spent half our time working on our pet projects." Tuttle had also bought a 6502 and was also burning the midnight oil, taking his prototype home and trying another approach. With their prototypes built, Tuttle, Wozniak, and another colleague approached their lab manager to suggest that Hewlett-Packard consider making microcomputers. Tuttle recalled, "It was one of those informal meetings. It wasn't a big deal. We just sort of asked for five minutes and showed Woz's board. We were told, 'HP doesn't want to be in that kind of a market.'"

When Wozniak took his unnamed computer to the Homebrew Club it received another cool reception. That wasn't surprising since a poll at one of the club's meetings in October 1975 showed that of the thirty-eight computers belonging to members, twenty-five were either Altairs or used an 8080 while only one used a 6502. Wozniak hooked his computer to a black-and-white television, connected a board of 4K bytes of memory chips that Myron Tuttle had lent him, and patiently typed in the BASIC. There was a certain amount of surprise that BASIC would run on a machine with so few chips, but most of the club members didn't even bother to inspect the computer. Wozniak passed out schematics to the few who were interested and later put his new machine in perspective. "It wasn't as difficult as some of the other computers I had designed."

"The time to completion is a constant,"
Andy Hertzfeld said.

The warm Sunday afternoon gloom pushed against the glass doors at the rear of the Mac laboratory. The air conditioning, which vibrated through the speckled ceiling tiles on weekdays, was turned off. The stuffy darkness was sliced in two places. A gentle light ballooned out of Andy Hertzfeld's programming cubicle and a cube of cold neon lit an engineer's bench where Burrell Smith was gnawing the skin of his knuckles. Hertzfeld slipped out of his cubicle and walked to the bench where Smith slid off his lab stool. Both stood lower than the head-light partitions that separated all the offices. They stared at a printed circuit board which, festooned with probes and wires, looked like a stomach pried apart with sutures, retractors, and hemostats. The probes were hooked to a logic analyzer and the rows of lines on its green screen monitored the signals emerging from the microprocessor.

Smith hadn't gone home the previous day until 11:30 P.M. and then had stayed up until 3 A.M. thinking about why the Mac's memory chips were not being recharged properly. Neither he nor Hertzfeld had worked on one project for quite as long before. The fatigue of designing a computer was printed on the pair and both were working harder than they had ever worked. Smith was twenty-six and Hertzfeld twenty-nine though both looked older. Behind his spectacles, Hertzfeld's eyelids looked like swollen leeches while his cheeks were unshaven and pale. The pallid circles around Smith's eyes bore the marks of late evenings. The same slack belts of fast food were strapped to their waists. Hertzfeld had found that developing a computer distorted time. "I used to think six months was a long time. But it's not. It seems like an instant."

Smith, his auburn hair tucked tight behind one ear and hanging in a thin curl beneath the other, tripped over his words in a frothy rush: "It's so weird," he complained to Hertzfeld. In a languid tone Hertzfeld asked, "How do you know that you've fixed it when you don't know how it occurs?" Smith replied, "It's so frustrating because I haven't proved that I cannot solve the problem and I haven't proved that I can solve it either." Hertzfeld sighed. "We're going to be getting into superstitions. We're going to see that it works but we won't be sure that it works."

Smith had been trying to solve the puzzle for a couple of days. He had first noticed the computer wasn't behaving properly while the rest of the engineers were celebrating what they thought was the completion of the first Mac prototype. Smith had ignored the champagne, which at Apple (and at the Mac group in particular) had a habit of appearing from behind even the thinnest milestone, and sat by himself looking at the computer. He had used a heat gun, which looked like a hairdryer, and a spray to heat and cool particular chips to temperatures where quirks were liable to appear more frequently. Smith had decided that the problem lay with the largest chip on the board, the Motorola 68000 microprocessor.

The 68000 and the other chips on the board were a tribute to the continuing advances in semiconductor technology. The 68000 was a sixteen-bit microprocessor, and consequently the Mac had about ten times as much computing power as the Apple II, though it used half as many chips. Smith compared the difference in complexity to watching an ordinary baseball game and then trying to follow the action in a game where eight batters hit simultaneously to fifty-four outfielders. He was perspiring and kept flicking frames onto the logic analyzer to inspect another frame showing the electronic signals from the clocks. He said, "You thrash around the design space long enough and you learn the idiosyncrasies."

Some at Apple thought the entire Mac project reflected a parade of personal idiosyncrasies rather than any grand design. There was no plan of Napoleonic proportions. False starts, diversions, mistakes, experiments, rebellion, and competition formed the stuff of the machine. The Mac, like other products that rely on technological advances, the uncertain swings of a fast-growing company, and the proclivities of different managers, was something that Apple had been groping toward for several years. For almost two years it was one of those projects that could have foundered with the departure of a programmer or the appearance of a faulty prototype. Hertzfeld, who had watched the ups and downs, the delays in announcement, had formed his own conclusion about how to measure progress: "The time to completion," he had decided, "is a constant."

The starting point turned into the only sure point of reference. In the middle of 1979 the manager of Apple's publications department, Jef Raskin, was asked to take charge of a small group that would build a computer to sell for $500, work through a television set, contain a built-in modem, and be able to run both the Pascal and BASIC languages. Raskin, misspelling the name of his favorite apple, code-named the project Macintosh and dreamed up his own idea for a computer. "I thought it was more important to give people a choice of case color than a choice between the number of bytes of memory. I wanted it to become an indispensable part of a house. I wanted something that people would become addicted to." Raskin suggested that Apple produce a battery-powered portable home computer that would sell for under $1,000. He built a cardboard mock-up and decided that the computer should have a built-in screen, should not contain any expansion slots, and should be accompanied by a thin manual. A year or so after starting work on the project he noted, "Apple II is a system. Macintosh is an appliance."

Raskin, a chunky, bearded man with a soft spot for model airplanes and music, set up shop in late 1979 and shuffled among several buildings, including Apple's original office suite near the Good Earth Restaurant. In early 1981 Raskin, as Hertzfeld re-called, ran afoul of Apple politics. "The Lisa team in general told Steve to fuck off. Steve said, 'I'll get this team that'll make a cheap computer and that will blow them off the face of the earth.' Then Steve saw that Raskin had critical mass: He had a hardware engineer and a software engineer. Since Steve was a bigger kid than Raskin, he said, 'I like that toy!' and took it."

Raskin quickly fell victim to Jobs, who wanted to impose his own imprimatur on the project. Jobs added veterans from the early days of Apple to Raskin's team. He tried to change the code-name of the project from Mac to Bicycle after reading a *Scientific American* article that described the personal computer as the bicycle of the twenty-first century. But he backed off when his group protested. After taking control of Mac, Jobs made his intentions clear. He bet John Couch, the head of the Lisa division, $5,000 that Mac would ship first.

At first, Smith and Hertzfeld eyed Jobs with suspicion. The former had been raised in upstate New York where he had studied literature at junior college and become interested in a UNIVAC computer and phone phreaking. The first electronic device he had ever built was a blue box, which he constructed on his mother's kitchen table. "I reckoned it was impossible to find it on the street and I wanted the satisfaction of building my own." For phone phreaking he adopted the name Marty, and when he first visited California he stayed with John Draper. He attended some Homebrew meetings and, on moving permanently to California, built an office control system for doctors and dentists and bought a Commodore Pet because he couldn't afford an Apple. Out of work, he helped a friend build a wall and was touring companies in a borrowed truck when he was offered a job as a technician in Apple's service department. He repaired Apple IIs by day and studied the schematics at night. "I wanted to find out how the board worked by myself. I had almost subconscious dreams that I'd be dealing with logical elements in some way. I was always driven down to the lowest level of the system. I don't like working on things if I don't know how they work."

Smith was fished from the service department by a programmer who recognized his talent and recommended him to Raskin. By the spring of 1980 Smith had designed a prototype based on an eight-bit microprocessor. For about six months, the computer languished with no software. A programmer hired to write some of the software placed unshakable faith in the computer languages used in artificial intelligence work and had little sympathy for the demands of microcomputers. Then Smith started working with the Motorola 68000 and by Christmas of 1980 had developed a second Mac. Hertzfeld, who was working on software for the Apple II, watched these changes with mounting envy. One night he stayed late and wrote a small program that produced a picture of Mr. Scrooge and the greeting: HI BURRELL.

Hertzfeld had grown up in Philadelphia and started programming when he was fifteen. "I was amazed you could get this typewriter to do such-neat things." He studied science and mathematics at Rhode Island's Brown University and moved to Berkeley because he wanted to live in California and preferred the prospect of graduate studies to corporate life. He bought an Apple II six months after it appeared and nursed an impatience with some of his fellow students. "They were people who didn't like programming. They liked talking about programming." He wrote an I Ching game and took it to a local computer club, designed a peripheral for the Apple II and was startled when he found out how much some of the computer companies were paying. "I didn't think it was the sort of thing you did for money. Now I've been corrupted by money and by thinking how much I can make."

Smith and Hertzfeld had gradually learned to live with Jobs and he with them. It was a delicate set of relationships glued together by the fact that they all needed each other. Hertzfeld and Smith worked around Jobs's unpredictable nature. Hertzfeld explained, "He'd stop by and say, 'This is a pile of shit' or 'This is the greatest thing I've ever seen.' The scary thing was that he'd say it about the same thing." The pair floated in the uncertainty of whether Jobs liked them or whether he just liked them for the jobs they were performing. And Hertzfeld, three years after the start of the project, admitted, "I like working for Steve because of Mac but I don't know if I like him."

Yet Jobs had instilled an urgency into the Mac project and his influence within the company had given it increasing prominence. One of the programmers who worked on the early stages of Mac had nicknamed Jobs "the reality distortion field" and the sci-fi moniker had stuck. Jobs had many of his group believing they were building another Apple II and his faith was almost strong enough to persuade them that they were working in a garage when all the tangible evidence suggested otherwise.

Like all employees, Smith and Hertzfeld had grumbled about their boss. They complained that Jobs forbade them to show Mac to their friends while he paraded visitors, including his one-time flame, folk singer Joan Baez, through the lab. Their irritation mounted when it took Jobs months to concede that the Mac screen and 64K bytes of memory were too small before he ordered a redesign. They mumbled some more when Jobs refused to give them permission to sell a mouse interface for the Apple II. When Jobs arranged for the programmer developing the word processor for the Mac to receive a royalty of $1 for every copy sold, tempers rose. It had not taken Hertzfeld and Smith long to figure that, given Apple's ambitions for the computer, the word processor would leave its author with larger tax problems than they were contemplating. Smith worried that Jobs wasn't thinking boldly enough about future computers and, on hearing that the Mac group would move into a building occupied by personal computer systems division, muttered, "It says, 'Thanks guys,' but now you're just like all the rest. You're just ordinary guys. Mac will become another PCS and we'll be just another big company." On several occasions Hertzfeld had threatened to quit but each time Jobs had persuaded him to stay.

Yet Jobs exercised many paternal touches. He had presented Hertzfeld and Smith and other members of the Mac group with medals and helped make a ritual out of outings to sushi bars. When a programmer fell ill, he called the hospital frequently. He dropped by the Mac lab over the weekends and took evident pleasure in personally delivering envelopes containing stock options. He had contemplated inviting actress Brooke Shields to attend a Christmas party and chuckled at how her appearance would make Hertzfeld and Smith blush. Jobs was shrewd enough to know that he could tantalize both Hertzfeld and Smith. "Andy," Jobs concluded, "is struggling with himself. He wants to make some money and he wants to be famous."

Fame and the notoriety that had come to surround Jobs and Wozniak and the programmers featured in Tracy Kidder's best-selling book *The Soul of a New Machine* worked as powerful stimulants. Smith's business card read HARDWARE WIZARD and Hertzfeld's SOFTWARE ARTIST and the two speckled their speech with the engineer's equivalent of fighter pilots' muscle talk such as kludge, glitch, and hairy edge. Hertzfeld, like Wozniak, talked about his audience and said, "The energy of all the people who will use Mac reverberates into the programming." To help ensure his prize duo and forty-five other members of the Mac group an encounter with posterity, Jobs had their signatures embossed on the inside of the mold for the case.

One result of this emotional fandango, the grueling work and the daliance with fame, was that Hertzfeld and Smith had become close friends. They enjoyed what Smith, with his tendency to reduce everything to initials, called a BFR: a Best Friend Relationship. Sometimes they daydreamed about leaving Apple and starting their own company. Yet every time Jobs asked for something, they worked day and night until it was completed. Smith had embarked on a six-month diversion to squeeze a lot of circuits onto one custom-designed chip. When the effort failed, he had to re-design Mac all over again. On one Friday evening Jobs had threatened to remove some chips that controlled the computer's sound unless they worked by the following Monday. Hertzfeld and Smith had straightened with alarm and worked through the weekend, and by the Monday morning the sound worked. These were the sort of management tactics (coupled with the difficulty of finding rewards to top riches and fame) that were calculated to burn out engineers.

Hertzfeld and Smith had suspended the rest of their lives until they completed Macintosh. They had no girlfriends, and they spent their Sundays hunched over a printed circuit board or behind a computer terminal. And on this one Sunday, Smith, as he had on dozens of previous occasions, had decided to abandon sleep until he had solved the problem. "Having friends," he said, "is orthogonal to designing computers. When they call, I find myself hanging up on them."

HALF RIGHT

While Wozniak completed the design of his computer, Jobs fluttered in the background, flitting in and out of Call Computer and continuing to work at Atari where he was asked to produce a device that would generate horoscopes from tidbits of information about dates and places of birth. The computing power needed to chart the progress of an individual with the course of the planets proved too much and the project fizzled. Jobs was uncertain about what he wanted to do and was unhappy about one obvious path. "I didn't see myself growing up to be an engineer." Though he nursed secret dreams of buying a BMW 320i he was uneasy about the prospect of being pulled into an orbit of cars and houses. Instead he fell back on his natural inquisitiveness and spent two semesters auditing a physics course offered by Stanford for gifted freshmen. Jobs left his mark on Mel Schwartz, the professor who taught the class. "Very few people turn up who say they want to learn something. I was impressed by Steve's enthusiasm. He was really interested and curious."

Unlike Wozniak, Jobs found the nitpicking technical debates of the Homebrew Club unappealing. He attended a few meetings but was bored by the chitchat about timing cycles, direct memory access, and synchronous clocks. Yet he kept close tabs on Wozniak's battles with his computer. When the two talked on the telephone, they almost always chatted about developments or problems with the machine. When they met, or when Jobs visited Wozniak's home, it was always the computer that formed the central topic of conversation. Jobs analyzed the reason why he and Wozniak, the proverbial odd couple who were separated by age, temperament, and inclination, could stay friends, and observed, "I was a little bit more mature for my age and he was a little less mature for his."

During January and February 1976 Jobs started to badger Wozniak about the possibility of making and selling some printed circuit boards so that others could build their own versions of the computer. Wozniak had not contemplated doing anything apart from handing out schematics of the machine to any Homebrew members who were interested. "It was Steve's idea to hold them in the air and sell a few." Jobs entertained the notion of a fleeting, informal venture that would be more of a partnership between friends than a proper company. There was no talk of Wozniak leaving Hewlett-Packard or of Jobs severing his casual arrangement with Atari. Jobs's thoughts about the possible market were limited to a few friends, members of the Homebrew Club, and one or two stores. The pair didn't consider permits, licenses, insurance contracts, and other legal demands because their idea of a company extended as far as the bylaw that required new partnerships to place a small formal advertisement in a local newspaper.

The two tossed around names for their company. One afternoon, driving along Highway 85, between Palo Alto and Los Altos, Jobs, summoning the shades of his dietary regime and his rural life in Oregon, suggested they call the company Apple Computer. Try as he might Wozniak couldn't improve on the suggestion. "We kept trying to think of a better name but every name we came up with wasn't any better." They played with the sound of names like Executek and Matrix Electronics but the simplicity of Apple always seemed more appealing. For a few days the two wondered whether their choice would land them in a legal wrangle with Apple Records, the Beatles' recording company, and Jobs worried that Apple Computer was altogether too whimsical for anything that even pretended to be a company. Eventually, anxious to place the partnership advertisement in the *San Jose Mercury* Jobs issued an ultimatum. "I said, 'Unless we come up with something better by five P.M. tomorrow, we'll go with Apple.'"

Jobs reckoned that it would cost about $25 to make each printed circuit board and that if all went well they might be able to sell a hundred for $50 apiece. They agreed that each would contribute half toward the $1,300 or so that Jobs reckoned the printed circuit board would cost. Neither had much money. Wozniak was earning $24,000 a year at Hewlett-Packard but was spending most of it on his stereo system, records, and the computer that had a way of gobbling up parts. His checking account at a Cupertino bank oscillated between black and red and his landlord, fed up with receiving checks that bounced, was insisting the rent be paid in cash. Jobs, meanwhile, was carefully guarding the $5,000 he had saved from his work at Atari.

To provide most of his share, Wozniak decided to sell his HP 65 calculator for $500. He knew that Hewlett-Packard was about to announce an enhanced version, the HP 67, that would be available to employees for $370. "I figured I had a profit and a better calculator." The buyer, however, paid Wozniak only half the agreed price. Jobs had a similar problem when he decided to use some of the $1,500 he made from selling a red and white Volkswagen bus. This particular piece of foreign machinery had never been given the parental seal of approval. Paul Jobs had accompanied his son on the original purchase mission, taken one look at the Volkswagen, and concluded, "It was a tired, gutless thing that wouldn't go anywhere." He told his son that Volkswagen vans tended to have problems with wheel bearings and the reduction-gear mechanism but his advice wasn't heeded. The younger Jobs planned to fix any problems and bought a book called *How To Keep Your Volkswagen Alive! A Manual of Step-by-Step Procedures for the Compleat Idiot.* Eventually, when the van proved too troublesome he buckled to his father's advice and sold the van after it passed some checks at an automotive diagnostic center. Paul Jobs chuckled quietly when "two weeks later the guy came back with the engine in a bucket." Steve Jobs promptly offered to share the cost of repairs and his $1,500 nest egg dwindled.

Jobs, never coy about offering his opinion, watched Wozniak make some modifications to the computer. Rather than rely on somebody else's board of memory chips, Wozniak decided to build his own. For the hobbyists the design of a reliable memory board was a persistent bugbear and the memory frequently came to mean the difference between a reliable and erratic machine. The memory chips were just as complicated to manage as the microprocessor and marrying the two—the most important parts of the machine—brought no end of trouble. A defective memory chip could blow out the computer and the quirks lurking in the rows of memory chips were notoriously tough to pinpoint. Wozniak was choosing his memory chips at a time when all the leading semiconductor companies were fighting to establish an industry standard for them. There were pronounced differences in technology, performance, and price among the chips, so picking the right chip was a bit like betting on a poker game. Wozniak plumped for a chip that he had spotted at the Homebrew Club, one that was made by American Microsystems Inc., a Santa Clara company. Jobs was appalled by the choice, thought Wozniak could do better, and embarked on a search for a brand-new Intel chip that hadn't filtered through to the electronics-supply stores.

Both the chips were dynamic RAMs and far superior to the static RAMs that were the standby of most hobbyists. Dynamic RAMs consumed less power than static RAMs and, in the long run, were also cheaper. However, they were far more complicated and most computer hobbyists clung to the adage, "Static memory works; dynamic memory doesn't." The crucial difference between the two parts was that information stored on dynamic chips would disappear unless it was refreshed with bursts of electricity every two thousandths of a second while the static RAMs didn't require regular shock therapy. The Intel chip was also compatible with the logic used by microprocessors, had fewer pins than the AMI chip, eventually became the industry standard—and Jobs's instinctive choice turned into a considerable triumph. Wozniak recalled long debates about the proper memory chip—"Steve was pushing to use the right part. We were lucky to be on the right track. It was one of the luckiest technology steps on the whole development. All the other hobby computers were using 2102 1K static RAMs."

While Jobs was pushing from one direction, Wozniak found that Alex Kamradt was tugging from another. In the spring of 1976 Kamradt and his small team were still trying to convert the terminal Wozniak had designed during the summer of 1975 into a reliable product for Computer Conversor. Kamradt telephoned Wozniak at work and at home and buttonholed him at the Homebrew meetings. But he found that Wozniak was more interested in adding features to his new computer than in completing an old design. Kamradt also had to contend with the full persuasive power of Jobs who was imploring Wozniak to place his faith in Apple rather than in the uncertain prospects of Call Computer. To add conviction to his argument, Jobs introduced Wozniak to Ron Wayne, a field sales engineer at Atari responsible for making sure that prospective video-game distributors were up to snuff. Wayne had casually agreed to help Jobs come up with a motif for Apple and to draw schematics to accompany the printed circuit board. Jobs argued that Wozniak's computer was doomed if he placed it in Kamradt's hands. He insisted that the prospects for the machine were far brighter if it was produced by an alliance of Wozniak, Jobs, and Wayne.

Wayne was in his early forties, a portly man with boyish curly hair that was turning gray. At the end of the sixties he had started a company in Nevada to design and build slot machines, but it had failed during the business recession in the early seventies. Strapped for money, Wayne had borrowed $600 to finance a trip to California and eventually earned enough to pay off his debts. By the time that Jobs approached him for advice about Apple, Wayne believed he'd "had enough failures to be a very smart fellow." He was also a strong believer in the permanent mark that engineers could leave on the world and liked to talk about "multifaceted, holistic engineering." A bachelor, Wayne lived alone in Mountain View where he was reading books about economic disasters and debasement of currencies. He had become convinced that the global economic system was on the brink of collapse and had started to protect himself from imminent doom by collecting rare stamps, old coins, and gold. He was also building an eight-foot-long replica of a Jules Verne nautical clock from carefully carved slices of cardboard. Though he found semiconductors and integrated circuits objects of complete mystery, Wayne was lassoed into helping Jobs muster arguments to prevent Wozniak from falling into Kamradt's grasp. Wayne consoled Wozniak and explained that the skilled engineer would always be remembered if he teamed up with the right marketer.

He pointed to the way Eiffel had left his name on a tower, and Colt his name on a gun.

Wozniak was not easily swayed. The trio sat up late into the night arguing about the form of the proposed partnership. Wayne suggested they should balance the equity of their investments with the merit of invention. It was an idea that appealed to Jobs, but Wozniak had problems coming to grips with twentieth-century notions of property. He wanted complete freedom to use his design tricks and was worried that Hewlett-Packard would assign him to a project where he would need to rely on some of the ploys he had used in the Apple. Wayne thought, "It was almost as if Wozniak would condescend to allow Apple to use these principles but he wanted to reserve the right to sell them to other people."

Eventually Jobs prevailed and Wayne drew up a ten-paragraph partnership agreement liberally sprinkled with "therefores," "herewiths," and "thereins." The agreement stated that none of the trio could spend more than $100 without the consent of another. It also laid down that Wozniak would "assume both general and major responsibility for the conduct of Electrical Engineering; Jobs would assume general responsibility for Electrical Engineering and Marketing, and Wayne would assume major responsibility for Mechanical Engineering and Documentation." Once Wozniak had been persuaded to agree to the venture, he had no qualms about giving Wayne 10 percent of the company and dividing the remainder with Jobs. He was convinced that if Jobs performed all the commercial donkeywork the split was equitable. What the agreement didn't say, but what they all understood, was that Wayne would act as tie breaker if Wozniak and Jobs couldn't agree on something. On the evening of April Fool's Day, 1976, at Wayne's Mountain View apartment, with Wozniak's friend Randy Wigginton looking on, the three signed the agreement forming Apple Computer Company. Jobs signed the document in a wide, faintly childish hand with all the letters in lower case. Wozniak scribbled a cursive signature, and Wayne's pen left his name illegible.

While they were sorting out formalities, Jobs had pressed ahead. He had used the $1,300 that he and Wozniak had pooled to commission the artwork for the printed circuit board. He visited

Howard Cantin, who had prepared the artwork for Atari's game boards (and had laid out the original Pong board) and asked him to prepare the board for the Apple computer. Cantin complied— "I did it as a favor for Steve." Once Wozniak had loaded the first printed circuit board with chips and completed the wiring, he and Jobs made a formal introduction of the Apple computer at the Homebrew Club in April 1976. Their remarks revealed the division of labor. Wozniak described the technical features of the machine: such things as the size of the memory, the BASIC that was available, and the clock speed of the memory. Jobs asked the members how much they were prepared to pay for a computer that, unlike the Altair, had all the essential features lodged onto a single printed circuit board. The overall reaction was muted. The majority of other engineers at the Homebrew Club didn't even bother to inspect the Apple. A few, like Lee Felsenstein, looked at the black-and-white computer with its 8K bytes of memory and concluded that "Wozniak might very well be heading for a fall. I thought if he was going to fail he was going to fail big and I wasn't going to step in the way."

Jobs, who by the spring of 1976 had taken to religiously attending meetings of the Homebrew Club, was busy sorting out people with a commercial bent from the engineers. That wasn't difficult since members were allowed to advertise their interests during the meetings. Paul Terrell was one of the more prominent salesmen and had become an influential figure in the murky world of distributors and kit suppliers. He had been selling peripherals for minicomputers until he had seen a demonstration of the Altair—after which he had quickly arranged to represent MITS in Northern California. At Homebrew meetings Terrell had pushed the Altair machines and ran afoul of the delicate sensitivities of the Homebrew members when he tried to charge $500 for a version of BASIC on paper tape.

Like others, Terrell had underestimated the enthusiasm of the hobbyists and when word of the Altair spread, he found engineers waiting outside his office door at the start of business while his regular customers started to complain that they couldn't negotiate his jammed switchboard. So Terrell buckled. "I decided we should go up on El Camino, open a store, hang out a shingle, and get all the guys who were sitting in traffic jams at four P.M." In December 1975 he transferred $12,700 worth of MITS inventory from his sales company to a computer store in Mountain View which he called the Byte Shop.

But Terrell's ambitions stretched far beyond the parish. He examined and planned to emulate Radio Shack's enormous chain of distributors and hoped someday to stock his stores with computers that he would manufacture. In private he chatted about a nationwide chain of Byte Shops like an enthusiastic goose breeder. He talked of "force-feeding the pipeline" and "pumping the product out" but he had to start somewhere and El Camino was a longer, if not better, strip than most. So El Camino, where almost every idea in search of a market was sure to find a temporary home, housed yet another. By the early summer of 1976 there were three Byte stores scattered along El Camino among the hot-tub emporiums, hi-fi stores, automobile dealers, and fast-food outlets. For the hobbyists, and for anybody hoping to sell a microcomputer, the imprimatur of the Byte Shop had become a seal worth having.

Terrell was one of the few Homebrew members with the means to buy more than one computer, so Jobs, hoping to obtain deposits before placing a firm order for one hundred printed circuit boards, visited the Byte Shop. Terrell had been wary of Jobs at Homebrew meetings. "You can always tell the guys who are going to give you a hard time. I was always cautious of him." Nevertheless, when Jobs slopped into the store, Terrell made time for him. Jobs showed Terrell a prototype of the Apple and explained his plans. Terrell told Jobs that he had no interest in selling plain, printed circuit boards and said that his customers didn't have any interest in scouring supply stores for semiconductors and other parts. Terrell said he was interested in buying only fully assembled and fully tested computers. Jobs asked how much Terrell would be prepared to pay for a fully assembled computer and was told anywhere between $489 and $589. The Emperor of the Byte Shops told Jobs that he would be prepared to place an order for fifty fully assembled Apple computers and would pay cash on delivery.

Jobs could not believe either his ears or his eyes—"I just saw dollar signs"—and rushed to telephone Wozniak at Hewlett-Packard. Wozniak, equally dumbfounded, told his colleagues around the lab who greeted the news with disbelief. Wozniak placed Terrell's order in perspective—"That was the biggest single episode in all of the company's history. Nothing in subsequent years was so great and so unexpected." Terrell's order entirely changed the scale and scope of the enterprise. The size of the business had expanded tenfold and instead of contemplating costs of around $2,500 for one hundred printed circuit boards, Jobs and Wozniak were looking at a bill of around $25,000 to cover the costs of one hundred fully assembled machines. Fifty would go to Terrell and the Byte Shop while Jobs and Wozniak would try to sell the other fifty to friends and members of the Homebrew Club. Wozniak recalled, "It was not what we had intended to do," and Terrell's order touched off a scramble for parts and a search for money.

Some ports of call were hopeless. Jobs strolled into a Los Altos bank, found the manager, asked for a loan, and was given a predictable rebuff. "I could tell that I'd get the same replies at other banks." He went to Halted and asked Hal Elzig whether he would take a share of Apple in exchange for some parts. Elzig declined the offer, recalling, "I didn't have any faith in these kids. They were running about barefoot." Jobs approached Al Alcorn and asked whether he could purchase parts from Atari. Alcorn agreed but demanded cash up front. Jobs turned to Mel Schwartz, the Stanford physics professor, who had formed a small electronics company in Palo Alto and had an established line of credit at an electronics distributor, and Schwartz agreed to buy some parts for Jobs.

Jobs then approached three electronics parts houses where he asked for credit arrangements that would allow them to assemble and deliver the computers to the Byte Shops, before paying for the parts. He was granted receptions that ranged from amusement to outright skepticism. At one shop Jobs persuaded the controller of the company to conduct a background check. Paul Terrell was surprised to find himself paged during a seminar at an electronics conference and summoned to the telephone where he assured the controller that the two characters sitting across his desk were not spinning fairy tales. Apple's biggest break came when Bob Newton, the division manager of Kierulff Electronics in Palo Alto, met Jobs and examined both him and the prototype. "He was just an aggressive little kid who didn't present himself very professionally." Nevertheless, Newton agreed to sell Jobs $20,000 worth of parts and explained that if the bill was paid within thirty days Jobs would not be charged interest. Jobs, unfamiliar with accounting rubric, recalled, "We didn't know what 'net thirty days' was."

Assured of a supply of parts, Jobs and Wozniak turned their attention to assembling and testing the computers. They were reluctant to rent a space in one of the parks of concrete and steel garages that dotted Sunnyvale and Santa Clara. Wozniak's apartment, ballooning from the early months of marriage, was too small to take the strain of a miniature assembly line. Wozniak's young wife, Alice, recalled, "The Apple was consuming all his time. I saw very little of him. He'd go off to HP and eat something at McDonald's on the way home. He wouldn't get home usually until after midnight. I was going nuts coming home from work and having things on the dining-room table that I couldn't touch." So with Alice resenting their presence, the founders of Apple resorted to the most practical spot which was the Jobs family home in Los Altos. Jobs, who was back living with his parents, commandeered the one unoccupied room in the three-bedroom house which had belonged, until she married, to his younger sister, Patty. The room was furnished with a single bed and a small chest of drawers and was fine for storing the plastic bags full of parts that arrived from the electronics distributors. The parts were assembled into Apple computers in that room and in Jobs's own bedroom, where dripping soldering irons left scorch marks on a narrow desk.

The incoming parts weren't subjected to exhaustive scrutiny. Jobs recalled, "We didn't evaluate them too much. We just found out they worked." The printed circuit boards were a great simplification over hand-wiring each computer. They sliced the assembly time for each machine from about sixty hours to about six. The boards also brought a new chore, known contemptuously in the electronics industry as "board stuffing," which required that semiconductors and all the other parts be inserted into specially numbered holes on the lime-colored board. Jobs delegated the task to his sister, who was expecting her first child. He offered to pay her one dollar for every board she stuffed, and after some practice, she found that she could finish four boards in an hour. She sat on the living-room couch, boards and parts spread out in front of her on a Formica-topped coffee table, with the Jobses' large color television providing background entertainment. The distractions of soap operas and programs like *The Gong Show,* along with telephone calls from her friends, meant that chips got plugged in the wrong way and some of their delicate gold pins wound up bent.

While the boards were being assembled, Jobs and Wozniak chewed over ideas for a retail price. Wozniak was prepared to sell the computers to his Homebrew chums for slightly more than the cost of the parts or for around $300. Jobs had larger thoughts and did some rough-and-ready reckoning. He decided that Apple should sell the boards for twice the cost of the parts and allow dealers a 33 percent markup. The arithmetic was close to Paul Terrell's offer and also happened to coincide with a retail price that had a euphonious ring: $666.66.

When Jobs turned up at the Byte Shop in Mountain View carrying twelve bulging printed circuit boards packed in thin gray cardboard boxes, Terrell was dismayed. "There was nothing. Steve was half right." The fully assembled computers turned out to be fully assembled printed circuit boards. There was quite a difference. Some energetic intevention was required before the boards could be made to do anything. Terrell couldn't even test the board without buying two transformers to power the computer and the memory. Since the Apple didn't have a keyboard or a television, no data could be funneled in or out of the computer. Once a keyboard had been hooked to the machine it still couldn't be programmed without somebody laboriously typing in the code for BASIC since Wozniak and Jobs hadn't provided the language on a cassette tape or in a ROM chip. Though Wozniak could type in 4K bytes of code in an hour, that was hardly a practical arrangement for even the most zealous hobbyist. Finally, the computer was naked. It had no case. Despite all the shortcomings and all his reservations, Terrell took delivery of the machines and paid Jobs, as he had promised, in cash.

Jobs was trying to balance everything, relying on instincts and common sense to cope with the daily rush of surprises. Aware of the importance of image he arranged for a polished corporate address by renting a mail-drop box in Palo Alto. He hired an answering service to help give the impression that Apple was a steady enterprise and not a fly-by-night operation. He also started to recruit some help and looked to familiar faces for support.

The steady, dependable Bill Fernandez had not been invited by Hewlett-Packard to transfer with the rest of the calculator division to its new base in Oregon and was looking around for work. Still living at home in Sunnyvale, Fernandez thought that Apple might someday offer him the chance to become an engineer. Jobs went through the pretense of an interview, asked some cursory questions about digital logic, and made his first job offer. Fernandez asked for a formal written contract and became Apple's first fulltime employee. "I was the only legitimate Indian. The rest were chiefs. . . . I was basically the gofer."

To keep track of the money Jobs asked his college friend, Elizabeth Holmes, who was working as a gem cutter in San Francisco, to monitor the Apple checkbook and keep a journal recording cash expenses. Holmes, who dropped by the Jobs household once a week and was paid the standard four dollars an hour, noticed that "Steve was working very, very hard. He was very directed and not very sentimental." Meanwhile, Jobs also kept Dan Kottke abreast of progress, invited him to Los Altos for the summer, and promised some work. When Kottke arrived, Clara Jobs turned the family couch into a bed.

As work started on the second batch of fifty computers, Paul Jobs buckled to reality and suggested Apple continue its business in the garage. "It was easier to empty out the garage than try and fight it out in the house. My cars could sit outside. Their stuff couldn't." Jobs temporarily retired from renovating cars, which in the summer of 1976 were Nash Metropolitans, and set about altering the garage. He cleared a long brown workbench that he had salvaged, years before, from an office in San Francisco. Loose parts were tucked into small drawers carefully labeled, MACHINE SCREWS, WASHERS, TOOTH-WASHERS, COTTER PINS, and RUBBER INSULATED CLIPS. Bulkier items were stored in a small loft above the garage along with items like dismantled lasers. Jobs lined the garage with plasterboard, rigged up extra lights, installed an extra telephone, and rehung a framed certificate that commemorated his first crossing of the equator in October 1944. He refused to move one item: a sparkling, firehouse-red trolley crammed with wrenches, pliers, spanners, and screwdrivers.

Gradually the garage started to fill. A large schematic of the computer hung on one wall. Paul Jobs built a "burn-in box" the shape of a long, plywood coffin to test the computers. It was large enough to house twelve boards which could run all night long under the uncompromising gaze of some heat lamps. The younger Jobs bought a metal workbench with a neon light from the firm that supplied Hewlett-Packard, a dispenser for three-inch-wide filament tape for the packing cartons, and a top-of-the-line postage meter. Bill Fernandez examined the purchases. "Steve was always very, very tight with money. He always wanted to get the best value for the least amount of money. Steve always wanted to make things of high quality and have high-quality equipment. He always wanted to do it right."

Clara Jobs, who scooted into the garage to use the washing machine, clothesdryer and sink, was recovering from a gallbladder operation. When her son occupied the kitchen table and turned it into a miniature office, she worked around him. When the answering service called with messages, she took notes or relayed them. When the doorbell rang she acted as receptionist, serving coffee to parts salesmen and prospective customers. She tolerated her son's infatuation with carrots and cleared up Wozniak's McDonald's hamburger wrappers and soft-drink cartons after some of the frequent all-night vigils spent chasing elusive bugs in the computer. When Wozniak's wife of six months called in tears, it was Clara Jobs who provided consolation. And when tempers flared in the garage Paul Jobs invariably provided some perspective. "What's the matter?" he would ask. "You got a feather up your ass?" Eventually Paul and Clara Jobs started joking to their friends that they were paying the mortgage in exchange for kitchen, bathroom, and bedroom privileges.

Steve Jobs asked Ron Wayne to draw schematics of the computer that would be suitable for a small manual and also to produce a logo for the company. In his apartment Wayne balanced a light table on a living-room table and produced a whimsical pen-and-ink drawing that had the tones of a monochrome engraving for a nineteenth-century college calendar. It was a portrait of Isaac Newton, quill in hand, resting against the trunk of a tree bearing one apple wreathed in an ethereal glow. Wrapped around the edge of the picture was a scroll that carried a line from Wordsworth's "The Prelude": NEWTON—A MIND FOREVER VOYAGING THROUGH STRANGE SEAS OF THOUGHT, ALONE. Wayne also started work on a four-page manual using an IBM electric typewriter which, with careful reckoning, could justify text at both margins. This spawned an argument over the use of background tones, with Jobs insisting that a gray shade be used for parts of the schematic. When the gray obliterated some of the detail, Wayne said, "We're both to blame. You for suggesting it. Me for listening to you."

Jobs displayed a similar concern for appearance when Kottke and he drafted Apple's first advertisement. The pair sat at the kitchen table with Jobs spitting out ideas while Kottke cleaned up the grammar. When the advertisement was set in type, Kottke recalled that Jobs was "meticulous about the typeface." Kottke meanwhile tried to immerse himself in electronics, reading manuals about the 6502 microprocessor and trying to catch up on what he'd missed during his adolescence. On one occasion he and Jobs tried to convert one of the computers into a makeshift clock. Unable to keep his friend in full-time employment, Jobs found him some extra work at Call Computer where Kamradt was still cursing the hidden quirks of Wozniak's Computer Conversor.

The prodding from the Byte Shop's Paul Terrell forced Jobs to pressure Wozniak to come up with an interface that could load BASIC into the computer from a cassette tape recorder. Wozniak, fully occupied with the computer, arranged for another engineer at Hewlett-Packard to design the interface in return for a royalty on sales. The design was unsatisfactory; it couldn't read the data properly from the tape and the duo had to buy out the engineer for $1,000. Wozniak flinched. "We weren't going to go ahead with our design and then pay him for each one we sold." Wozniak, who had no experience designing interfaces and had never dealt with data stored on cassette tapes, rigged up the simplest possible design: "It worked." Mounted on a small two-inch-high printed circuit board, the interface plugged into the main board.

As a sales incentive a cassette tape of BASIC was included with the $75 interface card and the Apple advertising copy stated: "Our philosophy is to provide software for our machines free or at minimal cost." The one-page advert carried the slogan: BYTE INTO AN APPLE and boasted about "A Little Cassette Board That Works," though it could be relied on to cope only with cassettes running on expensive tape recorders. There was a tentative tone about the ad that was reflected in the line "The Apple Computer is in stock at almost all major computer stores."

It was certainly in stock at the Byte Shops. It was almost always in stock. Despite the koa-wood cases that were supplied by a local cabinetmaker, Paul Terrell and his cast of refugee engineers and programmers found that the Apple computers weren't selling as quickly as the Altair or the IMSAI 8080, a computer that would run software written for the Altair and was sold by IMS Associates, another small company on the San Francisco Peninsula. Terrell, who was in the middle of a frantic eleven months during which he masterminded the opening of seventy-four Byte stores across North America, couldn't afford to stock $10,000 worth of slow-moving computers in shops that had monthly sales of only $20,000. At his headquarters he spent much of his time asking skeptical outsiders—who muttered about his precarious balance sheet and poked at the Formica counters—whether they could remember what the first one hundred McDonald's looked like. As for the Apples he recalled, "We had problems unloading them."

For a few weeks Jobs and Kottke tooled along El Camino, delivering the computers and encountering teenagers in the stores. Some, too young to drive, had discovered that if they timed it right they could catch the No. 21 and No. 22 buses of the Santa Clara Transit District and visit every Byte store in an afternoon. The teenagers formed a permanent part of the decor, playing with the computers laid out on the table, feeding paper-tape programs into the computers, and performing small programming chores in return for free magazines.

On these weekly rounds, Jobs typed into the Apple a demonstration program that paraded the message THIS IS AN APPLE COMPUTER across a television screen. Some of the Byte Shop managers found Jobs tough to handle. One, Bob Moody, said, "It was difficult at best. Steve wasn't the guy to deal with. He was very fidgety and very abrupt." Terrell was a bit more patient and reassured Jobs about the name of Apple Computer. "He came flying into the Byte Shop, buzzing at a hundred miles per hour. 'It's the goddamn logo. People think it's horseshit. We've got to change the name. Nobody is going to take it seriously.'" Terrell, who had endured similar taunts after he gave his store a name most people mistook for a sand-wich bar, passed on a piece of homespun wisdom: "Once people understand what the name means, they will never forget you. If it's difficult, people will remember it." The Apple price tags of $666.66 also brought trouble. They prompted a stream of angry telephone calls from a group of Sikhs who were convinced that the price had evil significance. When the horror movie *The Omen*, which also contained frightening references to strings of sixes, started playing in local theaters, the calls increased. After repeatedly explaining that there was no mystical reference in the price, Jobs utterly exasperated, finally told one irate caller, "I took the two most spiritual numbers I could think of: 777.77 and 111.11 and subtracted one from the other."

Ron Wayne was worried about more temporal matters. The size of the contract with the Byte Shops, which had gained a reputation for not always managing to pay bills on time, and the prospect of having to underwrite one tenth of any loss that Apple might incur, proved too much. Wayne left the partnership in the summer of 1976 and typed out a formal letter which he hoped absolved him of all responsibility. "I had already learned what gave me indigestion and I was beginning to feel the months running by. If Apple had failed, I would have had bruises on top of bruises. Steve Jobs was an absolute whirlwind and I had lost the energy you need to ride whirlwinds."

Though they had lost Wayne, by the time they decided to build a second batch of a hundred computers Jobs and Wozniak had established some credit. The local bank managers still refused to place any faith in Apple but there were others who would. Wozniak had an informal credit line with his pal Allen Baum who had bailed him out of previous scrapes. Jobs and Wozniak explained their predicament and asked for a $5,000 loan which they promised to repay as soon as the computers were sold. Baum and his father, Elmer, stumped up the money and wrote up a loan agreement for a year with the provision that it could be renewed quarterly. Allen Baum considered his money safe. "I had no doubt that it would be repaid. Steve Jobs had this silver tongue that could talk anyone into anything." Elmer Baum wasn't quite so sure. "I did it because he was Allen's friend. I was in pretty bad shape financially but Steve gave me a pitch. If I hadn't known him, I would have thought he was really good."

Most of the people connected with Apple were cautious, and contrary to the usual picture of small businesses, they were all wary of loss. Each had his own method for absorbing any risk that might crop up. Wozniak was supported by the regular paycheck from Hewlett-Packard. Ron Wayne decided he couldn't afford to take any chances while the Baums insured their gamble by charging a hefty interest on their loan. Bill Fernandez made sure that he received a contract. Steve Jobs risked something else—devoting years of his life to the business and becoming consumed by Apple.

The tension between mysticism and the business of assembling computers was caught in a gently sardonic correspondence with Dan Kottke who had returned to school in the East. On one occasion Kottke mailed Jobs a mystical photograph and enclosed a note which read in part: "After performing an extensive prana to the lotus feet of suchness, gaze lovingly upon picture with cosmic thoughts of cosmic relevance and profundity until phone rings. Answer phone, haggle furiously and refuse to sell for less than 2.3 million."

But there were some aspects of Apple that Jobs enjoyed. "I was getting a chance to do some things the way I thought they should be done. I felt I had nothing to lose by leaving Atari because I could always go back." For Jobs corporations were large and ugly and like Lockheed. They bribed senators. They arranged kickbacks. They paid for three-martini lunches. Jobs recalled, "I didn't want to be a businessman because all the businessmen I knew I didn't want to be like. I thought that living in a monastery had to be different from being a businessman." The private turmoil was the center of long discussions with those around him. Bill Fernandez padded along on midnight walks around Los Altos and Cupertino and provided a sounding board. Ron Wayne noticed that "Steve was searching. He seriously questioned whether he should pursue Apple." Wayne, for one, did not provide much reassurance, telling Jobs that he ran the risks of Frankenstein and predicted he would get swallowed in the maw of the company he was creating.

There was an older, wiser fountain of advice. Kobin Chino was a Zen monk whom Jobs met after he returned from India. Chino had been active in the San Francisco Zen Center as a student of Suzuki Roshi, author of *Zen Mind, Beginner's Mind,* a reflective handbook for followers of Zen. Chino lived at a small Zen center in Los Altos and Nancy Rogers, who had followed Jobs and Kottke to India, was living in a tent near the ranch, taking meditation courses. Jobs visited her frequently and talked both to her and to Chino about abandoning Apple and heading for a Zen monastery in Japan. Both Chino and Rogers listened. The former was amused at the dilemma and, in broken English, advised Jobs to pursue the business, telling him that he would find business to be the same as sitting in a monastery. Jobs did some more soul searching. "I had a sense that Apple would be consuming. It was a real hard decision not to go to Japan. Part of me was a little concerned because I was afraid if I went I wouldn't come back." Nancy Rogers felt "Steve was afraid of Apple. He thought he'd turn into a monster."

In the late summer of 1976 the managers and engineers at other computer, semiconductor, and video-game companies did not think that Apple posed a monstrous threat. At Atari, according to Nolan Bushnell, "We were up to our asses in alligators," so the hobby computer market would have been a peripheral distraction for a company whose central line of business revolved around entertainment and video games. At the semiconductor houses like National Semiconductor and Intel Corporation, some enthusiasts formed small task forces, pored over magazines like *Byte* and *Interface Age,* clipped advertisements of some of the small companies that were advertising single-board computers, and paid visits at predictable and appropriate ports of call. They knocked on the doors of companies like MITS. They were given demonstrations of the Alto Computer which was being developed at Xerox's Palo Alto Research Center. They talked to the editors of the People's Computer Company. They read industry surveys drawn up by research companies—which, in most cases, were little more than a man, a computer, and a cloudy crystal ball. They talked to some investment analysts at New York banks and were altogether thorough and dutiful. Then they retreated to their homes and offices to draw up arguments and marketing plans to convince their superiors of the bright future of microcomputers. They told them of the large number of hobbyists, of the puny competition, and of how semiconductors made up at least half the cost of a microcomputer.

Most of the chiefs were unimpressed. They thought the market for assembled microcomputers would be limited to hobbyists and most still bore the scars of earlier attempts to sell consumer items. Some years before, other young men had mustered similar arguments and had persuaded them to build digital watches and calculators. The results had been painful. The chiefs had discovered that expertise in one area wasn't something that could be transferred to another and that technical superiority wasn't enough to sway the consumer. Rapid price cutting and competition from the Orient had left some semiconductor companies with warehouses full of unsold calculators and watches.

The semiconductor houses were also faced with their own demands. William Davidow, a vice-president at Intel, remembered, "We had enough trouble keeping the wheels glued on our own machine without worrying about something else." Meanwhile, the minicomputer companies decided it made more sense to shrink their machines rather than to try to build microcomputers. Both Digital Equipment Corporation, which introduced the DEC LS1-11, and Data General with its microNova started to sell machines with switches on the front panels that looked like little sisters of the larger machines.

So small microcomputer companies were left in their anonymity. Most of the others had never even heard of Apple which was too small, too fragile, and too eccentric to be taken seriously. Those with a prophetic bent decided that the company was doomed by Wozniak's nonconformist decision to choose the 6502 microprocessor while most other companies built their computers around the 8080. Distributors and retailers like Paul Terrell had decided that the future lay with the 8080, the S-100 bus, and industry standards and were planning to discontinue stocking 6502 machines. The large advertisements in magazines like *Byte* were for companies like Southwest Technical Products, Processor Technology, and IMSAI. The Apple computer was an unconventional local curiosity.

Shortly before Labor Day, 1976, Wozniak and Jobs headed to the East Coast for a computer show that was being staged in a rundown hotel in Atlantic City. They packed a suitcase with Apple computers and a bundle of one-page advertisements. Along with the Apple computers, Wozniak carried another machine mounted in a case known to hobbyists as a cigar box. Like the engineers and salesmen of other California computer companies, Jobs and Wozniak took TWA's Flight 67 from San Francisco to Philadelphia. Much of the flight was consumed with the buzz of technical conversation, shop talk, gossip, and surreptitious peeks at new computers. The salesmen from Processor Technology were carrying a new machine named the Sol Terminal Computer, after Les Solomon, the editor of *Popular Electronics*. Dressed in a sheet-metal case with a built-in keyboard, it made the other computers look dated and amateurish. Its proponents were confident that their computer would savage the competition. They talked disparagingly of blankies—computers that had nothing but a switch on a front panel—and of blinkies, like the Altair, with just lights on the front panel. In their minds the Sol formed an entirely new category. Lee Felsenstein, who was a consultant to Processor Technology, leaned over Wozniak's headrest, glanced at the prototype of the new computer that rested on the fold-down tray, and formed his own conclusion, "It was thoroughly unimpressive. These two guys just had a cigar box. What the hell did they know?"

A LOT OF POOP

The cigar box that Wozniak and Jobs took to Atlantic City in the dog days of 1976 contained a savagely deformed Apple computer. The printed circuit board screwed to the wooden base was festooned with fresh wires that sneaked between the chips. Despite its forlorn appearance, Wozniak and Jobs guarded the machine carefully. During the daytime, while they tried to sell some Apple computers from a card table on the convention floor, it was locked in their seedy hotel room. In the evenings, after the crowds had disappeared from the fair, Wozniak, Jobs, and Dan Kottke (who had journeyed from New York to help his friends) slipped into a room dominated by a large television screen. Wozniak ran a cable across the carpet, typed some commands into the computer, and made it fling startling sprays of color across the television screen.

Wozniak had been working on enhancements to the Apple since its introduction at the Homebrew Club. In the give-and-take following the original announcement some members had asked what additional features were being contemplated. Wozniak mentioned that he was working on a circuit with a few chips that would convert the black-and-white machine into a color computer. It was an extravagant claim since at the time designers thought a color circuit would take at least forty chips. Wozniak's determination to add color to the Apple sprang from a demonstration at the Homebrew Club of a minicomputer that was capable of displaying color graphics. The Dazzler, a machine produced by Cromemco, a small company whose founders attended Homebrew meetings, also created color displays that left their mark on Wozniak. "It was so impressive to see colors whirling around. I knew I wanted to do color." So his announcement that he intended to design some color circuitry was virtually a masochistic challenge and completion amounted to a virility test. Wozniak's chief reason for adding color circuitry was practical. He wanted a computer that would play Breakout, the game that he and Jobs had designed for Atari.

Wozniak returned to his lab bench at Hewlett-Packard and started to attack two entirely different problems. One centered on devising a circuit that would display color. The other was devoted to reducing the number of chips on the board by simplifying the memory. The Apple computer had two sets of memory. One—an 8K-byte board of chips—served the microprocessor. Another—composed of shift registers (an older, slower form of memory)—served the black-and-white display. In an effort to reduce the number of chips, Wozniak wanted to find a way to let one memory serve both the computer and the display. He investigated the way a picture is displayed on a television and found that a raster scan spends two thirds of its time moving across the screen spraying the phosphor with electrons from left to right, and one third of its time whipping back from right to left. Armed with that knowledge Wozniak decided to force the microprocessor and the display to share the same memory. While the raster moved across the screen, taking bits from the memory, the microprocessor was barred. And while the raster whipped back, the microprocessor plunged in. It was the sort of approach that had been the subject of debate at the Homebrew and a writer in the newsletter had wondered in August 1975 whether the timing for a display might be solved for members if "a circuit could be published which read from a microcomputer memory while the computer isn't using it." To make the allocation work, Wozniak had to slow down the speed of the microprocessor. "All the computer was supposed to do was play games, so nobody would ever know. It was funny. Just by thinking of a couple of unrelated issues, out came a simpler design." Wozniak had virtually added color for free and designed a computer which, though it had about half the number of chips of the first machine, was more powerful.

Wozniak also wanted to expand the capacity of the Apple. Much of the power of minicomputers had sprung from slots in the motherboard that housed smaller printed circuit boards. The slots were a crucial part of the design because it meant that the computers could be expanded to perform a large variety of tasks. smaller printed circuit boards that plugged into the slots might contain more memory chips, a connection to a printer or to a telephone. Some of the most successful minicomputer companies had encouraged smaller firms to make peripherals that would work with the computer. So the slots tended to bring benefits to everybody: to the computer manufacturer who could boast about the machine's many attributes and the subindustry that it created; to peripheral manufacturers who would make a new product; and to the customer who came to own a machine that could do more than one job. Part of the reason the Altair made such an impression on the hobbyists was that it mimicked a minicomputer with slots. Wozniak liked the notion of slots—"I was used to computers with twenty slots that were always filled up with boards"—and decided that his color computer should have eight slots. Jobs disagreed, and the difference of opinion turned into one of their most protracted arguments. Wozniak recalled, "All Steve saw was a computer that could do a couple of things—write basic programs and play games. He thought you might add a printer and maybe a modem but you would never need more than two slots. I refused to let it go with two slots.

While Jobs and Wozniak wrangled about the number of slots, they made regular appearances at the Homebrew Club whose meetings ran like a motif through the development of the color computer. At the hobbyist sessions Wozniak collected a couple of teenage camp followers: Randy Wigginton who in the summer of 1976 was sixteen and fifteen-year-old Chris Espinosa. Wigginton had written some small programs for Call Computer and had encountered Wozniak and his dumb terminal, being more impressed by the latter than the former. Wigginton's father was a Lockheed engineer and the family home was in Sunnyvale. With a tongue that could be rough but with sunny, ice-cream looks, Wigginton had his share of growing pains. "I was strung out on drugs at junior high school." He watched while one of his acquaintances, a drug pusher, was arrested for murdering a slow-paying client who had been stuffed down a sewer. Wigginton was thirteen when he found a less dangerous diversion after encountering computers at a Homestead High School summer class where a Teletype terminal was linked to a computer at Hewlett-Packard. "Once I hit computers that was the end." Transferred by his parents to a private high school in San Jose, he became engrossed by computers. In his freshman year he organized a computer class and in his sophomore year taught BASIC to students two years his senior. He was nicknamed Computer Randy and when, embarrassed at having no date for the junior prom he tried to escape the clutches of a ticket seller, he was told to invite a computer. Wigginton found that Wozniak, who had endured similar taunts, was far more sympathetic. Wozniak provided parts and guidance and helped Wigginton, whose chunky soldering iron was giving him trouble, build his first piece of hardware, an Apple.

The Homestead summer computer course proved as infectious for Chris Espinosa as it had for Wigginton. "Once we were armed with elementary knowledge we knew more than the teacher." Espinosa had been raised in Los Angeles where he attended nine different schools in eight years but was caught in the Cupertino mill when his father started attending law classes at the University of Santa Clara. "Cupertino was a completely different atmosphere. In Los Angeles most of my friends grew up to be thieves, musicians, or drug addicts. In Cupertino I had new friends who were intelligent, academically inclined, middle-class and fairly progressive." During junior high school Espinosa was a student spokesman at town meetings that were convened to discuss plans to turn an orchard into a shopping mall. Thanks to an interest in public transportation, he also became a thorn in the side of the Santa Clara Transit District, arguing at public meetings in favor of an expansion of the local bus service and touting the merits of light railways. He took to riding buses for hours— "To me, the bus service was a large, intricate system"—and used them to visit Byte Shops where he learned how to program an Apple. Yet like Wigginton, who introduced him to Wozniak, Espinosa was too young to drive to Homebrew meetings. Since neither the tentacles of the bus system nor the inclination of their parents extended to the darker fringes of Palo Alto on Wednesday evenings, Wigginton and Espinosa were chauffeured to Homebrew meetings by Wozniak.

The two teenagers became Wozniak's acolytes. Espinosa persuaded Wozniak to give a computer to Homestead High School and displayed his bright, jaunty sense of humor by installing it in a box labeled IBM. On trips to Homebrew, they piled into Wozniak's car, making space on a backseat covered with magazines, newspapers, and hamburger wrappers and joking that the fungus growing on the upholstery was known, in botanical circles, as the Woz Effect. Espinosa, being of slighter build, carted books and manuals into meetings while Wigginton had the unenviable task of carrying Wozniak's nineteen-inch Sears color television. Wozniak carried the new computer in a wooden case designed and built by Wigginton's brother. After the meetings the trio adjourned to a local Denny's for more shoptalk. At one of the Homebrew sessions Jobs quizzed Espinosa, who was displaying his prowess by demonstrating the color, and offered him a job in exchange for a row of 4K memory chips which were the most sought-after parts for the Apple. Espinosa accepted but recalled, "Jobs never came through with the promise."

At every Homebrew meeting the Apple was set up on a card table alongside other hobby computers near the entrance to the SLAC auditorium. In the steeply raked hall, almost every major development in microcomputers surfaced while the club newsletter dutifully reported on the appearance of new products, the dates of fairs, the opening of the first computer store in Santa Monica, and the start of retail computer-kit companies like Kentucky Fried Computers. The newsletter's editors also taught the tinkerers some of the cruel facts of life. When Processor Technology's video display failed to appear as promised, the newsletter noted: "It would appear that patience is a necessary attribute of the computer hobbyist." There were frequent appeals for more software and an announcement of a journal whose editors intended to publish computer languages and programs and who gave it the whimsical title *Dr. Dobbs' Journal of Computer Calisthenics and Orthodontia.*

*   *   *

While Wozniak busied himself developing some programs for the Apple, the issue of software spurred a vigorous debate at the club. Most computer hobbyists considered software, if not a birthright, certainly something that should be provided free of charge to anyone who displayed the derring-do and moxie to build his own computer. The programmers who wrote software disagreed. In an open letter to hobbyists, published in the Homebrew newsletter, Bill Gates, one of the developers of the original BASIC for the Altair, complained that though most of MITS customers possessed a copy of BASIC, only about one tenth had actually bought the program. "Without good software," Gates wrote, "and an owner who understands programming a hobby computer is wasted. . . . As the majority of hobbyists must be aware, most of you steal your software." Gates's spirited defense of programmers' rights fell on deaf ears though one club member did respond: "Calling all your potential future customers thieves is perhaps 'uncool' marketing strategy."

Marketing was another thing that Wozniak couldn't be bothered with. Most of the features he gradually added to the Apple conformed to his personal wishes. He added circuits for game paddles and sound so that Breakout could be presented in its full glory. Letters appeared on the screen in upper case because most of the keyboards used by Homebrew members could only cope with capital letters. Wozniak even wrote a routine to convert lower case to upper case. "We weren't thinking very far ahead. We were going to put on a lower-case keyboard but we didn't have time to get to it." Similarly, the computer was designed to display only forty characters in a line because television screens couldn't cope with any more.

Wozniak was not even certain that he wanted Jobs to sell his color computer. At the time Apple was formed, Wozniak had reached a verbal arrangement with Jobs and Ron Wayne that he would own all the rights to improvements in the Apple. For a time he entertained the idea of selling his enhanced version to the manufacturer of the Sol Terminal, Processor Technology. "I wasn't sure that it was an Apple product." The entire Wozniak household was skeptical about Jobs. Leslie Wozniak heard about him as "this schlunky looking guy with bare feet and dirty hair," while her parents harbored more serious doubts about their older son's business partner. Jerry Wozniak encouraged his son to think about other allies and offered to put him in contact with some of his own acquaintances. "We wondered about Steve Jobs," Jerry Wozniak recalled. "We thought he was the type of person who felt he should always start right at the top and didn't care to work his way up."

These domestic clashes came to a head when, in the fall of 1976, two representatives from Commodore Business Machines arrived at Jobs's garage and offered to buy Apple lock, stock, and prototype. The prospective purchasers were familiar faces. Both Chuck Peddle and Andre Sousan had previously dealt with Apple, and the former had led the team that designed the MOS Technology 6502. (Wozniak had bought his first 6502 from Peddle's wife at the San Francisco trade fair.) While Wozniak made modifications to the Apple, Peddle had called at Jobs's garage and had demonstrated the KIM-1, a single-board microcomputer developed by MOS Technology to help train engineers who would use the 6502 in elevators and household appliances. In the interim MOS Technology had been acquired by Commodore Business Machines, where Andre Sousan was vice-president of engineering. Both Sousan and Peddle were convinced that a computer like a modified Apple would allow their new employer to jump into the microcomputer field. Jobs also had his price. He wanted $100,000 for Apple, some Commodore stock, and salaries of $36,000 a year for himself and Wozniak.

In fact, a sale would have brought more money than either had ever contemplated and also relief from a year of fourteen-hour workdays. But the more inquiries Jobs made about Commodore, the more suspicious he became. He asked about Jack Tramiel, Commodore's founder, who in the early seventies had been roundly cursed by the electronic-calculator industry for leading a savage price war and operating a chain of stores called Mr. Calculator. Jobs soon learned that when Tramiel started to bargain, he often fell back on a favorite saying: "There's one thing closer to me than my shirt and that's my skin." Jobs was unimpressed. "The more I looked into Commodore the sleazier they were. I couldn't find one person who had made a deal with them and was happy. Everyone felt they had been cheated." For their part, Tramiel and Commodore Chairman Irving Gould decided they did not want to acquire Apple. Sousan recalled: "They thought it was ridiculous to acquire two guys working out of a garage."

Yet Commodore's approaches were the subject of long discussions between Jobs and Wozniak and there were bitter disagreements about how any proceeds should be divided. Jerry Wozniak entered the arguments and made his feelings quite clear. Mark Wozniak recalled the strength of his father's opinions. "Dad got Jobs to cry a couple of times. He said he was going to make the little sonuvabitch cry and that'd be the end. He told him, 'You don't deserve shit. You haven't produced anything. You haven't done anything.' It came close to the end." Jobs felt miserable, was convinced that Jerry Wozniak sorely underestimated his contributions and told the younger Wozniak, "Woz, if we're not fifty-fifty you can have the whole thing." Eventually Jobs's instincts prevailed and Commodore and Apple went their separate ways.

While the founders of Apple were fending off suitors, they were also busying themselves with further modifications to the computer. Jobs thought a quiet machine without a fan would sell better than some of the noisier computers that used fans to cool power supplies that were as hot as toasters. Wozniak had never been that interested in power supplies: When he and Fernandez developed the Cream Soda Computer it was the power supply that failed. When he and Baum designed the Data General Nova, they hadn't even bothered to design a power supply. The power supplies for the Apple were afterthoughts. Power supplies were something to be plugged in at the last moment, something that could always be fished off a shelf at Haltek. The only time it was necessary to worry about a power supply was when it threatened to send a bolt of volts streaking through the computer—and blow out every sweetly tuned piece of digital electronics.

Power supplies belonged to an older, stodgier branch of electronics whose basic rules hadn't changed that much since the early days of radio. Power supplies, like regulators and transformers, were analog devices, and there was an emotional and intellectual division between analog and digital electronics. Youngsters like Wozniak were much more interested in digital electronics, where change was more rapid. Their conceptual world was framed in terms of highs and lows and 1s and 0s and their lives circulated around handling solutions that were presented to them by the semiconductor manufacturers.

General-purpose engineers tended to be more adept at analog electronics, which drew from a wide range of scientific disciplines and required a more thorough grounding in mathematics and physics. Analog designers worried more about completeness, aware that the addition of a screw or the placing of a wire might affect the performance of their design. They fretted about current losses and were altogether a more circumspect, patient breed. Unlike digital designers who would exclaim "It works," the analog designers would be more cautious, explaining, "It works within the bounds of the specs."

So Jobs drove to Atari and asked Al Alcorn to recommend somebody who could help design a power supply that wouldn't need a fan. He returned to the garage exploding with optimism, telling Wozniak and Wigginton that he had met the greatest analog designer in the history of the universe, an engineer who could design a power supply that would light up New York but still run off a six-volt battery. The subject of the excitement, Frederick Rodney Holt, was less confident about Apple. He met Jobs, surveyed all that was visible between hair and toe, and wondered whether Apple could afford to pay his consultancy fee. "I told him I was expensive. He said, That's no problem.' He just conned me into working."

Holt started spending evenings and weekends at Apple, and Jobs and Wozniak discovered, once again, that appearances were deceptive. Holt looked as if he might have been the chief designer of a sci-fi machine that fired bolts of swizzle sticks. His face was creased with pleats; he had jade-colored eyes, a thatch of hair, and a bony frame that was usually decked in a turtleneck shirt, slacks, and waffle-stomper shoes. Thin fingers almost always held a Camel cigarette and were stained with the nicotine that gave him a raspy cough. But he was no dried-out, middle-aged engineer. Though old enough to be the father of both Wozniak and Jobs, Holt had first become a parent at the age of eighteen, a year after he had left home to marry the first of several wives.

As a youth he had inherited the complete works of Lenin from his grandfather, a Revolutionary Socialist who ran for governor of the State of Maine on the Eugene Debs ticket. And though Lenin came to share his teenage bookshelf with the works of Darwin, Holt decided that the triumph of the proletariat was infinitely preferable to the survival of the fittest. He found graduate work in mathematics at Ohio State lonely—"It was like playing chess with yourself"—edited a free-speech newspaper, and explored the private jealousies of radical-left splinter groups. He became national treasurer for the student portion of the National Coalition Against the War in Vietnam and was invited by a small New York publisher to write a book about the Logic of Marxism. But he was diverted by the call of politics and in 1965, when John Lindsay ran for mayor of New York City, Holt managed the rival campaign of a black taxi driver who stood as a Revolutionary Socialist. The duo succeeded in drawing far more attention from the FBI than from the New York electorate.

Alongside his political forays Holt developed an interest in both electronics and motorcycles. He developed, built, and installed some low-distortion hi-fi sets "with a lot of poop" and for almost ten years worked at an electronics company in the Midwest where he helped to design a low-cost oscilloscope. During evenings and weekends Holt graduated from riding motor scooters to Harley Davidsons and Triumphs, and from flat-track to illegal road racing. As the years passed and racers bought the latest motorcycles, Holt's edge, which depended on his mechanical ability to modify stock machinery, began to evaporate. Nevertheless, when he moved to the West Coast from Ohio in the early seventies he installed his three motorcycles on a trailer and towed them across the country. In the spring of 1976 he abandoned racing because muscle-nerve damage in his thumbs prevented him from keeping a tight grip on the handlebars. The language of the motorcycle circuit still speckled his speech but his forced retirement and a bitter quarrel with a longtime friend at Atari nudged him toward Apple. "If I had still been racing motorcycles when Jobs came along, I probably would have told him to get lost."

Holt found that Jobs and the unruly Apple computer presented intriguing problems: "It was a challenge to do something on a commercial scale that had never been done before. It was the kind of problem that has a certain intrinsic appeal to me." However, Holt was not about to let any part-time consulting, no matter how interesting, interfere with his weekly game of pool. And Jobs and Wozniak soon discovered it was impossible to talk to Holt about any subject without finding that he was armed with something more than rudimentary knowledge. An off-the-cuff remark about the glaze on a piece of pottery was liable to provoke a discourse on chemical treatments. An admiring comment about a snapshot would prompt a discourse on photogravure techniques. Grumbles about the price of memory chips would spark a lecture on the evils of the capitalist system while a casual mention of poker was almost certain to produce a spirited card game. Holt, the youngsters at Apple soon noticed, was the sort of person who would want to be on speaking terms with an electron and was quite likely to sit down in a restaurant and, on the back of a napkin, prove that he didn't exist.

"It costs a helluva lot to have a revolution,"
Goldman said.

Beyond the windows a long maroon steel beam hung carelessly from a crane. From the ground some laborers flashed earthy semaphore signals at the crane driver. The white crowns of their construction hats made bouncing mirrors of the sun. For the two dozen people seated around a U-shaped table in an anemic ground-floor office the noise of the work on Apple's new corporate headquarters was sealed off by tinted windows. The drooping beam and the white hats were like a scene torn from a silent film on construction safety.

A few of the people at the meeting doodled and stared through the windows. About half were marketing managers from different divisions at Apple while the others came from the Chiat-Day advertising agency. John Couch, the head of the division making Lisa, sat anxiously on the edge of his seat. Fred Hoar, Apple's vice-president of communications, smoothed his carefully combed auburn hair and Henry Whitfield stood beside an overhead projector. Others concentrated on Fred Goldberg as he made some remarks about the campaign that he and his colleagues at the advertising agency had prepared for Apple. Goldberg described some of the preparations for advertisements that would appear simultaneously with the company shareholders' meeting where Lisa and the Apple IIes were to be formally introduced. He then started to outline a plan for advertising all of Apple's computers.

"We've got a job to cut through the confusion and make a brand a brand," Goldberg said. "We've got to build confidence among new users about which computers to use and when. Most people don't just buy the computer. They buy the company, its size and the confidence it inspires." He expressed some faith in the effect of the advertisements. "The running of around an announcement offers much less chance of backfiring than PR. When you run advertising you know what you're going to get. Spending corporate money demonstrates corporate confidence in the product. It makes a statement when you spend your own money."

Goldberg introduced the agency's creative director, Lee Clow. A tall man with a faint stoop and a beard, Clow inhaled deeply on a cigarette and propped some poster-sized advertisements on a table. He pointed at the posters and said, "The second coming is the tenor of what we think this piece should be." He read a chunk of the copy: "Evolution. Revolution." He paused. "It's very delicate to say that everything everyone else makes is obsolete, but that's what we are trying to say. It's very important that the Lisa introduction show that everyone else is an also-ran." Clow finished reading the ad copy and some of the people from Apple voiced their concerns.

"We don't want the ads to step on the editorial," Fred Hoar said. He pointed out that news reports would appear for a few days following the introductions of Lisa and the Apple IIe. "This is going to be a skyrocket. I want to give the PR some impact."

Alan Oppenheimer, an Apple marketing manager with a generous smile and steel-framed spectacles, touched on a running sore. Though Mac and Lisa both relied on a mouse and on visual symbols, programs written for one wouldn't work on another. So the marketers had their hands full trying to conceal the fact that Lisa and Mac might have been designed by different companies. "Maybe the master plan is not quite appropriate," Oppenheimer said. "Mac and Lisa aren't compatible. The technical press can see through it. They could take us apart."

"The master-plan harmonic wouldn't be something we'd ram home," Hoar said, "but we'd like to dispel the idea that Apple is opportunistic, haphazard, and uncoordinated."

John Couch rocked on the edge of his chair and commented sharply, "What we really want to say is 'Here's a personal office system. There's been a hardware revolution in the seventies and there will be a software revolution in the eighties.' That's the message."

A few seats down the table, Linda Goffen, who worked for Couch, nodded vigorously and added, "We have to preempt that terminology and make it our own."

As the debate subsided Clow described the advertising agency's proposal for linking advertisements for Lisa and Mac. He recited the tag line: "Introducing computers you don't have to be afraid of even if you have to hold a mouse in your hand."

"I think that's almost technical suicide," said Paul Dali, the tousle-haired head of marketing for the Apple II and Apple III. "Apart from the mouse interface they're not similar. We shouldn't be trying to create a family."

"The only people that'll beat us up on compatibility will be the *Fortune* 500," Couch said in a soothing manner. 'They'll say, 'Why can't I take my word processor home from Lisa and plug it into Mac?' They'll think we're a bunch of dummies."

"It's an issue." Henry Whitfield sighed. "These things are incompatible. People are going to find out sooner or later that they're not going to talk to each other. Most of the *Fortune* 1000 companies think we should have more compatibility. We'll say we've tried to keep the price down to get back into more of a consumer marketplace."

John Couch returned to the central theme of the meeting: how Apple could persuade people in large companies to buy Lisas and Macs. He started to complain about the data-processing managers who were used to controlling the computer power at large companies. "They're more concerned about putting barriers up to prevent computers from getting to the rest of the world. They didn't like Apple IIs running all over the place and now they've got IBM calling on them. We cannot compete with IBM from a sales and service standpoint so we've got to rely on technology. We've got to say, 'It's new technology. There's a revolution out there. If the technology doesn't meet your needs, still buy Apple because they're way out in front of everybody.'"

"We've got to plant the flag right," Paul Dali emphasized.

"There just isn't enough money," Fred Goldberg said, spreading his hands in a resigned way.

"We've been banging our heads against the wall to get more money," Henry Whitfield observed. "We're significantly underspending. We just don't have enough money."

"You cannot have a revolution and approach it with quarterpage ads," the advertising agency's Maurice Goldman agreed. "It costs a helluva lot to have a revolution."

MERCEDES AND
A CORVETTE

Apple Computer was caught in a thin, flimsy world of amateurs. It was a comfortable place that many microcomputer companies were content to occupy. The engineers could argue into the small hours about circuits and clever pieces of code. The founders could revel in their newfound authority, snipe at the staid ways of large companies, place large advertisements in small publications, lick their lips at the sight of several thousand dollars, and generally conduct themselves like tinpot emperors of banana republics. Many of these people never understood what they didn't know and were either too wary, or too cocksure, to seek advice from others more experienced in the ways of the world.

These receptacles of wisdom sat in dozens of low-slung buildings with steel frames, concrete walls, and blank panes of glass. By the mid-seventies these monotonous industrial barns had largely replaced the mosaic of fields and orchards that had once stretched over the plain alongside the western fringes of San Francisco Bay. They were home for the dozens of companies that had been founded during the sixties and seventies as the center of electronic novelty drifted south from Sunnyvale toward San Jose. There was a clinical frailty to these buildings that were sometimes called "tilt-ups" because the walls were made from prefabricated blocks of poured concrete which were tilted into position. The buildings looked as if they had been supplied by a builder with a florist's yard. There were fresh curbstones, gleaming black asphalt, and cropped grass that had all the smoothness and allure of Astroturf. It was an industrial Levittown.

A quick drive around Santa Clara or Mountain View brought a blur of logos and signs that seemed to be contractions or combinations of about five words: Advanced-Digi-Integrated-Micro-Technologies. The similar sounding names that stood by the driveways were familiar to any regular reader of *Electronics News,* but to say the companies were all the same was about as perceptive as observing that most shirts come with collars, sleeves, and buttons. Life behind the walls had a transitory flavor and the old seasonal rhythms of rural life had given way to a pattern associated with young companies that was almost biological. It tended to run through a cycle of ambition, enthusiasm, exhilaration, complication, disillusion, and frustration. An electronics association had taken to publishing a corporate genealogical chart, and chroniclers of the electronics industry would patiently explain to newcomers how Fairchild Semiconductor begat Intel Corporation and National Semiconductor and how they, in turn, spawned other companies. The chart, which grew longer and more entwined over the years, had its share of corporate divorces, second marriages, stepsons, and illegitimate offspring, and the breeding patterns were so incestuous that in humans they would have led to birth defects.

The founders and managers of these companies were fond of saying that there was nothing they might need that wasn't within an hour's drive. There were lawyers to draw up incorporation papers, venture capitalists to provide money, contractors to lay foundations, interior designers to decorate offices, accountants to check the books, distributors who stocked parts, job shops to perform tedious chores, public-relations agencies to court the press, and underwriters to prepare stock offerings. Many of these men had grown up in the semiconductor industry. They hopped between companies, left to form their own, and kept loose track of one another. They were mobile reservoirs of experience who knew whom to trust and steered business toward one another.

It was a small place where word and rumor traveled fast, where people frequently wound up working for someone they had once hired and where allegiances were to people rather than to companies. All these men worked or invested in the companies whose products eventually trickled down to Haltek and Halted and to the likes of Wozniak and Jobs. But for all the physical proximity, there was still a considerable distance between the professionals and the amateurs.

Jobs, with his keen internal gyrocompass, began to bridge the gap and called the marketing department at Intel to find out who was responsible for their distinctive advertisements. To the irritation of many Intel engineers, these weren't cluttered with dull charts or black-and-white technical drawings and didn't dwell on the esoteric strengths of a new chip. They used color and wraparound type and relied heavily on symbols to explain the potential power of the electronics. Poker chips meant profits, race cars, speed, cleavers, cost cutting, while hamburgers showed that chips could be made to order. Jobs discovered that the ideas and look came from an advertising and public-relations agency in Palo Alto that bore the name of its founder, Regis McKenna. Jobs rang the agency and was funneled toward Frank Burge who took informal responsibility for screening new businesses. Burge wasn't about to be harried by some youngster who announced that he wanted to prepare a color brochure and said, "You guys do good stuff; I'd like you to do my mine." Burge listened and told Jobs he would speak to him within the week. Jobs called Burge several more times. "There were always a pile of messages on my desk and Steve wouldn't let his get to the bottom of the pile. I didn't want to be rude to him so I finally said, 'Yeah, I'll come take a look.' As I was driving over to the garage I was thinking, 'Holy Christ, this guy is going to be something else. What's the least amount of time I can spend with this clown without being rude and then get back to something more profitable.'"

After Burge saw Jobs emerge from the kitchen with his jeans, sandals, unwashed dank hair, and thin beard, his discomfort grew. "I forgot about being rude. For about two minutes I was just thinking of escaping. In about three minutes two things hit me. First, he was an incredibly smart young man. Second, I didn't understand a fiftieth of what he was talking about." Impressed, Burge checked Jobs's credentials with another agency client,

Paul Terrell of the Byte Shops. Terrell told Burge, "They have overextended themselves and need some organization. Jobs isn't very comfortable in a marketing role." A couple of weeks later, another of the McKenna executives met Jobs and suggested that the agency might be prepared to handle Apple's entire marketing campaign for a share of the company's sales revenue. He added that they should all await the result of Apple's first advertisement and also subject the computer to some closer scrutiny. An agency memo noted the extent of Jobs's progress: "Though he moved a quantity into retail distribution, there is as yet no evidence that the retailer(s) are successful in finding customers." The memo concluded that "Steve is young and inexperienced," but the final line cautioned: "Bushnell was young when he started Atari. And he claims to be worth $10,000,000 now."

Eventually Jobs and Wozniak were introduced to the head of the agency, Regis McKenna. His business card, which carried the impish line REGIS MCKENNA, HIMSELF, sounded sturdier than the bearer whose fragile appearance offered a clue to his chronic diabetes. McKenna had careful eyes, thinning fair hair, and a soft manner of speaking that concealed some tough bones. But the business card did reveal his stock-in-trade, which was to make companies appear larger, more stable, and more imposing than they were. As one of seven sons, McKenna had grown up in the blue-collar shadows of the Pittsburgh steel barons, hadn't bothered to graduate from college, and had moved to California at the start of the sixties as an advertising salesman for a family-run magazine company. He moved to the Peninsula during its hush-hush, super-super secret days, slipped into the electronics industry, and wound up at Fairchild. When National Semiconductor was taken over in the late sixties by some disenchanted Fairchild employees, McKenna also defected. He helped build National's image by using ploys that included the distribution of pictures and profiles of the executives on baseball cards.

When McKenna started his own company in 1970 he won the business of Intel which had been founded by yet more refugees from Fairchild. For some time McKenna looked after the account by himself, wrote the advertising copy, and arranged for interviews with journalists. He suffered all the pains of starting and building a business and won some clients by keeping an eye on activity at new buildings around the industrial parks. Every now and again when he rewarded himself with a pay raise, he wound up putting the money back into his business. McKenna's own taste was often reflected in his clients' advertisements. His cashmere jackets came from Wilkes Bashford, a swank outfitter in San Francisco, while he paid for a work by the French surrealist Joan Miró by mortgaging his home in Palo Alto.

Yet the image of Intel, which formed the keystone of McKenna's business, was probably shaped more by public relations than advertising. McKenna had taken pains to step beyond the electronics trade journals and cultivate reporters and editors at magazines like *Business Week, Fortune,* and *Forbes.* He had the cunning to make most journalists believe he was confiding secrets, and he was far more patient with journalists than the electronics executives who would invariably find some reason to complain and grumble about reporters and press coverage. Andrew Grove, then the executive vice-president of Intel, said, "He taught us to build relationships with the press rather than firing off press releases and hoping for wonderful things to happen." McKenna had earned a reputation with reporters for being straightforward and not resorting to subterfuge. He liked to share industry gossip, made no secret of his pet likes and dislikes, and always practiced his wife's advice: "Don't pick a fight with anyone who buys ink by the barrel." He seemed to gain more satisfaction from seeing a page-long story about one of his clients than an advertisement, but would occasionally sound like a Madison Avenue account executive—as in "We rolled out the Byte Shops with a full page in *Business Week.*"

By 1976 McKenna already had some experience with marketing microcomputers. His agency was responsible for the general image of the Byte Shops and had also designed some advertisements for Intel's single-board computers, which featured a young boy with a sunny, all-American look. So when Jobs and Wozniak appeared in his office McKenna was heading an agency that, like some of its clients, had built a reputation far beyond its size. The meeting was uncomfortable. McKenna asked to take a look at an article about the Apple computer that Wozniak was writing for a trade magazine and stressed that it should not be too technical. Wozniak, with all an engineer's ruffled pride, retorted: "I don't want any PR man touching my copy." To which, with a stubborn rush of Irish blood to the face, McKenna replied, "Well, you better both get out." Jobs played peacemaker and negotiated an uneasy truce.

Apple's encounter with McKenna revealed a hint of grander plans. But those plans were useless without money. The rest of the microcomputer industry was growing more quickly than Apple, and Jobs didn't have enough money to match his expanding ambitions. Apple was not in the same league as Processor Technology which was regularly buying five pages of color advertising in magazines like *Byte*. Jobs returned to Atari and asked Nolan Bushnell for advice about where he should turn for more money. Bushnell gave him a tutorial on the world of venture capitalists, men who would supply money in return for a stake in the company, and told Jobs, "The longer you can go without having to go to those guys the better off you are." But Bushnell also suggested he call Don Valentine, an investor in Atari.

When he drove his Mercedes Benz from his office in Menlo Park to the Jobses' garage, Valentine was embarking on one of those inspection trips that usually didn't pay off. But it was a tribute to his curiosity—as well as to his nose for profit—that Valentine even bothered to make the drive. Valentine was the son of a New York truck driver and a venture capitalist who looked like a weathered version of the frat brother who organized the weekend football pool. He had worked during the sixties as the marketing head of Fairchild, helping sell the virtues of integrated circuits first to the military and then, when the prices started to drop, to commercial customers with military connections like General Dynamics, Hughes Aircraft, and Raytheon. He had run the marketing department at National, was frustrated by the growth of a corporate bureaucracy, and left to start a venture-capital firm which he named Sequoia Capital. He specialized in maintaining an impassive, impenetrable exterior, leaving even his friend Regis McKenna with the impression, "He can be a hard-nosed rug merchant if he's trying to buy or sell from you." All in all, Valentine wasn't likely to be softened by sentimental appeals. He frequently took refuge in one of his favorite aphorisms: "If a man comes into my office and says he wants to be a millionaire, I'm bored to death. If he says he wants a net worth of fifty to a hundred million dollars, I'm interested. If he says he wants to make a billion dollars, I say, 'Tell me about it,' because if he comes close we're all going to clean up."

Valentine had brushed up against Jobs while he was considering investing in Atari and also knew that the McKenna Agency, where he was a member of the board, was dallying with Apple. Valentine wore button-down shirts and regimental ties and thought Jobs looked like "a renegade from the human race" and his meeting with the Apple duo was not a success. The younger pair explained, in a stumbling manner, that if the market for single-board computers was going to be as large as some people were predicting, they would be more than content to nibble at the edges and make a couple of thousand boards a year. That was not a line guaranteed to win Valentine's heart; he thought, "Neither one knew anything about marketing. Neither one had any sense of the size of the potential market. They weren't thinking anywhere near big enough." Valentine resorted to yet another of his pet sayings: "Big thinkers often do big things. Small thinkers never do big things," and told the younger pair that he was not prepared to invest since nobody connected with Apple had any marketing experience. Jobs immediately asked Valentine to suggest some candidates who might fill the bill. Valentine returned to his office, riffled through his Rolodex, selected three names he knew from his days in the semiconductor industry, and checked their progress with people he trusted. One, Mike Markkula (who became irritated when addressed by either of his given names, Armas or Clifford), had worked for Valentine in the mid-sixties at Fairchild.

On Valentine's urging, Markkula (whose last name was Finnish) arranged to meet Wozniak and Jobs. Markkula was thirty-three years old and lived in youthful retirement in Cupertino. He was one of dozens of men who had made money from a young company's public stock issue only to decide that there was more to life than becoming a corporate vice-president. In Markkula's case the company had been Intel where he had worked for four years after leaving Fairchild. He had made no secret of the fact that one of his goals in life was to become a millionaire by the time he was thirty, and when he managed to do so, he also didn't bother to conceal his satisfaction. Markkula was, in the words of one of his wealthier Intel colleagues, "a multimillionaire but a small multimillionaire". He had been raised in Southern California, had earned both a bachelor's and a master's degree in electrical engineering from the University of Southern California, and after graduating, had joined Hughes Aircraft Company where he worked in a research and development laboratory.

After leaving Fairchild and joining Intel Markkula was buried deep in the ritual of the semiconductor industry. He worked on the pricing strategy for new chips, composed data sheets, helped solve customers' problems, and was considered steady and reliable but not a rising star. His main claim to fame was guiding the development of Intel's computer system for processing customer orders, where he immersed himself in the nitty-gritty details of the programming. He watched the growth of Intel's line of memory chips and realized the importance of good financial contacts and the need for reliable distributors and dealers. Intel's technical edge, the strong demand for its chips, and keen attention to promotion and public relations helped make the marketing department's task easier.

In an industry where salesmen like to boast of, and if the opportunity presents itself practice, cocksmanship, Markkula was Mister Squeaky Clean. He preferred to curl into the lap of his own family, was uncomfortable with small talk, was punctilious and level-headed, and played his cards close to his chest. He managed his financial affairs quietly and borrowed money to buy stock before Intel went public. One of his colleagues, Richard Melmon, said, "He wasn't one of the boys. A lot of people couldn't stand him. He wasn't a hell raiser. He was a fussy fellow who always had to know the answer even when he didn't." Peeved when a vice-president of marketing was appointed over him, Markkula surprised his workmates and left Intel. He retired to the warmth of Cupertino, muddled about his house, watched his two young children grow, splashed about in his swimming pool, installed garden sprinklers, built cabinets for his stereo system, strummed a guitar, and learned the ins and outs of oil and gas shelters. His body still had the trim look of the high-school gymnast and he openly admired Jerry Sanders, the flashy founder of Advanced Micro Devices, who, unlike most semiconductor executives, said he liked the expensive things of life. Markkula's taste leaned toward the conspicuous, like the prominent watch he wore on his wrist and the gold-colored Chevrolet Corvette he drove to Jobs's garage.

Markkula talked to Jobs and Wozniak, inspected the computer, and was enthralled by the gadgetry. "It was what I had wanted since I left high school." He also sought Don Valentine's counsel in a two-story wooden office building in Menlo Park set around a courtyard and studded with the discreet brass nameplates and thin lettering that were sure signs of the presence of several venture-capital firms. Valentine and Markkula chatted about Apple's prospects in an office brimming with advertisements, prospectuses, and Lucite blocks that commemorated some of the venture capitalist's more visible coups. It was also decorated with sepia photographs of the Sundance Kid and a sign that read ANYBODY CAUGHT SMOKING ON THE PREMISES WILL BE HUNG BY THE TOENAILS AND PUMMELLED INTO UNCONSCIOUS-NESS WITH ORGANIC CARROTS.

Bolstered by his chat with Valentine, Markkula offered to give Jobs and Wozniak advice about how to organize Apple. They got together in the evenings and over weekends and Markkula gradually became more enchanted with the business. He talked matters over with his wife, promised that he would give Apple only four years of his life, and eventually told Jobs that to help pay for the development and introduction of the Apple II, he would underwrite a $250,000 bank loan: an amount less than one tenth of his net worth. Markkula called McKenna, said he was about to invest in Apple, and asked him to tolerate Jobs and Wozniak. Jobs, Wozniak, and Holt all trooped to Markkula's house and in a cabana alongside the swimming pool spent several evenings mulling over Apple's future shape and prospects. In return for investing in Apple, Markkula wanted to own a third of the business, though distributing the shares caused some ill-feeling when Wozniak questioned whether any company would be prepared to pay Jobs what he himself was earning at Hewlett-Packard. Markkula rose to Jobs's defense and Wozniak was taken aback. "He had a lot of confidence in Steve. He saw him as a future executive, as a future Mike Markkula." Holt listened to the conversations and, with the practical bent of a Revolutionary Socialist, decided he would fare well if he wound up with one tenth of the shares Jobs received. Holt also harbored some doubts about Markkula. "He had a certain arrogant bearing and the subtle self-confidence of those people who have a lot of money and believe that somehow or other they have a birthright to it. I was suspicious." Holt was also suspicious that Markkula would help draw up a business plan and then leave the company. The suspicion was mutual. Markkula checked all of Holt's references back to high school.

Wozniak considered Markkula's confidence entirely misplaced and predicted to his parents with steadfast assurance that Apple's bigtime investor would lose every penny. Wozniak did not share Markkula's enthusiasm and was wondering whether to accept Hewlett-Packard's invitation to transfer to Oregon. Nor was his wife, Alice, very enthusiastic about the business that consumed so much time and hadn't produced much money. She said, "I liked security and the paycheck coming in." When Markkula made it a condition of his investment that Wozniak join Apple full time, matters came to a head. Markkula, Jobs, and Holt discussed whether they could muddle through without Wozniak and issued all sorts of threats. Holt recalled, "We told him if he didn't come to work full time for Apple Computer he was out. Even then he didn't come waltzing through the door. He moaned and groaned and puttered around for a couple of weeks." Jobs staged a fierce campaign to persuade Wozniak to join Apple. He called Wozniak's friends, moaned that he was at his wits' end and asked them to place persuasive telephone calls. He went around to Wozniak's parents' house, broke into tears, and begged for their help. Markkula provided a quieter pressure, patiently explaining to Wozniak, "You go to a company when you want to turn an idea into money." Wozniak said, "Once I decided I was doing it to make money, it made the rest of the decisions easy."

There were a few practical considerations. The Apple Computer Company was officially formed on January 3, 1977, and in March 1977, bought out the partnership for $5,308.96. To avoid any possible complication Markkula insisted that the company purchase Ron Wayne's share of the partnership. Wayne was delighted when he received a check and discovered that it was worth $1,700 more than the paper it was printed on. There were also some larger matters. Since Markkula had never expressed any desire to run the business, there was also a pressing need to find somebody who would look after the nuts and chips. Wozniak recalled, "Mike said if he was putting money in, he wanted someone to mind the pennies."

Markkula's idea of a penny minder was Michael Scott whose career had been interwoven with his own. When both started work at Fairchild on the same September day in 1967, they were given adjoining offices. For a short time Markkula worked for Scott who was a year his junior. They did the sorts of things contemporaries did. They joshed about company chitchat and predicted to each other the speed with which prices for semi-conductors would fall. After they discovered that they shared the same birth date, February 11, they made it a point to have an annual celebratory lunch. It was at their ritual meal in 1977 that Markkula asked Scott whether he would be interested in becoming president of Apple.

Scott, like Markkula, was an engineer at heart. He had grown up in Gainesville, Florida, and in his teens had spent afternoons and weekends playing around in a university data-processing department with an IBM 650—which, in the late fifties, had been the most popular computer in the world. He chose the California Institute of Technology over MIT because he preferred sun to snow, and he specialized in physics. After graduating he spent a couple of years as an engineer at Beckman Instruments Systems Division in Southern California which was building ground instruments for checking Saturn rockets. Beckman happened to be a regular port of call for Fairchild salesmen anxious to meet quotas and targets set by Don Valentine. Scott joined Fairchild (where he was lured partly by the promise of a $100 reward for leads to other recruits). He stayed a couple of years, was disillusioned by corporate politicking, and left to join National Semiconductor.

On his thirty-second birthday Scott was running a $30 million a year manufacturing line which made chips that combined analog and digital electronics. It was not the most glamorous place to be at National but Scott's position as a director of a line was one of the keystones in the company's system of management, and he was, in effect, running a business that employed eight hundred people. He prospered, endured table-pounding sessions with the company's president where coffee cups were known to bounce, turned down an offer to run a plant in the Far East, and decided he wanted to stay in California. By the time he lunched with Markkula, Scott said, "I was bored. I had been doing the same job for four years." He saw the formation of a company in engineer's terms: "It's like a chess game except the moves continue to happen. The challenge is to put together a whole system that works without being minded and that has its own checks and balances. I wanted to see if I could build a system from scratch." He was a tubby man who walked with his fists clenched. He wore spectacles, had short hair that he would curl with his fingers, usually wore T-shirts that bulged over his belt, and on a good day looked like the benevolent proprietor of an automobile wrecking yard. There was about him more than just a hint that he would have been happy running an automated factory from a seat behind a computer terminal, with a can of Budweiser at his side while "The Ride of the Valkyries" thundered in the background.

Markkula, who was diplomatic and disliked imposing demands on others, asked Jobs and Wozniak to consider Scott as a possible president for Apple. Wozniak, anxious not to be burdened with any corporate drudgery, was impressed by Scott and flattered by his obvious infatuation with computers. "I felt very comfortable knowing that somebody else besides Steve would be around to manage production." Jobs, however, was far less sure about this tumbling man who didn't seem to care about Eastern philosophy and who preferred pizza to salad. He spent hours at a Bob's Big Boy with Holt and Wozniak, ruminating about Scott. Holt recalled, "Jobs didn't know whether he wanted to run the show or not. He didn't have much confidence that Woz had much business acumen and was going to speak with him and help, if push came to shove, to keep the company on the right course. He was left in the uncertain position of not knowing how much power he was giving up." If Scott proved unsatisfactory, Jobs also wanted to be free to repurchase his share of the stock. Markkula once again exercised his persuasive influence and explained to Jobs that it was not a question of power but whether Apple would be better managed.

Jobs listened. He balanced the promise of future contributions against the tangible loss of power. He was strong enough to admit what he didn't know and pugnacious enough not to get bowled over by men who were many years older. He was prepared to relinquish the sweat of a year, but was also consoled by simple arithmetic. Since any combination of Wozniak, Jobs, and Markkula controlled the majority of the company's shares, they could unseat Scott at any time. It was a peculiar arrangement and Scott, who had become a guardian of other people's investments, recognized reality. "I wondered whether I could really get anything done or whether we would argue all the time. My biggest concern was whether Jobs and I could get along.

He was concerned that I wasn't doing consumer stuff. I was concerned that he didn't know what he was doing." Since Scott was the nominal boss, he was paid $20,001 for the first year, one dollar more than the members of the triumvirate.

Though, to one degree or another, they were all tekkies, Jobs, Wozniak, Holt, Markkula, and Scott had virtually nothing in common. They differed in age, appearance, background, and ambition. They were attracted to different sorts of lovers and had varying attitudes toward fidelity, pleasure, aesthetics, religion, money, and politics. A couple speckled their speech with obscenities while others almost blushed at the sound of a four-letter word. They were so different that a biologist presented with five chromosome specimens would probably have been surprised to learn the donors were all male and bipedal.

There was Jobs who, though he certainly liked money and relished power, virtually fell into Apple for want of anything else to do; Wozniak, for whom the binary difference between one thousand and one million was far clearer than the monetary, derived his chief delight from displaying the power of his machine; Holt, who had never owned thirty thousand dollars in his life, was attracted by the prospect of making a quarter of a million dollars in five years; Markkula, who could not conceal his interest in the computer or his desire to bolster a personal portfolio; and Scott who, more than anything else, wanted to be the president of a company that would leap over the moon.

"In China it could be marvelous," Paola Ghiringelli exclaimed.

An Apple II, an Apple III, a Lisa, and a Macintosh were lined up in battle order on a pair of steel tables. Two Mac marketing managers, Michael Murray and Michael Boich, were sitting in front of the computers, putting the finishing touches to a presentation they were about to give to the Belgian-born artist Jean-Michel Folon. Some months before, Steve Jobs, in his role as Apple aesthete, had been impressed by the bridge between romance and surrealism formed by Folon's work. He had decided to marry the European artist with the California computer and, for a time, wanted Apple's advertising to reflect Folon's image of Mac. Jobs had contacted Folon, attended one of his shows in New York, and invited him to Cupertino. For Jobs the triple combination of art, New York, and Europe was irresistible. Folon, in turn, had sent some sketches of his ideas, which Jobs had been keeping on a chest of drawers in his bedroom.

So it was no accident that Murray and Boich inhabited a Folonesque world. The gray felt walls of the conference room were draped with mock-ups of advertising posters, instruction manuals, and diskette sleeves devised by Apple's graphics department from the slants, shades, and recurring figures of Folon's work. A five-foot-high cardboard cutout of a Folon character with a melancholy demeanor, frumpy hat, and angular overcoat was propped against one wall.

Murray had decided to offer Folon a royalty of a dollar for each Mac sold which, given that Apple eventually hoped to sell over a million Macs a year, was a lucrative contract. Boich was playing with the Lisa when the screen suddenly became a jumble of scrambled letters and numbers. He took a look and said, "I'm going to see if we can do something about this; otherwise we're going to end up with a dead Lisa when Folon arrives." Murray glanced at the mess and muttered, "We have a history of messing up presentations at Apple. We want to get this one right." He returned to the Mac where he finished drawing a miniature version of one of Folon's characters with a cartoon bubble enclosing the greeting BONJOUR MONSIEUR.

When Folon arrived he brought a Parisian palette to Cupertino. A tall, rumpled man, he wore creased royal-blue painter's pants, narrow crimson suspenders, a checkered Viyella shirt, a scuffed cotton jacket, and round, horn-rimmed spectacles. He was accompanied by Paola Ghiringelli, who was dressed in an orange corduroy waistcoat and fawn trousers, and Marek Millek, who worked as a graphic artist for Apple in Paris and was acting as Sherpa and interpreter. Folon immediately upset the carefully laid plans when he decided to investigate the computers.

"*Oh, regardez!*" said Folon as he spotted Murray's drawing.

He was drawn to the machine and sat down for a demonstration of Macintosh and, as it turned out, a quick lesson in how computers worked, with Murray explaining things in short, clipped Pidgin English which Millek, in a Cockney accent, then translated into French. Murray started sketching some more.

"Go to his eyes and put some eyeballs in," Boich urged.

"We can put freckles on his face," Murray explained.

Folon sat down and started to draw with the mouse. He looked at the picture that appeared on the screen and winced. "Ah. He doesn't know how to draw now," Ghiringelli exclaimed in a husky Italian accent. She turned to Murray and asked, "This will only be for drawing?"

"No, no, no," Murray said earnestly. "For writing, for typing as well."

They gathered around the long conference table with Murray standing by a flip chart covered with five basic questions about Macintosh.

"*Celles sont des bonnes questions,*" Folon said as he slid a small tape recorder onto the table.

"Macintosh," explained Murray, "is a code name. But it has taken on a personality of its own. It is more than a fruit. Mac means the machine. The man. The Personality. The Character."

"What is a Macintosh?" asked Ghiringelli.

"It's an apple," answered Murray.

"An apple?" Paola Ghiringelli asked again.

"Yes," said Murray. "There are Golden Delicious, Pippins; there are probably ten kinds of apple."

"Ah! Macintosh is a kind of apple," Ghiringelli exclaimed.

Folon spoke with his hands. "In Europe," Millek translated, "the word *mac* makes people think of machine. He thinks of speed. He thinks of a big guy. He thinks of macho."

"I think it's a nice name," Folon said quietly, "but in Europe it's far from apple."

Murray explained the differences among all Apple's computers and said, "We do not want to sell it as a technology machine. We want the product to have a personality and we want people to buy it because of its personality. We want to make it a cult product. We want people to buy it for its image as well as its utility."

He pointed to another question on the chart and asked rhetorically, "Who will use it? It will be used on desks. The desks are in offices. The desks are in big offices . . . little offices . . . big cities . . . little cities . . . in colleges . . . . in the U.S. . . . in Europe . . . all over the world."

Millek exhaled and turned to Murray. "Wait a minute," he said. "This is getting a bit complicated. In French when you say *bureau* it means 'desk' and 'office.' When you start saying *desk* in an *office*, it gets complicated."

"Is it secret?" asked Ghiringelli.

"Very," said Murray.

"We have many friends at Olivetti and IBM," Ghiringelli added.

"It's very, very secret," Murray repeated.

"Don't talk to me about it," Folon shivered.

Suddenly Murray paused. "I don't know how to say this."

"What?" asked Millek.

"User interface," said Murray.

"Don't say that, for God's sake," Millek said.

"I want to say it's easy to use," Murray continued.

"That's better." Millek sighed.

Murray continued with a brief history of Apple, annotated with sales numbers and employee count. He and Folon talked about the possibility of Folon's designing posters and a series of postcards and working alongside one of the programmers to produce a game to accompany the computer. He described what he thought would be the eventual world market for personal computers. He then checked off the countries where he thought Apple wouldn't find buyers for Macs and concluded, "Not China, not Russia, not India. Well, maybe one or two people in India."

"In China it could be marvelous," Ghiringelli said with assurance. "They are very lazy. They count with an abacus. They will like it very much."

WHAT A MOTHERBOARD

The push to complete the successor to the Apple computer was given greater urgency by the immovable threat of the First West Coast Computer Faire. There was an indignant tone to early advertisements for the fair. It was almost as if the Silicon Valley hobbyists felt their rightful place in the world of microcomputers had been usurped by a string of exhibitions held during 1976 in godforsaken spots where people weren't supposed to be able to tell the difference between a microprocessor and a shift register. There were glum faces at Homebrew Club meetings as fairs took place in cities that were thousands of miles away from microcomputer's Bethlehem—Detroit, Michigan, Trenton, New Jersey. So there was some relief when, shortly after Jobs and Wozniak had taken their cigar box to Atlantic City, word began to spread that a large fair was planned for San Francisco's Civic Auditorium in the spring of 1977.

The chief organizers of the fair were both Homebrew Club members and had originally envisaged a swap meet at Stanford but were turned down by the university authorities. Forced to look elsewhere and encouraged by the crowds that the Atlantic City show had attracted, they scrimped enough money to pay for the rental deposit on a large convention hall in San Francisco. Advertisements promising a large attendance and plenty of exhibitors had appeared in the Homebrew Club newsletter and Jobs, in September 1976, was one of the first to make a commitment to have a display. With grand promises about the size of the show, the number of exhibitors, and the conference panel, it was a natural forum to introduce a new computer. And for Wozniak, Jobs, and their newly acquired professional collaborators, the months leading up to the Computer Faire were a hectic scramble.

Jobs thought the cigar boxes that sat on the SLAC desk tops during Homebrew meetings were as elegant as fly traps. The angular, blue and black sheet-metal case that housed Processor Technology's Sol struck him as clumsy and industrial, "I got a bug up my rear that I wanted the computer in a plastic case." No other microcomputer company had chosen that course. A plastic case was generally considered a needless expense compared to the cheaper and more pliable sheet metal. Hobbyists, so the arguments went, didn't care as much for appearance as they did for substance. Jobs wanted to model the case for the Apple after those Hewlett-Packard used for its calculators. He admired their sleek, fresh lines, their hardy finish, and the way they looked at home on a table or desk. He drove to Macy's department store in San Francisco and lingered in the kitchen and stereo departments looking at the design of household appliances. He was a very careful observer with a sensuous taste who knew what he liked and was determined to get what he wanted.

Jobs approached a former workmate at Atari and the original Apple tie breaker, Ron Wayne, and asked them to come up with sketches for a case. His Atari chum produced some water-wash drawings full of angles, swoops, and compound curves. Ron Wayne's design might have come from Rube Goldberg's garage. The case had a removable Plexiglas top that was fastened to wooden sides by metal straps. To protect the computer against strands of hair, drops of coffee, and flecks of dust, Wayne incorporated a tambour door that slid down over the keyboard like the hood of a rolltop desk. As the door moved it tripped a switch concealed in a runner that turned the computer on and off. Jobs had little time for either of the designs and started a search for a more sophisticated approach.

Jerry Mannock was recommended as a possible savior by one of Wozniak's colleagues at Hewlett-Packard. At the beginning of January 1977 Jobs called Mannock, explained his dilemma, and suggested he attend a meeting of the Homebrew Club. Mannock had once wanted to be an electrical engineer, discovered that he preferred the concrete to the abstract, and for several years worked as a product designer at Hewlett-Packard. Bored with designing cases calculated to appeal to electrical engineers and alarmed by the sound of young men talking about retirement, he quit, joined a company that made devices for the handicapped, and almost immediately started to feel that he was being treated as a draftsman. "My stomach was in a knot going to work." He quit once more, sold his cars, traveled around Europe with his wife, and when he returned to California, started his own firm. At the time Jobs called, Mannock was trying to build a clientele out of his home. A firmly built man with dark hair, Mannock took any project he could land. During his first year in business he had designed a solar home in New Mexico, accepted some small contracts for packaging, and scraped a $100 profit.

Mannock found Jobs in the SLAC lobby standing beside a card table that carried the computer and talking to some other people. "He was time-sharing a conversation with three other people and he was doing a good job keeping up with all three conversations. I'd never run into anybody who did this." Mannock discovered that Jobs wanted several plastic cases within twelve weeks in time for the formal introduction of the Apple II at the First West Coast Computer Faire. Mannock wasn't discouraged by the tight deadlines. "I hadn't done this before so I didn't know any better." When Jobs offered to pay $1,500 for mechanical drawings of a case, Mannock agreed but wanted to be paid in advance. "These were flaky-looking customers and I didn't know if they were going to be around when the case was finished." Jobs convinced him that Apple would be around to pay its bills and was virtually as safe as the Bank of America.

Much of the design of the case was dictated by the computer. It had to have a removable lid, be high enough to house the cards that would slot into the motherboard, and be large enough to let some of the heat from the power supply dissipate. Mannock completed the drawings within three weeks. "I did a very conservative design that would blend in with other things. I wanted a good, honest statement in plastic and the minimum amount of visual clutter." Once the general shape was settled there were only a few changes. A pair of indented handles on the side were eliminated because the whole case was slim enough to be gripped between thumb and pinkie. While Jobs was enthusiastic about the drawings Mannock presented for the case, he steadfastly refused to pay for a $300 foam-core mock-up produced for an advertisement.

Just as Ron Wayne's design for the case was set to one side, so was his original logo with its academic overtones. At the Regis McKenna Agency Rob Janov, a young art director, was assigned to the Apple account and set about designing a corporate logo. Armed with the idea that the computers would be sold to consumers and that their machine was one of the few to offer color, Janov set about drawing still lifes from a bowl of apples. "I wanted to simplify the shape of an apple." He gouged a rounded chunk from one side of the Apple, seeing this as a playful comment on the world of bits and bytes but also as a novel design. To Janov the missing portion "prevented the apple from looking like a cherry tomato." He ran six colorful stripes across the Apple, starting with a jaunty sprig of green, and the mixture had a slightly psychedelic tint. The overall result was enticing and warm. Janov recalled Jobs's demands: "Steve always wanted a very high-quality look. He wanted something that looked expensive and didn't look like some chunky model airplane." Jobs was meticulous about the style and appearance of the logo, buzzing to the agency and fretting at Regis McKenna's home in the evening. When Janov suggested that the six colors be separated by thin strips to make the reproduction easier, Jobs refused.

To manufacture name plates for Apple's computers, he hunted down the company that made Hewlett-Packard's labels and came away with embossed logos on strips of thin aluminum. He rejected the first set of labels because the bands of color bled into each other. Most of the other computer companies settled for a plainer look: stamping their names onto sheet metal and refusing to pay the few extra cents to go first class.

Meanwhile, Holt was busy taming the computer. He felt, from the moment Jobs had enticed him to work for Apple, that the only way to produce a reliable, lightweight power supply that would stay cool was to resort to an approach that hadn't been used by any of the other microcomputer companies. Instead of settling for a conventional linear power supply that hadn't changed much since the twenties, Holt decided to take a more elaborate tack and adapt a switching power supply he had previously designed for an oscilloscope. A switching power supply was substantially lighter and considerably more complicated than a linear power supply. It took an ordinary household current, switched it on and off with dizzying rapidity, and produced a steady current that wouldn't blow out any of the expensive memory chips. For computer hobbyists who cursed the heat of the chunky linear power supplies, a switching power supply was something to admire from a distance. "Beware of switchers," they warned one another. Wozniak admitted, "I only knew vaguely what a switching power supply was." Holt's final design was eminently reliable and smaller than a quart carton of milk.

As Holt completed his work and the final size of the computer became clearer, Jobs returned to his former Atari workmate Howard Cantin, who had produced the artwork for the Apple I printed circuit board, and asked him to do the same for the Apple II. This time Jobs had more strenuous demands. He rejected Cantin's first layout and insisted that on the second the lines linking chips be soldier straight. Cantin recalled the tussle. "He just drove me up the wall. I tried to tell him that there was a point at which a drive for perfection is nonproductive. He irritated me so bad I swore I'd never work for him again." Jobs relented only when Cantin reduced the layout of the printed circuit board to the size of a lawyer's scratch pad. Instead of taking the taped artwork directly to the printed-circuit-board manufacturers, Jobs insisted that the layout be fine-tuned, or digitized, by computer even though that caused a delay.

As the West Coast Computer Faire drew closer, there were other humdrum concerns. The business cards weren't returned from the printer until two days before the fair opened. A few printed circuit boards were stuffed with chips before they had been coated with their glossy silk screens. Jobs meanwhile had plumped for a brown keyboard after gauging the reaction of people like his parents to a variety of colors. Though the computers were working, the keyboards went dead every twenty minutes because of a chip that was sensitive to static electricity.

Meanwhile, Wozniak was busy trying to squeeze the programming code for an abbreviated form of the BASIC language into a ROM chip. He had hoped to use a new chip from AMI but when the part failed to appear on time he had to revert to a chip made by Synertek. He, Espinosa, Wigginton, and Holt wrote some small demonstration programs that highlighted the computer's way with color and sound. The demonstration programs were duplicated hurriedly onto cassette recorders and every time the supply of tapes was exhausted, Espinosa was dispatched to the nearby Gemco discount store to buy some more.

More important, there was uncertainty about whether the case would be ready for the opening of the fair. After the mechanical drawings had passed muster, Mannock and Jobs had been presented with a choice between two molding processes: reaction injection or structural foam. In the former, a chemical reaction forces polyurethane to fill a mold but leaves bubbles in the finish. The latter is more elaborate, requiring pressurized foam to be injected and heated, but it also leaves a more polished result. Since nobody expected that Apple would sell more than five thousand of its second computer, Jobs and Mannock chose the reaction injection method which used epoxy tools rather than the more durable, and far more expensive, metal used for long production runs.

The first cases that were extracted from the molds were rickety. The surfaces were uneven, the lids were bowed, and the edges lapped over the keyboard. At Apple half a dozen people used trimming knives, sandpaper, and putty to camouflage the worst blemishes and sprayed the cases with a beige paint which gave a light look. They decided to muddle though the fair without air vents on the sides of the cases that weren't cut cleanly. With most of the preparations over they adjourned on the evening before the fair to the St. Francis Hotel on San Francisco's Union Square. Scott and Markkula were used to large hotels but for the younger members it was their first taste of the big time. Espinosa, who had traded his newspaper route for an hourly wage at Apple of three dollars, was startled to receive a cash advance and expense-account privileges.

Apple's color computer was named with the same sort of reflex with which other, larger computer companies had named their machines. Just as Digital Equipment Corporation had given each successive PDP computer a progressively higher serial number, so Apple named its machine the Apple II. The computer that appeared at the West Coast Computer Faire was not one person's machine. It was the product of collaboration and blended contributions in digital logic design, analog engineering, and aesthetic appeal. The color, the slots, the way in which the memory could be expanded from 4K to 48K bytes, the control of the keyboard and hookup to the cassette recorder, and the BASIC that was stored in the ROM chip—in effect the motherboard—was Wozniak's contribution. Holt had contributed the extremely significant power supply, and Jerry Mannock the case. The engineering advances were officially recognized when, some months later, Wozniak was awarded U.S. Patent #4,136,359 for a microcomputer for use with video display, and Holt was given Patent #4,130,862 for direct current power supply. But behind them all Jobs was poking, prodding, and pushing and it was he, with his seemingly inexhaustible supply of energy, who became the chief arbiter and rejector.

In January 1977 when the Homebrew Club newsletter had reached a circulation of fifteen hundred, a survey of membership revealed 181 computers of which 43 were IMSAIS, 33 Altair 8080s, and 6 Apple 6502s. Apple was in eighth place with a share that one hobbyist calculated, using a specially written computer program, of 3.2967 percent. Even if they didn't talk about it in quite this way, the men at Apple knew that the West Coast Computer Faire could help change that pecking order. They also understood the power of first impressions. The combination of Markkula, Jobs, and the McKenna Agency turned Apple's public bow into a coup.

Because Jobs had made one of the first commitments to appear at the show, Apple had pride of place in the front of the hall. Markkula organized the design of the booth—ordering a smoky, backlit, large and illuminated Plexiglas sign carrying the new company's logo and a large television screen to display the computer's capacity. Three computers lay on two counters. These gave the impression of substance and bulk even though they were Apple's only fully assembled machines. Meanwhile, Markkula and McKenna paid attention to sartorial graces, guiding Jobs to a San Francisco tailor and persuading him to buy the first suit of his life. "We all agreed to dress nicely," said Wozniak. So at the start of the fair they all looked vaguely respectable even if Jobs found his three-piece suit and tie less comfortable than jeans and Birkenstock sandals.

The harried preparations were worthwhile for the First West Coast Computer Faire was a giant hybrid—an enthusiastic Homebrew Club meeting crossed with some of the professional aspects of mainframe computer shows. A hundred or so speakers presented seminars and papers on subjects like the shirt-pocket computer, robots, computer-controlled music, computers for the disabled, high-level languages, networks, graphic speech-recognition devices, electronic mail. Some of the wheeling and dealing and back-room handshakes typical of larger fairs took place and at some of these Markkula courted potential dealers and distributors.

There was also some critical scrutiny of the competition. A prototype of another personal computer, the Commodore PET, was shown though it was displayed at a booth under the name of Mr. Calculator. John Roach, a vice-president of Tandy Electronics, best known for selling electronic devices like CB radios under the Radio Shack label, was touring the fair and subjecting both the Apple and the PET to close inspection. There was also another undercurrent. Small notices were pinned up on bulletin boards and word was passed about surreptitious meetings where phone phreaks pored over the latest issue of the TAP newsletter and whispered to one another about some new advance in telephone switching equipment.

For the thirteen thousand who teemed through the doors and who strolled the floor with plastic tote bags stuffed with advertisements and promises, the Apple display, opposite the main entrance doors, was inescapable. Yet it was only half the size of the Processor Technology booth, smaller than the Cromemco booth and far less popular than the IMSAI stand. But Apple dwarfed other booths which had the unmistakable look of hobbyists. Little booths sold plug-in boards, flimsy magazines, and T-shirts. Companies no larger than Apple had rented sad card tables and written corporate names in felt-tip pens on paper signs. Stacked up by the flimsy yellow backcloths were half-opened cardboard boxes. They looked like what they were: exiles from the Homebrew Club trying to sell a few single-board microcomputers. One of these modest booths belonged to Computer Conversor Corporation where Alex Kamradt was still trying to sell the terminal Wozniak had designed and was advertising the Conversor 4000 as "an affordable alternative to high-priced computer terminals."

Apple's booth, with its counters draped in dark cloth and piled with stacks of brochures, had the desired effect. The dozen or so people who manned the booth and distributed brochures were surprised by the interest in the computer. Some prospective customers refused to believe that a computer was housed in the plastic case and were only made believers when they were shown that the space hidden by the tablecloths was empty. A few engineers were impressed that a printed circuit board with so few chips could include color circuitry. Lee Felsenstein admired the approach. "It was highly simplistic and bold in its crudeness but it worked." The display prompted about three hundred orders over the following few weeks, surpassing by a hundred the total number of Apple Is sold. Nevertheless, despite the folklore that built up in succeeding years, Apple didn't take the fair by storm. Jim Warren, the show's chief organizer, said, "I didn't feel Apple was the strongest exhibitor," while the issue of Byte that later carried a report of the event failed even to mention Apple.

Wozniak, staggered to learn that the booth cost $5,000, was preoccupied with a more entertaining diversion. Along with Wigginton he was putting the finishing touches to a spoof which they had been planning for several weeks. Wozniak had composed an advert promoting a new computer called the Zaltair: a hybrid play on a new microprocessor, the Z-80, and the Altair computer. The copy described the computer in effusive terms and offered trade-in terms for owners of existing Altairs. To avoid trouble Wozniak arranged with a friend to have the leaflets printed in Los Angeles. The morning of the show, while everybody else was hovering about the booth, Wozniak surreptitiously distributed cartons of brochures around the hall. The lime-colored advertisement described the computer in extravagant and convincing terms.

The advert left no misunderstanding about the ideal microcomputer:

> Imagine a dream machine. Imagine the computer surprise of the century here today. Imagine Z-80 performance plus. Imagine BAZIC in ROM, the most complete and powerful language ever developed. Imagine raw video, plenty of it. Imagine autoscroll text, a full 16 lines of 64 characters. Imagine eye-dazzling color graphics. Imagine a blitz-fast

1200-baud cassette port. Imagine an unparalleled I/O system with full Altair-100 and Zaltair-150 bus compatibility. Imagine an exquisitely designed cabinet that will add to the decor of any living room. Imagine the fun you'll have. Imagine Zaltair, available now from MITS, the company where microcomputer technology was born.

Wozniak described the computer's software BAZIC: "Without software a computer is no more than a racing car without wheels, a turntable without records, or a banjo without strings. The best thing of all about BAZIC is the ability to define your own language. . . a feature we call perZonality. TM." And there was a glowing portrait of the hardware: "We really thought this baby out before we built it. Two years of dedicated research and development at the number ONE microcomputer company had to pay off, and it did. A computer engineer's dream, all electronics are on a single PC card, even the 18-slot motherboard. And what a motherboard."

With its corporate logo on the spoof and a coupon offering prospective customers trade-in allowances on their Altairs, the MITS management was not amused. It frantically stamped FRAUD and NOT REAL on all the brochures it could find. Finally, despite the $400 he had sunk into the prank, Wozniak began to get nervous, and worried that thousands of computers would be returned to MITS, he and his accomplices dumped cartons of dummy ads down stairwells.

Jobs picked up one of the advertisements and started to examine the details of the surprising new competitor—which Wozniak had plotted in a chart against machines like the Sol, IMSAI, and Apple beneath the line: "The mark of a microcomputer champ is performance." Wozniak and Wigginton, who couldn't smother their giggles, slid out through a side door, leaving Jobs inside gasping, "Oh, my God! This thing sounds great." Jobs looked at the detailed rankings given in a performance chart on the back, discovered that the Apple II ranked third behind the Zaltair and the Altair 8800-b, and with an air of intense relief, sighed, "Hey, look! We didn't come out too bad."

UP TO SPEC

The spray of a public splash is made of facades, gestures, and illusions. At the West Coast Computer Faire in 1977 Apple Computer, Inc., appeared a lot larger than the actual little business that moved out of the Jobses' garage into a shingled office building at 20863 Stevens Creek Boulevard in Cupertino. The office, Suite E-3, was smaller than a tract home and was barely a mile from the homes of Jobs's and Wozniak's parents. It was separated from Homestead High School by Interstate 280 and was a stone's throw from the crossroads where the Cali Brothers' muddy-colored silos were corralled by stores and subdivisións. Apple's neighbors were a Sony sales office, an employment agency, a weight-loss clinic and a teachers' organization. A plasterboard wall was run down the center of Apple's rented quarters to separate half a dozen desks from the lab and assembly area. It was in these cramped surroundings, two hundred feet from the Good Earth Restaurant, that Apple's founders and their hired hands turned their attention from the cosmic to the parochial.

For almost a year the men in Cupertino concentrated on controlling Apple's bodily functions. They were building everything from scratch and had to settle on details and procedures which they had either never encountered or had always taken for granted. To provide some sort of framework, Markkula, for the first three months of 1977, concentrated on Apple's business plan.

He turned for guidance to John Hall, a group controller at Syntex, a Palo Alto pharmaceutical company. Markkula and Hall were casual acquaintances. They had met at a couple of parties, shared some common friends, and bumped into each other on ski slopes in the California Sierras. Markkula knew that Hall had helped other young companies with their business plans and he asked him to do the same for Apple. Hall took a two-week vacation from Syntex and holed up with Apple's principals for hours of meetings at the local eateries: the Good Earth Restaurant and Mike's Hero Sandwiches. Scott helped Hall cost out a bill of materials and project manufacturing costs. Jobs provided details of contracts with parts suppliers and Wozniak and Holt were consulted for advice on engineering matters.

For grander marketing strategy Hall and Markkula rubbed a hazy crystal ball and decided that the Apple II would launch a three-pronged assault. They thought the machine would be sold to home-computer hobbyists and to professionals like dentists and doctors who had previously shown a weakness for gadgets like programmable calculators. They also planned to develop the Apple as a control center for the home, linked to comforts like automatic garage doors and lawn sprinklers. Hall recalled, "We felt that we needed three tenets for a business plan. But I didn't believe the business plan and Mike Markkula didn't believe it. I felt it was a weak plan strategically." Hall's skepticism was so great that when Markkula asked him to become Apple's vice-president of finance, he declined. "I couldn't afford the risk of joining a screwy company like Apple." However, he did ask Markkula whether Apple would pay in stock for his consulting work. When Markkula demurred, Hall accepted a check for $4,000.

As the business plan took shape, Scott turned to familiar faces for help. Apple's first receptionist, secretary, and general factotum was Sherry Livingston, a perky, bright woman who had worked for him at National Semiconductor. Uncertain about Apple's prospects, Livingston was only convinced of its staying power after Markkula tugged open a drawer stuffed with orders. Gene Carter, who had been Scott's boss for a while at Fairchild, was looking for a job and became head of Apple's sales and distribution. When Scott wanted somebody to mind the books he turned to Gary Martin, a cheerful, gossipy accountant who had also worked for him at National. Martin took a look at the Apple II and thought, "Who the hell is going to want this thing? I felt so sorry for Scott I tried to buy him lunch." Eventually, Martin decided to try Apple for a month, knowing that his boss at National had promised not to turn in his security badge.

Others came of their own accord. Wendell Sander, a shy engineer-cum-sleuth at Fairchild, had become intrigued by Apple after adding some memory chips of his own design to the Apple I. He wrote a *Star Trek* program to amuse his children, demonstrated it to Jobs while Apple was still in the garage, and eventually, after thirteen years with Fairchild, decided to let his passion guide his star. "If they had folded I could have got a job the next day. There wasn't much personal risk apart from the chance of getting a bruised ego. My career would not have vanished." Jim Martindale, a colleague of Jobs's at Atari, was hired to look after production while Don Bruener, a high-school pal of Randy Wigginton's, became a part-time technician. Jobs's college friend Dan Kottke graduated from college and became Apple's twelfth employee, and Elmer Baum started working in the final assembly area. Scarcely anybody considered that the decision to join Apple was risky. Instead they all seemed to feel that the greatest risk was to stay put and do nothing.

As the newcomers arrived, through the late spring and summer of 1977, they found themselves in a small business that had bound itself to some visible public promises. An advertisement in the February 16, 1977, issue of the Homebrew newsletter promised delivery of the Apple II no later than April 30, 1977. Markkula had also decided that Apple could save itself a lot of bother by offering Apple I owners a choice between a full refund or replacement with an Apple II. The arrival of age, or at least what passed for age in Silicon Valley, brought a sense of rigor to Apple. Blending experience with exuberance proved to be a troublesome task, but it was also a fortunate combination. Experience helped temper impulse and instill a sense of discipline while innocence inevitably questioned convention and authority.

Wozniak, Jobs, Holt, Markkula, and Scott were all alert to technical matters and tended to understand the size and implications of electrical problems that cropped up. But they also had serious differences and had to work through the clashes that occurred between men whom a Hollywood screenwriter might have labeled The Hobbyist, The Rejector, The Fixer, The Pacifier, and The Enforcer. At the outset, they shared none of the experience that comes from surviving mistakes and weathering trouble. Holt felt, "There wasn't much trust at all. The question was not of trusting each other's honesty but each other's judgment. You might score seventy percent all round. It was a business not a family affair."

Almost from the start Scott and Jobs irritated each other. Scott, in his curious position as corporate caretaker and the guardian of Apple's internal affairs, became Jobs's first encounter with an unbending authority. Before Scott's arrival Jobs had done anything he wanted. After Scott became president, Jobs found his boundaries were prescribed. The pair approached life from different angles. Scott thought experience was more valuable than native wit while Jobs was convinced that most problems could be solved with a proper application of intelligence. Scott admired Jobs's optimism, his exuberance and energy and gradually learned to appreciate his sense of style. But he also decided, "Jobs cannot run anything. He doesn't know how to manage people. After you get something started he causes lots of waves. He likes to fly around like a hummingbird at ninety miles per hour. He needs to be sat on." Scott squelched Jobs at every turn and one of the earliest mechanical chores provoked a clash. Scott handed out official employee numbers to go along with some laminated-plastic security badges. Since, in Scott's mind, the computer gave birth to the business he assigned Wozniak number one, Jobs number two, Markkula number three, Fernandez number four, Holt number five, and Wigginton number six, reserved number seven for himself, and gave Espinosa number eight. Everybody, apart from Jobs, was satisfied with the order.

"Am I number one?" he asked Scott.

"No. Woz is number one. You're number two."

"I want to be number one," Jobs insisted. "Can I be number zero? Woz can be number one. I want to be number zero."

Number Zero and Number Seven also found much to differ about in the diurnal flow. Wigginton watched from the sidelines.

"Jobs had strong ideas about the way things should be done, and Scotty had the right way, which didn't happen to be Jobs's and there was the inevitable fight." They differed over the way materials should be moved from one section to another, how the desks should be positioned, and what color laboratory benches should be ordered. Jobs wanted white because he felt it would be better for the technicians and engineers. Scott wanted gray because he knew those benches would be cheaper and easier to get. Gary Martin, the accountant, watched another spat shortly after he joined Apple. "They got into a roaring argument over who should sign some purchase orders. Jobs said, I got here quicker than you. I'll sign them.' Then Scotty said, I've got to sign them,' and then he threatened to quit."

In the quieter moments following Scott's arrival Jobs looked after purchasing and some of the fixtures and continued to press for quality. When an IBM salesman delivered a blue Selectric typewriter instead of the neutral color he had specified, Jobs erupted. When the phone company failed to install the ivory-colored telephones Jobs had ordered, he complained until they were changed. As he arranged delivery schedules and payment terms, Jobs humiliated a lot of suppliers. Gary Martin watched. "He was very obnoxious to them. He had to get the lowest price they had. He'd call them on the phone and say, That's not good enough. You better sharpen your pencil.' We were all asking. 'How can you treat another human being like that?'"

Elsewhere a natural division occurred between the older engineers with experience of some of the headaches of manufacturing and the younger ones who were eager to get a prototype running and content to leave the duller polishing and finishing to others. One programmer recalled, "There wasn't any sense of fear. Anybody could call anybody an asshole. It wasn't assumed we were doing the right thing. We had to prove we were doing the right thing." Wozniak never had much of a reputation for finishing the last part of anything. For him and some of his younger accomplices the difference between a prototype dangling cords and trailing wires and a completed machine verged on the academic. Anyone worth his salt, they argued, would obviously be capable of fixing a computer that was a little bit flaky.

Holt, on the other hand, was like a mother hen, pecking and scratching until he was convinced everything worked and he knew what it would cost to build. It was Holt who insisted everything be "up to spec." It was Holt who accompanied Jobs to Atari to find some modulators, little devices that connected a computer to a television set. It was Holt who clipped an oscilloscope to the computer to check the signals running from the microprocessor to the memory chips and the cassette recorder. It was Holt who insisted, after Wozniak had dreamed up some new approach, that he explain, demonstrate, and draw diagrams of the design. Holt said, "I hardly ever trusted Woz's judgment." Holt also discovered the way to Wozniak's heart. "The only real trick to get Woz working on something was to become his audience or get him an audience."

Meanwhile, Markkula and Scott had exerted his own pressure on the engineers and programmers. When the young programmers were more interested in cobbling together short demonstration programs to illustrate the power of the computer, Markkula insisted that they start work on programs people could use. To show the depth of his concern, Markkula did much of the tedious work on a program that would let people balance their checkbooks. He also brought a quieter style. When Wozniak was compiling a scoring system for Breakout and wanted to include BULLSHIT as a comment for low scores, Markkula persuaded him that there was a call for something more refined. When the first computers were ready to ship, Scott forced the youngsters to tack together an abbreviated version of BASIC so that Apple could start to ship machines accompanied by a computer language.

Scott had similarly unsentimental ideas about both production and finance. He had a strong dislike for automated manufacturing and expensive test machinery. He was also determined that outsiders should help pay for Apple's growth and that they should suffer the discomforts of swings in business. His ideas about the growth of the company were the equivalent of Wozniak's ideas about the chips in a computer. Both were talking about productivity. Scott wanted to design a company that did the most amount of work with the least number of workers. "Our business," he said, "was designing, educating, and marketing. I thought that Apple should do the least amount of work that it could and that it should let everyone else grow faster. Let the subcontractors have the problems." Scott had an undying commitment to letting outside manufacturers make anything that Apple couldn't produce more cheaply. He also felt that a fast-growing business had no time to master some of the rudimentary skills needed to produce reliable components. It was easier, for example, to expand the quality tests for printed circuit boards stuffed by outside suppliers than to contemplate expanding the work force and mastering all the techniques needed for production of decent boards.

So for help with board stuffing Scott relied partly on Hildy Licht, a Los Altos mother and the wife of one of Wozniak's acquaintances from the Homebrew Club. Licht operated a cottage industry. Parts were delivered to her home and she distributed them to hand-picked assemblers scattered around the neighborhood, tested the finished work, and returned it to Apple in the back of her brown Plymouth station wagon. She was flexible, could make revisions on boards, and offered overnight service. Scott also turned for help to a larger company that specialized in turning out larger quantities of printed circuit boards. Both were the sort of services designed to relieve small companies of time-consuming chores.

Scott also kept a close eye on Apple's cashbox. He arranged for Bank of America to provide a payroll system to relieve Apple of the chores of withholding tax, deducting Social Security payments, and issuing paychecks. Along with Gary Martin, who acted as his fiscal fist, Scott monitored the most expensive components like the 16K memory chips. The pair arranged to buy the chips on forty-five days' credit and the keyboards on sixty days' credit. Meanwhile, they tried to collect money from customers within thirty days of all sales. Martin paid close attention. "My job was to collect money from customers before we paid our vendors. We kept our customers on a very short leash." Martin, who had once worked for a freight company that went bankrupt after turning its accounts receivables from fact to fiction, also tended to veer toward the conservative. His natural impulses and the need to give Apple a respectable seal helped him select auditors from one of the country's largest accounting firms. Like other accountants in Silicon Valley, the people from Arthur Young offered a discount on the cost of their first year's work. Apple and its accountants also took full advantage of Uncle Sam. By deciding to end Apple's first fiscal year on September 30, 1977, they effectively received a fifteen-month interest-free loan from the government for the tax owed in the final calendar quarter, which was always the consumer industry's largest quarter.

Wigginton watched Apple's president at work and decided "Scott's motto was let's make some money. Let's get something out the door." Scott didn't mind getting his hands dirty. He would happily muck about in the manufacturing area helping pack computers into shipping cases. After the computers were packed, he often took them in the back of his car to the local UPS office. When cassettes had to be duplicated, Scott operated the tape recorders. Whenever production outran orders, Scott stacked piles of printed circuit boards behind Markkula's desk to make his point.

When it became clear that Jobs's plan to ship a polished manual with the computers would cause a long delay, Scott started to assemble his own. All along he had favored distributing plain data sheets, so Apple's first manual contained listings of codes and instructions for hooking up the computer. It was copied by a duplicating service in a local shopping mall. The instructions were then slipped between report covers purchased at McWhirter's stationery store in Cupertino and packed with the computer. Some months later Scott cobbled together a slightly more elaborate manual which Sherry Livingston typed. Wozniak recalled, "We just decided to include as much as we could because we didn't have much." Devotees who couldn't find the answer in either manual and made inquiries were sent a bulky package of routines and listings known as The Wozpack, which sprang from Wozniak's insistence that the sort of information he had been sent when he investigated minicomputers should be available to Apple owners. The rush to ship was evident in the opaque explanation that accompanied a demonstration *Star Trek* program. It contained the single line of instruction COO. FFR. LOAD. RUN.

Gradually, as 1977 progressed, a sense of community began to develop. It was certainly helped by the fear that acted as a strong social glue when, five months after the formal introduction of the Apple II, the business came close to folding. The subcontractor who had turned out unsatisfactory cases for the West Coast Computer Faire continued to do so. Part of the fault lay with Jobs's decision to rely on soft tooling, but most of the trouble was caused by the men who manufactured the cases and who were, in Holt's acerbic view, "a bunch of plumbers." The lids continued to sag and the lid from one case wouldn't fit another. The paint refused to stick.

In September 1977 the main tooling broke, and customers who had placed orders were beginning to get impatient. Apple was within inches of earning a reputation for being unable to meet its commitments. Dozens of printed circuit boards started to pile up, suppliers demanded normal payment, and Apple's thin cushion of cash was running low. Without tools Apple would have been stuck without any revenue for about three months. There were a few rumors that Apple would close and Holt even delayed hiring Cliff and Dick Huston, a fraternal combination of engineer and programmer, until he was certain that Apple would be able to issue paychecks. "It was life and death for us," Scott recalled. "We'd have had a good product and not been able to ship it." Jobs scurried off to a Tempress firm in the Pacific Northwest that specialized in producing molds for clients like Hewlett-Packard. He explained Apple's predicament to Bob Reutimann, a Tempress vice-president, who recalled, "I thought to myself 'Does he know what the heck he's doing?' I was a little afraid of going ahead with the project. I thought, 'Here comes another guy with big ideas.'" Jobs's exuberance paid off as did his offer of a bonus of $1,000 for every week that the new mold was brought in ahead of schedule. The new tooling was delivered toward the end of 1977.

As Apple's founders and managers made fumbles and learned to sense each other's weaknesses, they gradually built a mutual trust. The trust was derived from a sense of their colleagues' frailties as much as from their complementary strengths. Markkula's early sales forecasts were quickly shown to be pessimistic, but it also became clear that he wouldn't scuttle back into retirement. Jobs's choice of technique for the manufacture of the case, Wozniak's unwillingness to finish a design, Scott's refusal to fret about aesthetics, and Holt's habit of nitpicking all revealed private weaknesses.

The mixture of pedigrees came to the fore in discussions over important details like the system used for numbering parts in engineering. They all had their own ideas for a system which, if poorly designed, could cause horrible complications. Scott observed, "When you're working on big topics which you don't know all the answers to, it's easy to switch to something else really teeny that everyone can get their teeth into." Jobs, for example, dreamed up his own phonetic system in which an item like a 632 Phillips head screw would be labeled "PH 632." It was a charming notion but didn't have the flexibility to cope with oddities like different lengths and distinctions between black-oxide, nylon, and stainless-steel screws.

Jerry Mannock, the case designer, suggested adopting a system like the one used at Hewlett-Packard. Somebody else wanted to copy Atari's procedures. Others wanted parts to be numbered from the outside of the computer toward the inside. A few considered it more natural to work from the inside toward the outside. Finally Holt wrote a five-page paper detailing a formula based on seven digits which divided parts into categories like nuts, washers, and custom semiconductors. It became the object of religious attachment. "If there wasn't an engineering print and a specification associated with a part number, then it wasn't an engineering part number. Then they could go to hell."

They began to tolerate quirks and idiosyncrasies and solved some of the small pieces of mechanical confusion. After telephone callers kept asking for Mike—not making clear whether they wanted to speak to Markkula or Scott—the former kept his name while the latter became known as Scotty. When a cranky line printer broke down they all knew who guarded the jar of Vaseline that was used to grease the roller. They all learned to endure Holt's chain-smoking and Bill Fernandez's piping bird whistles and occasional departures for Bahai holidays. They worked around Jobs's temperamental car and his complaints that Apple's first Christmas party couldn't be catered with vegetarian food. Scott was also delighted to learn about Jobs's personal cure for relieving fatigue: massaging his feet in the flush of a toilet bowl.

The fishbowl existence brought immediate gratification. Most of the employees tended to hear or see what was going on. When somebody strolled in off Stevens Creek Boulevard and counted out $1,200 for a new computer, Apple's teenagers could scarcely believe their eyes. Sherry Livingston felt that it was like "a big octopus. Everybody did a bit of everything. I didn't feel as though there were presidents and vice-presidents. I felt as though we were all peers." Workdays often started before 8 A.M. and lasted until late into the evening, with breaks for sandwiches.

Many of the two dozen or so employees worked part, or all, of weekends. Gary Martin, for example, dropped by over the weekends to sift through the mail for checks. Don Bruener, who helped troubleshoot the printed circuit boards, enjoyed the unpredictable nature of the work. "Each day there was something different to do. Since everything was new there were no real routines." When a demonstration program was completed or some quirk in the computer had been pinned down, the entire entourage would inspect the progress. Wigginton recalled, "There would be a big brouhaha and everybody would get excited." Scott, who took special delight in the absence of a formal bureaucracy, explained, "There was no time for paperwork. We were so busy running just trying to keep up." Apple's anonymity also tended to strengthen ties and provoked blushes for the likes of Don Bruener. "I told my friends I worked at this little company called Apple and they laughed."

There were also the amusing peculiarities of regular visitors. One of the most frequent callers was John Draper who had emerged from a minimum-security prison in Lompoc, California, after being convicted for phone phreaking. At Apple he soon arrived at a casual arrangement with Wozniak to design a printed circuit board that could be plugged into one of the slots of the Apple and turn the computer into a grand, automatic telephone dialer. It was nicknamed The Charlie Board, was capable of producing dial tones, and could be left overnight to scan banks of toll-free telephone numbers and match them with customer code numbers. The codes could then be used to charge calls. The results of these laborious tests were typed out on a printer. Wozniak thought "it would have been one of the great products of all time" and programmed an Apple to remorselessly dial a friend's house. Though Wozniak helped modify the design, Markkula, Scott, and Jobs didn't want anything to do with Draper who concluded, "They were chickenshit and paranoid about having me on the premises." There was good reason. Draper took an Apple and a plug-in board to Pennsylvania and was arrested. He eventually pleaded guilty to stealing over $50,000 worth of telephone calls and was jailed again.

The utilitarian setting formed a backdrop for a business that filled some emotional need for many of the employees. For the teenagers, the computer held the main allure. Wigginton, who spent most of his time working on software with Wozniak, kept the nocturnal hours of a youthful engineer. He worked between 3 A.M. and 7 A.M., disappeared for school and a sleep, and returned to Apple late in the evening. "My parents weren't super-crazy about it but they were starting to split up. Apple definitely replaced my family." When he graduated from high school a year early, in June 1977, almost the entire company took the afternoon off to attend his graduation and present him with a fifty-dollar gift voucher.

Chris Espinosa, meanwhile, started to cut Homestead classes and graduated with a grade-point average barely adequate for entrance to a decent university. He abandoned his paper-delivery route, which paid one cent a paper, in favor of three-dollar-an-hour part-time work at Apple. After one of his first all-night sessions working on some software with Wozniak, his mother (who herself later joined Apple) forbade him to work for a while. Espinosa soon returned, helping Markkula demonstrate the computer at nearby stores and deciding that when he needed a new pair of spectacles, they would be rimless like Markkula's.

For Wozniak and Jobs, Apple also was a refuge from private turmoil. Wozniak, who was either working on his computer in the office or on another at home, saw little of his wife. The pair went through a couple of trial separations and Wozniak took to sleeping on a couch at the office. Eventually talk of separation turned to talk of a permanent split, and Wozniak, for whom divorce was a miserable blot, found himself unable to work until he resolved some critical matters. "I didn't want my wife to have stock. I just wanted to buy it out." He turned for guidance to Markkula, who steered him toward a lawyer who drew up a separation agreement giving Wozniak's wife of seventeen months 15 percent of his Apple stock. Alice felt ostracized. "Steve was told not to bring me to Mike Markkula's home in case they discussed company business."

Jobs had his own troubles. In the summer of 1977 he, Dan Kottke, and his high-school flame, Nancy Rogers, toured Cupertino, inspecting houses and giggling at the types they called Rancho Suburbio. Eventually they found a four-bedroom house belonging to a Lockheed engineer, which was scarcely a fifteen-minute walk from Apple. It was a Rancho Suburbio Special with wall-to-wall beige shag carpeting, aluminum windows, and an all-electric kitchen. Jobs moved his belongings, which consisted of a mattress and meditation cushion, into the master bedroom while Kottke slept in the living room on a foam pad next to an old piano. It wasn't an entirely conventional existence. Kottke filled a small bedroom thigh-deep in fist-size chunks of foam packing material and let the neighborhood children romp in the stuff.

Nancy Rogers was unsettled. "I was really insecure and young men in their early twenties are not very good with women. They need to prove themselves. I was afraid to go out. I didn't have enough money. I didn't paint." Rogers took to calling Jobs at the office, asking him to return and help fix broken light sockets. She hurled plates at Kottke and Jobs, toppled books off shelves, scrawled obscenities with a charcoal briquette on Jobs's bedroom walls, and slammed a door so hard it punctured a hole in a wall. She became pregnant, took a job at Apple helping with assembly, spurned an offer from Holt to learn drafting, and finally left Apple and moved out of the house. "Steve didn't care that I was pregnant. I had to get away from Steve, Apple, and people's opinions."

For Jobs it was a difficult time and Holt reacted to the emotional whirlgig. "Sometimes I felt like his father; sometimes I felt like his brother." Jobs, who had always tried to mimic a surrogate elder brother, was also starting to understand that he didn't have to pattern his behavior on another person. "I saw Mike Scott and I saw Mike Markkula and I didn't want to be like either one and yet there were parts of them that I admired a lot." He was coming to grips with the difference in pace that exists between a garage operation and even a small business. The discomfiting fact was that the output of a dozen people (let alone one hundred) wasn't predictable and such imperfection, for somebody who always demanded the best, was enormously difficult to tolerate.

Jobs was also adjusting to the idea that computers and software could not be completed in a few weeks and that progress was not something that could be easily measured. Like managers in other companies whose future revolved around taming technology, he found that progress was invisible until it could be made to work on a tabletop. When Wozniak started writing a floating-point version of BASIC, he felt the tension. "Steve had no idea what it takes to write that sort of code. If something seemed wrong, he'd quickly go and make a change. He would always want to have an influence and change whatever came up."

Yet Jobs contributed much. He was always the company dynamo and the house personality. He started adding zeroes to Apple's gross sales before some of the others were even thinking in hundreds, and started to talk about millions before his colleagues had contemplated thousands. When Markkula thought that color logos on the cassettes were too expensive, Jobs won the day. When Scott threw up his hands in horror at the notion of offering a one-year warranty on the computer when the industry standard was ninety days, Jobs burst into tears, had to be cooled off with what became a standard ritual (a walk around the parking lot), but eventually won his way. When Gary Martin discovered a $27,000 check that had been forgotten, Scott wanted to use it to buy a new mold, Markkula wanted to spend it on an advertisement in *Scientific American,* and Jobs wanted to do both. Apple bought a mold and an advertisement.

Jobs's and Scott's squabbles and arguments were such a constant in Apple's life that they became known as The Scotty Wars. But the quarrels also took whimsical turns. On Jobs's twenty-third birthday he was startled to find a funeral wreath decorated with white roses propped up in his office. It carried an unsigned card with the message R.I.P. THINKING OF YOU. Jobs didn't discover for some time that the perpetrator was Scott who took to using a white rose as his personal seal.

Markkula stood between the twin volcanos. He dealt with Jobs much as an uncle would nurture a favorite nephew but he allowed Scott to handle him. Scott and Jobs found it far easier to make tough decisions than did the milder-mannered Markkula. Perhaps helped by the quiet of a family life Markkula was more cordial, punctual, and polite. He avoided tying his fate as closely to the company as Scott and Jobs did. As Apple grew he was prepared to delegate. "If it doesn't work," he kept repeating, "fix it." he was also ready to let people fail. Jean Richardson, who joined Apple in 1978, said, "He didn't want to come down and beat the heavy hand. He wanted people to work it out among themselves. He would always say, 'You two go and work it out.'" A programmer said, "He seemed to have a strong desire for people to like him. He was so subtle in the way he worked that it was impossible to pin any bad deed on him." Others found him imperturbable and a perennial optimist, important qualities in a position where managers usually spent most of their time coping with problems.

Trip Hawkins, an Apple marketing manager, recalled, "Markkula absorbed stuff like a sponge. He could also make you see a unicorn in a field."

As individual characteristics started to become clear, work proceeded on a project that melded all the strains in the business. It was a mini-reprise of the development of the Apple II computer and blended developments in technology with an inventive bent and uncompromising pressure: It was an interface that connected the computer to a disk drive rather than to a cassette recorder.

Disk drives were not new. Mainframe computers had used them since 1956. But as the evolution of electronics led to the microprocessor, so disk drives also got progressively smaller. When they were first used on mainframes the disk had a diameter of about two feet and were stacked inside cabinets the size of dressers. The disk drives were linked to the computer by a device enclosed in a large box known as the controller. Even so, disk drives offered enormous advantages over the reels of magnetic tape that had previously stored information. Instead of waiting for hundreds of yards of tape to pass by a fixed point, information could now be plucked by a little "head" that floated above a rapidly spinning disk. In 1972 IBM announced a further advance in disk-drive technology when it displayed a pliable disk that was no larger than a birthday card and which quickly became known as a floppy disk. The disk drives were boiled down into boxes no larger than a concise dictionary and the controller from a cabinet onto a single-printed circuit board. The floppy disk was an advance that IBM publicists didn't hesitate to compare to a jumbo jet flying one tenth of an inch above the ground for several miles without scorching its tires.

Cassette tapes hooked to microcomputers had the same sort of deficiencies as the magnetic tapes connected to mainframe machines. They were so slow that loading a language like BASIC could take ten minutes and finding data was a hit-or-miss proposition. By comparison, a disk drive could find data in seconds. Gary Kildall, the founder of Digital Research, a software company, had written to Jobs and complained about Wozniak's cassette interface. "The cassette subsystem is particularly frustrating. I used two different recorders and found them both equally unreliable. . . . I must consider the backup storage subsystem as low-end hobbyist grade."

At Apple there was a united push to hook a disk drive to the computer. Jobs paid weekly visits to Shugart, a Silicon Valley company that was one of the first to make disk drives, and implored its executives to supply Apple. Meanwhile, Wozniak studied the circuitry used by IBM engineers who had developed a disk controller and also the approach employed by a Berkeley start-up, Northstar. But Wozniak only started work in earnest shortly before Christmas, 1977. His tendency to procrastinate made life uncomfortable for Scott who, anxious to ship, said, "Woz would take a product right up to the crisis point and do it. It was almost as if he needed the adrenaline spike of almost being late in order to really create." But once Wozniak started working on the disk controller he didn't stop until it was complete. Holt, who again played taskmaster, thought, "It was close to insanity for him to get his mind so close to the machine." Jean Richardson also kept a maternal eye on him. "He was a ghost that came and went at odd hours. He worked through the night. I would meet him going out as I came in in the morning. Eating and sleeping didn't seem to matter." Wozniak worked furiously for a couple of weeks, accompanied by Wigginton who wrote programs to test the drive and Holt who badgered him until he was convinced that the device would really work.

When the drive was announced at the Consumer Electronics Show in early 1978 and subjected to more careful scrutiny some weeks later at the Second West Coast Computer Faire, the reaction was uniform. The disk-controller card used far fewer chips than any competing device and Wozniak considered it "the favorite design of my life." Fellow engineers also applauded. Lee Felsenstein, who a year before had been so skeptical about Jobs and Wozniak and the computer in a cigar box, took a look at the controller and recalled, "I nearly dropped my pants. It was so clever. I thought, 'We better keep out of the way of these guys.'" At Commodore Chuck Peddle was guiding a design team that was also working on a disk drive but was beaten to the finish line. He thought about Wozniak's design in geopolitical terms and said, "It absolutely changed the industry." Until the drive was announced, Apple, Commodore, and Radio Shack had all been working out teething problems with their manufacturing and nothing much separated the companies.

Apple also always had computers in stock and when suppliers visited Cupertino they weren't taken into the part of the building where the inventory was piled up. Once the drive was announced matters changed.

After the design was completed and Apple coaxed the disk drives to life, Scott brought his remorseless pressure to bear. The drives that arrived from Apple's only supplier, Shugart, which was a Xerox Corporation subsidiary, were unreliable. So the engineers and technicians in the laboratory cannibalized parts to produce working drives and buckled to Scott's implacable demands. He insisted that Apple start shipping the disk drives even though there hadn't been enough time to complete a comprehensive manual. The results of Scott's pressure and the quality of the flimsy leaflet that accompanied the early disk drives were revealed in a complaint that a Southern California customer mailed to Markkula. "You fucking bastards. I bought an Apple with floppy and nobody, I mean nobody, in L.A. or San Diego knows how to use the sonuvabitch for random access files. I really feel 'ripped off.' Everybody talks about this great manual in the sky that is coming out soon??? Shit! Shit! Shit! I need this computer now in my business not next year. Fuck you. I hope your dog dies."

"The Star is an incredible pig," Hertzfeld said.

An oblique comment on the way of life at a large company was pinned to a notice board in the Mac engineering laboratory. It was one wag's jaundiced view of the development of a computer and the bureaucracy at Apple. To the rhetorical question "How many Apple employees does it take to change a light bulb?" the anonymous skeptic answered:

> One to file the user input report for the bad bulb.
> One to revise the user interface specifications.
> One to redesign the lightbulb.
> One to build the prototype.
> One to approve the project.
> One to leak the news to the press.
> One area associate to coordinate the project.
> One project manager.
> Two product marketing managers.
> One to write the lightbulb product-revision plan.
> One to analyze the lightbulb's profitability.
> One to negotiate the vendor contract.
> Seven to alpha-test the lightbulb.
> One to revise the lightbulb operating system.
> One to obtain FCC certification.
> One to write the manual.
> One to do the foreign translations.
> One to develop the lightbulb product-training pack.
> One to design the artwork.
> One to design the package.
> One to write the data sheet.
> One to write the self-running lightbulb demo.
> One to copy-protect the lightbulb.
> One to write the ECO.
> One to forecast use.
> One to enter the part number in the computer.
> One to place the order for each lightbulb.
> One to QC the lightbulb.
> One to distribute the lightbulb.
> One to seed vendors with the revision.
> One to organize the product introduction party.

One to make the press announcement.
One to explain the lightbulb to the financial
   community.
One to announce the lightbulb to the sales force.
One to announce the lightbulb to the dealers.
One to train service.
And one service technician to swap out the
   lightbulb.

A few of the Mac group were hovering around a Lisa proto-type. Programmer Andy Hertzfeld provided a commentary as Michael Boich fiddled with features of the machine. "I couldn't work at Lisa," Hertzfeld said to no one in particular. "The only thing that gets done there is by committee and politics. Lisa equals competent engineering."

Boich and Hertzfeld eyed the performance of the Lisa with the critical air that men once used to inspect tappets and pistons. Boich pressed a button on the mouse and Hertzfeld said as he watched a list appear on the screen, "They've got a really ugly font for their menu. I've seen it take five minutes to make a menu."

Boich chuckled. "It thrashes pretty badly."

"It's a total misuse of the menu," Hertzfeld insisted with the air of an offended monk.

"It's in one of those thrash modes," Boich said as he waited for a file to appear on the screen. "They've got a lot of things to do."

"We're never going to have these performance problems," Hertzfeld said, "but our programs are never going to be this big."

Engineering manager Bob Belleville, who was watching the scene from the entrance to the cubicle, cautioned quietly, "'Never' is not a word I feel real comfortable with." He said that the comments reminded him of a time when some former colleagues at Xerox, who were developing a laser printer, had greeted the appearance of a machine from a competitor with the comment, "Our specs are much better than that."

Boich continued to play with the machine, looked at Hertzfeld, and mentioned the Xerox computer that bore some similarities to Lisa. "It's still as fast as the Star."

"The Star is an incredible pig. It's a disaster. It's unusable," Hertzfeld said. He pointed at the Lisa and added, "To see how slow it is you should try opening another application."

"I'm almost afraid to do it." Boich grinned.

"It's a tribute to three years of programming when it works," Hertzfeld said.

THE BEST SALESMEN

The custodians of Apple quickly learned the art of making friends and influencing people. Markkula, who guided Apple's early contacts with outsiders, used precisely the same technique that Scott employed to manage the internal affairs of the company. Markkula made others help Apple grow. More than any of his colleagues Markkula understood the importance of appearance. The tone of his strategy was summed up in the way he kept prodding Jobs to spruce up his dress. "You judge a book," Markkula kept repeating to his younger partner, "by its cover." He recognized the power of gilt-edged associations. He knew that it was more important to lavish attention on a few people rather than many. He understood that reputable investors lent a sheen to a business that was difficult to acquire in any other way and the Regis McKenna Agency demonstrated that a magazine story was cheaper and far more influential than a splashy, multicolored gatefold.

Apple was more a production of the whispering grapevine that linked investors and reporters in a gossipy circle than any great marketing triumph. In the ugly jargon of the trade, Apple concentrated on opinion makers. They sensed that others without the time, inclination, or wit to investigate the odd assembly that made the Apple II would rely on the judgment of people who were already wealthy or knew a thing or two about computers. For investors and reporters share at least one trait: Both money men and scribblers usually behave like sheep.

Off the bat Markkula knew that alliances with a couple of experienced financiers were worth far more than the weight of their investments. Though his personal investments had been successful enough, Markkula had no direct experience dealing with any of the 237 or so firms that made up the venture-capital industry and which, in exchange for stock, provided financing to young companies. Originally, Markkula had wanted to wait until Apple had proved that it could produce its computer before turning to the venture capitalists, knowing that he would get a better price for the company stock if he could demonstrate that Apple wasn't in desperate need of money. In the fall of 1977, the troubles with the quality of the case threatened to exhaust Apple's credit line and left Markkula with no choice. Even the profit from sales of the computer were barely sufficient to keep Apple in business. The company's needs were so dire that Markkula and Scott supplied an injection of almost two hundred thousand dollars to bind things over until negotiations for more money could be formally concluded.

Once again Apple turned to familiar faces. Hank Smith had been one of Markkula's colleagues at both Fairchild and Intel. He was an exuberant man with bouncy ginger hair who had left Intel and moved to New York to become a general partner of Venrock the venture-capital arm of the Rockefeller family. In the informal hierarchy of venture funds, Venrock, ranked among the best, and there was the additional advantage that it had not yet financed any microcomputer companies. Markkula first approached Smith in the spring of 1977 and for several months Venrock monitored Apple's progress. John Hall, who had helped write the business plan, called on Venrock and discussed Apple's prospects with two of the partners. When Smith was on the West Coast, visiting other Venrock investments, he made a point of dropping by Apple's Cupertino office. The venture-capital firm made about seven investments a year, but there was nothing apart from a personal relationship that drew its people toward Apple. Hank Smith said, "We probably wouldn't have looked at Apple had I not known

Mike Markkula." Eventually, in the fall of 1977, Markkula was invited, along with Jobs and Scott, to meet Venrock's other partners and present their projections for Apple.

Though the earlier plan had been considered aggressive, Apple, despite all the problems with the quality of the case, had been beating its projections. The presentation concealed much of the rush that had preceded it. Though Markkula had written a prospectus and based much of his forecast on financial projections supplied by Gary Martin, touch rather than science carried the day. Sherry Livingston watched while the forecasts were made. "It was a joke the way they came up with projections. There were so many projections they'd almost flip a coin."

Nevertheless, the business plan reflected the semblance of order and sense of focus that Markkula and Scott brought to Apple. The night before the presentation to the Venrock partners in New York, Scott remained in Cupertino with most of the rest of the company munching slices of pizza and helping to copy, staple, collate, and bind the prospectus. Clutching a dozen copies he caught a red-eye flight to New York, took an early morning nap at the Hilton, and then accompanied Hank Smith, Markkula, and Jobs to the Venrock offices. With the arrangement tentatively closed, the trio made for the airport. Scott saw some former colleagues from National Semiconductor queuing for standby tickets and decided to treat himself and his companions to first-class seats.

While dealing with the Venrock partners, Markkula had also been talking to Andrew Grove, executive vice-president of Intel. Grove, a wiry Hungarian refugee with an expressive face and curly hair, had earned a reputation for being as noisy and remorseless as a steam hammer. (At Intel he had insisted that all late arrivals enter their names in a sign-up book and was notorious for dispatching "Grove-Grams"—bullet-sized reprimands.) Markkula hoped that Grove would lend Apple some of the experience he had acquired building Intel's factories. Grove swallowed the bait and bought fifteen thousand of the twenty-five thousand shares that Markkula offered but decided not to become a director, feeling that he had enough to worry about at Intel without becoming involved with another young company. In later months Scott recalled, "Grove kept calling. He'd say, 'I'd like you to stop stealing my people,' and then he'd say, 'Do you want to sell some Apple stock?'"

Another member of Intel's board of directors, Arthur Rock, happened to see a demonstration of the Apple II given by Markkula. As a result, a few days before Apple was due to sign its agreement with Venrock, Rock telephoned Hank Smith at Venrock and Mike Scott at Apple expressing his interest in the offering. In the mid-seventies a telephone call from Arthur Rock was viewed by other venture capitalists, underwriters, commercial bankers, and stockbrokers as the financial equivalent of white smoke emerging from a Vatican chimney. Rock, who was in his early fifties, had made investments in companies that bridged the years between the disappearance of the vacuum tube and the arrival of the integrated circuit. As a New York financier, he had helped arrange the financing for the start of Fairchild Semiconductor. Along with a partner, he participated in the rise of the minicomputer industry by investing in Scientific Data Systems which was sold to Xerox Corporation in a 1969 exchange of stock for $918 million. Rock's stake was worth $60 million. In 1968 when a couple of senior managers left Fairchild to form Intel, they turned to Arthur Rock for advice and money. Rock invested $300,000 of his own money, arranged for another $2.2 million and became the company's first chairman. He had offered critical advice at several points, and when Intel's management was dithering about whether to try to develop markets for its first microprocessor, Rock's advice proved decisive.

Rock shunned publicity, had never been the subject of a long newspaper or magazine profile, hardly ever appeared at meetings of venture-capital associations, was formidably discreet about his investments, and conducted most of his business either from an office on San Francisco's Montgomery Street or from a $450,000 three-story condominium in Aspen. He had an austere look and the neat physique of a man who spent an hour exercising every morning. He was an avid baseball fan and frequently braved the winds of San Francisco's Candlestick Park where he had a front-row seat seventy feet from home plate. He was also an enthusiastic supporter of San Francisco's ballet and opera and a collector of works by, among others, the modernists Robert Motherwell and Hans Hoffman. He was quite old-fashioned, believing that television was the curse of modern society, that marijuana addled the mind, and that there had been no significant developments in literature or art for a couple of decades. A fellow venture capitalist said, "He can be charming and endearing and a cold sonuvabitch."

Provided they could lure Rock away from his office in San Francisco or his ski lodge in Aspen, the managers of young companies took great pains with their presentations to him. Like most experienced venture capitalists, Arthur Rock was not a gambler. He usually made only three or four investments a year and generally supplied only a small amount of money until he was convinced that the company would succeed or that he would get along with the management. He had a reputation for being easily bored, had little patience with corporate contributions to charities like the United Way, and was also known for saying little during board meetings. He would frequently cut short suggestions with the question: "What purpose would it serve?" Tommy Davis, Rock's investment partner for much of the sixties, said, "He only wants the right answer." Andrew Grove thought Rock was "like the pilot of a plane who sees the geography far better than the people who are driving around in it." So when Rock called Apple he gained admission on the strength of a gilt-lined reputation.

The investment of Don Valentine, the venture capitalist who first allied Markkula with Apple, was partially a result of coincidence. When Valentine spotted Markkula, Jobs, and Hank Smith dining together one evening at Monterey's Chez Felice Restaurant, he sensed what was being discussed. He dispatched a bottle of wine to the trio with a note reading "Don't lose sight of the fact that I'm planning on investing in Apple."

When the financing was eventually completed in Janaury 1978, and all the papers signed and notarized and share certificates swapped, Apple was valued at $3 million. The financing brought Apple $517,500 of which Venrock invested $288,000, Valentine, $150,000 Arthur Rock, $57,600. In return Markkula and Scott asked for an informal agreement from their investors that their financial commitments last at least five years.

Within six months word of Apple had begun to scep out and when Michael Scott and the others appeared at the Consumer Electronics show in the summer of 1978, they were buttonholed by investors from Chicago's Continental Illinois Bank who wanted to invest $500,000 in Apple. The price of the shares was about three times what it had been six months earlier. The Venrock partners grumbled about the increase in the price of the stock but eventually made an additional investment and wound up owning 7.9 percent of the company while Valentine complained the price was far too steep and refused to add to his original stake.

Some months after the initial financing Scott took another call but this time from a close friend of Rock's, Henry Singleton, chairman of Teledyne Inc., one of the companies that had helped make *conglomerate* a fashionable word during the sixties. Rock had helped start Teledyne and served on the company's six-member board of directors. Scott was astonished that the chairman of a two-billion-dollar company which sold life insurance, made tank engines, shower massages, oil drilling equipment, and an ill-starred electronic device for measuring a dieter's bites was calling Apple Computer to find out about the internal quirks of the Apple II.

Like Rock, Singleton had not gained a reputation for sentimentality. He was reputed to manage Teledyne's subsidiaries as if they were items in his personal stock portfolio, was said to have a head for detail, a devotion to cash, and no problem with ordering summary closures. Scott patiently answered Singleton's questions and later asked Rock whether he thought that his investment partner would be interested in becoming an Apple director. Rock thought it impossible, saying that Singleton served on only one other board and was trying to rid himself of that obligation. He told Scott, "If I ask, the answer will only be no."

Scott persisted and when Apple announced its disk drive he arranged to hand deliver one at Singleton's Century City office. He found that Singleton not only had an Apple in his office but also had one at home and was busy programming in assembly language. The appointment turned from half an hour into the whole day, with a lunch at the Beverly Hills Country Club where Singleton impressed Scott by paying in cash rather than resorting to credit cards. When Rock discovered that Scott had been invited to Singleton's home, he knew the knot was tied: "You've got him nailed." Singleton bought $100,800 worth of Apple stock and in October 1978 became a director.

As Venrock, Arthur Rock, and Henry Singleton were recruited, Markkula showed that he wasn't squeamish about selling parts of the company to properly qualified people. Unlike some of the other microcomputer companies who were wary that investors or directors would grab control or turn into bullies, the men at Apple recognized the help they could offer. More important than the injections of cash were the intangible benefits of the financier's experience and reputation. They had monitored the growth of other small companies, had lived through dark days, were aware of some of the likely pitfalls, and could lend some weathered perspective to the pellmell pace of life in a start-up. They could offer advice about limiting the company's tax liability, help sort out a distribution strategy, provide connections to people who could be helpful and help lure experienced managers. Recognizing this, Apple was careful to make life easy for its investors. It arranged board meetings to coincide with the day Rock traveled down the Peninsula to attend Intel's board meetings while Scott often chauffeured Henry Singleton to and from the San Jose airport.

Though Apple's early stock sales were wreathed in anonymity, the reputations of the early investors were too large to hide. Their interest in Apple was precisely the sort of thing that provided snippets of gossip for venture capitalists. It was just the stuff that would make the rounds at the monthly lunches of the Western Association of Venture Capitalists, or be shared among bankers in the first-class section of the wide-bodied jets plying between San Francisco and New York, or for others who would breakfast at Rickey's Hyatt House on El Camino Real in Palo Alto. The more industrious could ferret out the information by sorting through the files in the meanly furnished lobby of the California Department of Corporations office in San Francisco.

Investors who laid their money on the table were one sign of confidence. Stock analysts who put their opinions on paper were another. In the late seventies one of the most influential Wall Street electronics analysts was Ben Rosen. Rosen had followed the electronics industry for years. He was fond of gadgets. He spent several weeks a year industriously traipsing around trade shows, kept an eye on new products, wasn't swept away by the accounts of senior managers, and would patiently solicit opinions of middle and junior managers.

Markkula and Scott were just two of the younger managers Rosen had run across. He had known them both while they were still at Fairchild and on one of his inspection tours of Intel had taught Markkula how to operate a programmable calculator. Apple's managers took care of Rosen, who started using an Apple in April 1978. Rosen was given the sort of customer service reserved for sheikhs and princes. When he didn't understand some feature of the Apple and couldn't find an adequate explanation in the manual, he called Jobs or Markkula at home. Markkula even offered to sell Rosen some Apple stock but was politely rebuffed. However, he would visit Apple and was almost always given straight answers to straight questions. Scott said, "Ben always had the data two or three years in advance of what was actually going on." The attention paid off.

Many of the journalists who followed the early years of the microcomputer industry were the people who had monitored the semiconductor industry and they had learned to trust Rosen. Among a crowd of men who made it their business to boost companies and tout stocks, Rosen they considered impartial. He always returned telephone calls, offered comprehensive reports on companies, and would provide pithy quotes based on shrewd observations which often wound up in *The Wall Street Journal*, *The New York Times*, *Business Week*, *Fortune*, *Forbes*, and the news-weeklies. The reporters who trooped through Rosen's New York office found that he was using an Apple. So Rosen became, in some ways, Apple's most influential sponsor. Regis McKenna, Apple's publicist, who was given an introduction to *Time* at a luncheon organized by Rosen, thought "Ben gave Apple real credibility," while the venture-capitalist Hank Smith felt he was "one of Apple's best salesmen."

Apple's select financial following was important and started to feed off itself. When Rosen and another Morgan Stanley analyst, Barton Biggs, lunched with Arthur Rock in San Francisco, their conversation was summarized in a two-page memo circulated around the New York banking house. Written by Biggs, it had a breathless tone: "Arthur Rock is a Legend with a capital 'L' like Ted Williams or Fran Tarkenton, Leonard Bernstein and Nureyev. . . . In his line of business he is a player who is several orders of magnitude better than anyone else who has ever been in the game." Biggs dutifully reported Rock's comments about Apple to his colleagues at Morgan Stanley. "The people running this company . . . are very bright, very creative and very driven." Words like those were guaranteed to make readers (and investors) froth at the mouth.

The early descriptions of Apple's marketing campaign were hardly guaranteed to have the same effect as tips from one of the country's most experienced venture capitalists. In set speeches and formal presentations, Markkula was given to describing Apple's grand plan in three words: "Empathy. Focus. Impute." The muddle of nouns and verbs provoked giggles among the advertising account executives but Markkula was expressing, in a peculiarly modern way, an old idea. In the 1940s, for example, IBM had used a similar strategy when it opened a lavish showroom on New York's Fifth Avenue, and the company founder, Tom Watson, had later explained. "We were carrying the corporate image far out in front of the size and reputation of the corporation."

At the start, Apple's marketing strategy was not the result of any clearheaded vision. Notions of product life cycles resembled the sort of patterns that were common in the semiconductor industry where chips were liable to be superseded within twelve months of introduction. The early gaffes were concealed by the forgiving nature of an expanding market. At first there was great uncertainty at the Regis McKenna Agency about Apple's prospects. The account executive, Frank Burge, explained, "People who knew Markkula and Apple wondered whether they would make it. We kept saying 'These guys are flakes. They're never going to make it.' Jobs and Wozniak looked as if they were on something. It was counter to everything we believed in." The agency people looked at Markkula, whom they didn't consider to have much of a reputation for marketing, and Scott with his manufacturing instincts, and worried that nobody at Apple had any experience selling to consumers.

To hedge his bets McKenna took on another computer company, Video Brain, which at the start of 1978 announced a non-programmable computer named The Family Computer, with the hope that people would plug cartridges in and use the machine at home. The product was greeted enthusiastically by the press and by buyers for major department stores who felt that consumers wouldn't want to learn how to program. Eventually consumers balked at the price, which kept creeping up, aided by the company's ambitious decision to make the semiconductors for the machine. Video Brain failed.

However, for some months McKenna had a tough time trying to decide whether to dump Apple in favor of Video Brain. Though the agency chose to stand by Apple, its caution was reflected in the size of the advertising budget it proposed for the company's second year. McKenna proposed that Apple spend $300,000. Markkula insisted that the budget be doubled. Markkula was convinced that it was futile for Apple to try to eke out a living on a small share of the microcomputer market and steadfastly insisted that Apple had to look imposing and pretend to be large if it was ever to become a force in the industry. McKenna explained, "I'm always conservative with very young companies. I don't want to be stuck with unpaid bills of one hundred thousand dollars. Markkula kept saying 'We must develop a position early.' He really pushed for that. It was a very important decision."

The advertisement that introduced the Apple II showed a kitchen with a woman merrily at work beside a chopping board while her husband sat at the kitchen table using the computer to attend to more worldly chores. The copy was unequivocal about what the computer could be used for: "The home computer that's ready to work, play and grow with you . . . You'll be able to organize, index and store data on household finances, income taxes, recipes, your biorhythms, balance your checking account, even control your home environment." The advertisement also carried a lot of technical specifications which were aimed at the ardent hobbyist but were not calculated to appeal to the layman. Keen hobbyists with agile hands and a technical bent were told they could buy the Apple II in the form of a single printed circuit board for $598.

A large poster which started to appear in computer stores about the same time carried the distinctly equivocal slogan APPLE II: THE HOME/PERSONAL COMPUTER. Markkula was quoted at the time as saying that Apple would not be an exhibitor at the National Computer Conference, the traditional showcase for manufacturers selling to businesses, but would concentrate its efforts on the Consumer Electronics show. Apple's advertising manager, Jean Richardson, admitted, "There was not a lot of sophisticated strategy. They thought they were selling to people in a home."

The magazines in which the advertisements appeared were more important than the copy or the look. Compared to companies like Compucolor, a Georgia company that produced a color computer, Apple's earliest advertisements were wan. As well as buying space in hobbyist magazines like *Byte,* Apple, during its first year, also advertised in *Scientific American* and *Playboy.* They were expensive places to advertise but the nature of the magazines helped lift Apple above the crowd of other small computer companies. Apple also placed little adverts, designed to boost the corporate image, that didn't say much about the computer but were bright and perky and written by McKenna himself. One of the most popular began: "A is for Apple. It's the first thing you should know about personal computers."

At the end of 1977 Digital Research's Gary Kildall again wrote to Jobs and among other subjects politely recited his concerns about Apple's marketing: "From our earlier discussions I believe you want to address the consumer market. . . . The Apple advertising is somewhat misleading. . . . The Apple II is not a consumer computer and, even though I have had 'previous computer experience,' I had some difficulties getting parts together, and making the system operate. . . . Further, commercial appliance manufacturers do not advertise products which do not exist. . . . Your advertisement implies that software exists (or is easily constructed) for stock market analysis and home finance handling. Do these programs exist? Secondly, a floppy disk subsystem is promised by the 'end of 1977.' Where is it?" Kildall was right on all scores, and the program that allowed an Apple to connect to the Dow Jones ticker appeared a year after it was first announced. All told, Apple's early ads reflected Markkula's own hobbyist bent.

Though the line of the early advertisements missed the mark, there was a change in strategy within six months of the Apple II announcement. It was the sort of luxury given to a tiny, invisible company in an industry that was too small to be taken very seriously. Apple was able to take advantage of its obscurity and the forgiving nature of an expanding market and consequently had much more freedom to maneuver than a large company whose blunders would be magnified.

A memo to Apple from the McKenna Agency in early 1978, outlining a marketing strategy, demonstrated a clear understanding that the time when consumers would use computers in the home was far away. It also reflected McKenna's anxiety that Apple not ruin a consumer market by making promises that couldn't be fulfilled. The agency also began to identify its targets, recognizing the differences between the hobbyists, the "programmable calculator market," and the markets in schools and universities. And within thirty-six months of its earliest advertisements, Apple started running television commercials that tried to remove the impression that the Apple II was a plaything or home computer. The spots featured talk-show host Dick Cavett posed with housewives who were using their Apples to run a small steel mill or trade in gold futures.

Apple's advertisements were devised for an industry where small companies drenched their computers in superlatives. For skeptics there wasn't much room to argue. There was no authoritative market research. MITS had taken out full-page advertisements with the copy shaped in the form of a large figure 1, boasting that the Altair was the leading computer: "When you buy an Altair, you're not just buying a piece of equipment. You're buying years of reliable, low-cost computing. You're buying the support of the NUMBER ONE manufacturer in the micro-computer field." Vector Graphic called its machine "the perfect micro-computer"; the IMSAI 8080 was dubbed "the finest personal computer"; Radio Shack announced "the first complete, low-cost micro-computer system." Processor Technology named the Sol "The Small Computer." Apple trumpeted its machine as loudly as the rest.

In July 1978, barely a year after the first Apple II was shipped, a double-page advertisement in the trade magazines carried the banner headline WHY APPLE II IS THE WORLD'S BEST SELLING PERSONAL COMPUTER, a boast that just proved that numbers can be dredged up to support any claim. About the same time another advertisement, which also stretched reality, read "No wonder tens of thousands have already chosen Apple." Chuck Peddle, who worked on the Commodore PET, thought "Apple consistently overstated their position and contribution."

The corporate image was also reflected on the counters of computer dealers. Many of the stores were in a fragile state. They were strapped for cash and managed by hobbyists who sometimes seemed more interested in the computers than they were in their customers. Apple had a hunger for dealers. Some prospective independent dealers trooped to California, were antagonized by officials at Commodore, and found far more affection at Apple. From the start Apple also understood that the attitude and appearance of its dealers were important. For instance, it forced a dealer in San Francisco to switch his company's name from Village Discount to Village Electronics and modeled the dealer agreements on those used by Sony.

When Computerland, a franchise chain of computer stores, started to open outlets around the country, Apple tagged along, Markkula was the linchpin for setting up the original arrangements with Computerland. He took to attending store openings and giving computer demonstrations. Ed Faber, the head of Computerland, said, "It was one of those mutually advantageous relationships. Apple had a product; we had the beginnings of a retail distribution system. The more success we had, the more success they had. The more success they had, the more succcess we had." Apple, however, also used it dealers to help a limited amount of money go a long way. It was the first company in the personal-computer business to start a co-op advertising program where factory and dealer shared the costs of advertisements. Faber said, "It frightened other manufacturers. They thought we were so closely allied with Apple that they wouldn't get any recognition in our stores."

Some of Apple's success could be put down to the advertising campaigns that were paid for by other companies. After Commodore and Radio Shack introduced their computers, they wasted no time before taking out large newspaper advertisements. At the beginning of 1978, a memo sent to Apple by the Regis McKenna Agency candidly noted that "Commodore and Tandy . . . have popularized the personal computer." But few of Apple's competitors proved to be particularly competent and none of their machines reflected the delicate balance of expertise and exuberance that was being knit together in Cupertino—even though almost every company that, at one time or another, announced or was rumored to be on the verge of announcing a computer was larger, richer, and stronger than Apple. Radio Shack, with its thousands of stores and a twenty-five-million-name mailing list, was supposed to have an edge in distribution. But Radio Shack's TRS-80 black-and-white computer was tarnished by a low-quality image and proved difficult to expand. This allowed Apple's adverts to play on the Apple II's expandable nature. Commodore's PET had a pleasant name, but the company was dogged by a lack of funds, management by fiat, a keyboard that looked like an upgraded calculator, and a case made in a Canadian metal-bending factory because the company chose not to pay for plastic cases. It was also black and white, which compared unfavorably with Apple's color. Atari and Mattel, with their stronger names in consumer electronics, were slow to produce a computer, and when they finally did, their machines were inferior to the Apple II. Smaller companies like Ohio Scientific and Cromemco, despite having reliable computers, had not sought venture funding. Kentucky Fried Computers was too whimsical a name for a computer company, but by the time it was changed to Northstar Computers, much of the damage had already been done. Meanwhile, MITS—the number-one name in microcomputing—was swallowed by Pertec, a large Chatsworth, California, company that made peripherals and minicomputers.

But looming behind the small fry was the massive specter of Texas Instruments. And in 1978 and 1979, it was Texas Instruments that inspired knee-knocking fear. The company was 327 million times the size of Apple, made its own semiconductors, had gained experience selling consumer products with a line of calculators that had severely damaged other competitors, and along the way, had gained a reputation for remorselessly pursuing profit. In his newsletter Ben Rosen warned that Texas Instruments had a corporate commitment to personal computers and "when TI has a corporate commitment—watch out."

While the prospect (more than the eventual appearance) of a Texas Instruments computer stirred up fear in Cupertino, Apple was quietly working with the press. Regis McKenna recalled, "We thought the way to beat TI was with the press. TI had always had an adversarial relationship with the press and Apple had a chance to develop a friendly relationship. The press was the equalizer." McKenna understood how to handle the press better than any of the senior managers at Apple did. Scott grumbled that he had never been quoted properly; Markkula was not always easy to understand and was likely to rile reporters by presenting them with Apple button-pins or informing them that the story they were about to write would be very important for the company or insisting that buyers would be able to learn how to use the Apple II within half an hour. Jobs, meanwhile, carried away with his own enthusiasm, was always liable to blurt out every secret detail of Apple's plans. Yet Apple was also something of a dream for a public-relations man. It was a cheerful story that, once told, was difficult to forget and revolved around the sort of distinctive personalities that, at least for journalists, always help give companies a clear image.

McKenna was far more patient and didn't expect an interview or telephone call to generate a story immediately. He told his clients that they had to build long-term relationships with the press, preached the virtues of patience, and took a more dispassionate view of the stories that eventually appeared. While Apple started to get occasional coverage in trade magazines like *Interface Age*, it took several years to crack the skepticism and suspicion at better-known magazines where the name of the McKenna Agency wasn't even recognized. The account executives at the McKenna Agency spent several years wooing the press, answering reporters' calls, providing background material, arranging photo sessions that never ran, answering questions that never appeared in print, and checking facts. He also coached his clients—trying to anticipate the questions that would be asked, or rehearsing lines that they wanted to etch on an editor's mind.

McKenna arranged for several busy two- and three-day trips to New York with Apple and endured plenty of snubs and disappointments. He, Markkula, and Jobs visited what they called the "verticals"—magazines that appealed to a narrow audience—and "horizontals"—magazines that had a general readership. They carted an Apple about New York, plodding from magazine to magazine, waiting in lobbies, lugging the computer up elevators, snatching quick breakfasts with journalists from one magazine before dashing off to keep morning and lunch appointments. It was exhausting, tiresome, repetitive work that didn't lead to many immediate payoffs.

*   *   *

Apple's early, favorable press coverage had more to do with the inescapable elegance of the computer than with any minutely planned public-relations campaign. There was no stronger advertisement than satisfied owners and quietly, almost imperceptibly, whispers and rumors about the performance of the Apple II began to spread. Daniel Fylstra, the head of what was then Personal Software, a small software company in Boston, talked to other hobbyists and was surprised at what he found. "I began to find people who bought Apple computers and the things actually worked. They worked right out of the box!" Some squibs about the Apple started to appear. In January 1978 *Penthouse* magazine, in a review of personal computers, noted, "The Apple II is, in many people's opinion, the Cadillac of home computers."

Three months later, in the first major review of the Apple II, Carl Helmers, writing in the computer magazine *Byte,* called it "one of the best examples of the concept of the complete 'appliance' computer." That amounted to a bold endorsement in a magazine that treated the arrival of other computers with a certain amount of circumspection. *Byte's* review of the Commodore PET, which appeared in the same issue, concluded: "The Pet is far from the only alternative in the marketplace today. But it is a strong contender." The reviewer also made the ominous observation: "For several weeks I was unable to get anyone at Commodore on the phone and was left to fend for myself." *Byte* greeted Radio Shack's TRS 80 with what sounded like a familiar refrain: "The TRS 80 is not the only alternative for the aspiring personal computer user but it is a strong contender."

The importance of blue-chip financial backers and the way in which business journalists often look to canny investors for guidance only became apparent when stories started to appear in general-interest magazines. About the time the Apple II disk drive was introduced, the syndicated financial columnist Dan Dorfman paid a call in Cupertino. His glowing account in *Esquire,* beneath the headline MOVE OVER, HORATIO ALGER, included this assessment: "Apple has some mighty impressive believers. . . . One is Venrock Associates, the venture capital arm of the Rockefeller brothers; another is Arthur Rock, one of the country's premier venture capitalists."

While Apple, two years after it was founded, made the cover of *Inc,* a magazine specializing in the coverage of small businesses, cracking the skepticism at the major magazines proved a much tougher proposition. Apple was more than three years old before it made the pages of *Time*. Even then, under the headline SHINY APPLE, the firm was given only one column.

If McKenna was helpful with the mechanical aspects of dealing with the press, Apple's own managers looked after other parts of the company's image. The general look of the company was tied up with the owner's instruction manual. Scott was more eager to ship computers than to fuss over the graphic design of a manual and felt that all the company needed to distribute was data sheets. Jobs thought otherwise. Jef Raskin, who managed the production of Apple's first comprehensive manual, said, "Jobs wanted good manuals and he fought very hard for them." When the manual eventually appeared in August 1979, it set a standard that competitors like Commodore, Radio Shack, and Atari publicly admitted they would have to match.

It was Markkula who guided the formation of alliances that Apple used to great purpose. The company allied with larger companies to give a durable sheen to its image. It joined with ITT, for example, to distribute computers in Europe (though the relationship eventually foundered) and with Chicago's Bell & Howell, which had a strong reputation among teachers, to help place Apples in schools. "Markkula was the driving force who made these things happen," Trip Hawkins, an Apple marketing manager, recalled.

Markkula was receptive to approaches made in 1977 by Andre Sousan, the Commodore official who had once wanted to buy Apple. Sousan recalled: "I said to the two Steves and Markkula, 'Listen! You're not going to make it on the scale you want to make it if you don't go immediately to Europe. I'll set up the operations as if they are a part of Apple and I'll write up a formula which will allow you to buy it out.'" Apple, stretched to the limits, agreed and Sousan became a member of the Executive Staff.

In March 1978 Markkula called Dow Jones's Princeton, New Jersey, offices, spoke to Technical Director Carl Valenti, and asked for an appointment. Valenti recalled: "I told him I had a space on my calendar for nine the next morning. He said, 'Fine.'

I didn't realize he was calling from Cupertino. So next morning in walks Mike Markkula with bloodshot eyes, having come on the red-eye." Markkula showed Valenti how he had programmed an Apple II to fish stocks off the Dow Jones News Retrieval Service and the pair agreed, on a handshake, that the two companies would jointly develop software programs. "The other companies," Valenti observed, "came in and tried to tie us up ten ways to Sunday. Apple didn't do that."

Closer to home Apple was one of the first microcomputer companies to recognize the importance of users groups. When the company drew up plans to organize its first international users group, a memo stated: "A major element in our strategy would be to draw heavily upon outside resources in planning and executing this meeting." It continued: "There is no one who sells as well as a committed, involved user who cares about his vendor and his product." In San Francisco a group was formed to help solve a practical problem. As one of its founders, Bruce Tognazzini, explained, "We couldn't figure out how to work the damn computer." These groups, which gradually started in dozens of cities along with local and regional chapters and their own publications, not only helped spread the word and promote software development but also served as a way of keeping track of owners, maintaining a pool of guinea pigs for testing new products and providing bodies to recruit.

Markkula recognized better than any of his colleagues the way in which appearances could affect business. When, in 1979, Apple rented a large booth at the National Computer Conference in New York, it was calculated to impress the financial analysts who, sooner or later, would make judgments about what Apple was worth as a public company. Occasionally Markkula's taste for splash got the better of him and a foray into the sponsorship of automobile races where Apple spent more than one hundred thousand dollars backing a Southern California team was a flop. "It was the worst thing we ever did," said Jobs. Scott's far simpler and cheaper idea of a balloon decorated with the Apple logo, inspired by some beer commercials, was far more successful. The moral seemed obvious: Relatively small expenditures could bring a disproportionate amount of publicity.

As happened with minicomputers, outsiders developed dozens of uses for the Apple II which had not even been contemplated in Cupertino. Little companies started to make attachments that plugged into the machine. The printed circuit boards that slid into the expansion slots of the computer would turn it into a clock or a calendar or allow letters to run across eighty columns rather than forty. Rows of extra memory chips were designed to boost the Apple's memory; other cards allowed the computer to connect with a telephone. One of the most popular cards, Microsoft's Softcard, allowed the Apple to run programs originally written for computers built around Intel microprocessors that used the CP/M operating system. There were light-pens and graphic tablets, calculator keypads, fans to cool the machine and small devices that protected it from surges in energy.

Apple recognized that software would help expand the market for its computer and gave large discounts to programmers who promised to write programs. Time and again programmers discovered ways to stretch the limits of the computer. Apple was receptive to programmers, particularly since most of the programs that were demonstrated did not always work properly. And Apple was also seen by some programmers operating off a shoestring as a large company that could bankroll their diversions. When programs were completed and Apple chose to buy them, Jobs frequently did seat-of-the-pants calculations and arrived at a price by counting the lines of code. Exchanging software or copying some interesting new program became the most important part of many Apple user-group meetings. In 1979 when Fred Gibbons, who had started Software Publishing Corporation, needed an Apple, he picked it up at Jobs's home. Others relied on their own steam. Phone phreak John Draper developed a word-processing program, Easywriter, for the Apple and then hawked it to San Francisco Bay Area computer stores.

Others were attracted by the computer. Bill Budge, then twenty-two, had declined job offers from Intel and was studying for a doctorate in computer science at the University of California at Berkeley when he saw an Apple II. He promptly spent $2,000 of his $5,000 teaching-assistant salary. "It was the best toy I ever had." Necessity became the mother of programs and Budge said, "There was no way to get enough software to keep you occupied." When Budge, at the end of 1979, took his first game, Penny Arcade (an adaptation of Pong), to Apple he traded it for a $1,000 printer. Within six weeks Budge had written another three programs. In 1979 Apple also published a word-processing program dubbed

Apple Writer. The program was written by Paul Lutus, a graduate of San Francisco's hippie movement and a one-time panhandler who had helped design lighting systems for the space shuttle *Columbia* before turning to programming. Lutus wrote the first version of his word-processing program, Applewriter, in a twelve-by-sixteen-foot log cabin on Eight Dollar Mountain in a remote part of Oregon.

But the one program that did more for Apple than all the others combined was Visicalc. At a time when nobody at Commodore would take his telephone call, Daniel Fylstra, the head of Personal Software, a pint-sized company based in Boston, managed to gain a hearing at Apple. Jobs offered Fylstra an Apple II at dealer price to ensure that Personal Software, which was selling a chess game, would develop programs for Apple. At the time, two acquaintances of Fylstra's were working on a program to simplify budget forecasting. Daniel Bricklin, a Harvard MBA student, wanted a program that would eliminate the tedious recalculating required after revising financial budgets and enlisted his friend, Robert Frankston, a fellow computer programmer, to help make it work. A finance professor scoffed at the commercial prospects for Bricklin's idea but did suggest he contact Fylstra. Bricklin wanted to borrow a computer from Fylstra and because the Commodore and Radio Shack machines were being used, wound up with Personal Software's Apple. Bricklin wrote a prototype program in BASIC for an Apple with 24K bytes of memory and then, said Fylstra, "We all decided he might as well continue on the machine he had started on." Visicalc—the name derives from *visible calculator*—was demonstrated to Markkula and to officials at Atari in January 1979, Fylstra recalled: "He interpreted it as a checkbook program. I don't think Markkula or the others had an inkling of what it could be but they did encourage me." But the electronics analyst Ben Rosen, impressed by the power and speed of Visicalc and the way in which it gave the user more control over the computer, was more impressed and reported to readers of his newsletter: "So who knows? Visicalc could someday become the software tail that wags (and sells) the personal computer dog."

Visicalc did wag. And because it was available, at first for $100, solely on the Apple for twelve months after its formal introduction in October 1979, it wagged harder for Apple than for any other manufacturer. Visicalc was what helped Apple creep into small and large businesses. It was an electronic spreadsheet which could calculate the effect of changing one number in a tabletop of numbers. It offered the precision of a good accountant, the sprightly touch of a bright financial planner, and the plodding steadiness of a reliable bookkeeper. It also provided another compelling reason for Apple to shift even farther away from the home market. Fylstra tagged along to dealer training sessions to demonstrate Visicalc on a wide-screen television. Business users were convinced. Fritz Maytag, president of San Francisco's Anchor Brewing Company, was ecstatic: "I trust Visicalc more than my own financial statements. It's just a miracle." Of the 130,000 computers sold by Apple before September 1980, Michael Scott estimated that 25,000 were sold on the strength of Visicalc.

"You've got to play guts ball," Morris said.

Early breakfast meetings were an inescapable fact of life for almost everyone at Apple. So one morning at 7:30 sharp the waitress at the Good Earth Restaurant was filling large brown mugs with coffee. The trimmings of the restaurant belied its name. There were plastic menus, vinyl bench seats, veneer tables, and the baroque wicker chairs that importers like to say are made in Thailand. The only trace of the good earth was a smell of cinnamon that seemed to come from the wallpaper.

Anthony Morris, an Apple dealer from Manhattan, was having breakfast with the Mac marketing manager, Michael Murray. Morris, in a blue pinstripe suit, starched white button-down shirt, and silk tie, let out an early morning sigh as the waitress disappeared. "Cleavage this early in the morning. Cupertino is getting decadent." A Stanford MBA, Morris was considered one of Apple's better dealers and was among two hundred invited to Cupertino for a preview of Lisa. There was some industry chatter as Morris passed on scuttlebutt that another computer company was going to avoid complying with FCC regulations governing new products by introducing an entirely new disk drive but giving it a name belonging to an existing series. "The sales rep was all over town boasting about this. But last year she took a year off to finish her master's in arts and dance so that tells you a lot."

Morris, who sold only Apples, mentioned that he was about to start carrying computers made by IBM and DEC. "We could not survive selling only Apples," he explained, "so there's been a loss of faith or what some would call the emergence of sound business practices." He paused. "Apple has to start thinking about the business customer. Those buggers are demanding."

Murray raised his eyes from his breakfast plate and asked, "What would it take to make you cancel IBM?"

"I probably won't," Morris replied. "First, the Apple III was going pssss. We've got twenty-eight people. I cannot feed them when sales are going down. It's scary how quickly your business goes down. Second, my clients want IBM and nobody has ever got fired for buying IBM. IBM's goddamn thorough. They have done a lot of thinking. They understand the business user. The message from IBM is if you take 'em on you can double your sales in ninety days." Morris mentioned a fellow dealer in New York City. "He did a million dollars in a month. He didn't do that with Apple."

Murray countered, "We're going to hang Mac out in front of the dealers and make them salivate and see if we can get some momentum away from IBM. We've got so many different kinds of dealers. How do we understand our best one hundred dealers? How do we get you really excited?"

Morris argued that many of Apple's promotional pieces weren't suitable for dealers whose customers were businesses. "The people in Cupertino don't leave Cupertino enough. They don't know what the world is about. We've got to systematically reduce the number of decisions a customer has to make in order to get them to make the decision we want. We shouldn't be saying, 'Here's a candyland. Make your choice.'"

Murray nodded and reverted to the nagging prospect of IBM. "It's scary to think how small we are and how slick IBM is."

Morris replied with assurance, "You've got to play guts ball. You will fail if you're only as good as IBM. It's just like women in business. You've got to work twice as hard to get half the recognition."

Some mornings later a group of marketing managers from all the Apple divisions gathered for their monthly meeting. Joe Roebuck, a marketing manager, placed his Styrofoam coffee cup on the table near an overhead projector and surveyed his companions. "This place is beginning to look like IBM. Everybody's got ties. No blue shirts yet. But we're getting there." The chief topic of discussion was the avalanche of magazines, brochures, newsletters, buyers' guides, flyers, catalogs, and data sheets—the "pieces"—that Apple published to help persuade customers to buy its products. Phil Roybal, who headed Apple's marketing publications, showed a series of slides about the importance of these publications and said, "Literature is not an event. It's part of a process. We have to sell prospects what they want"—he paused for effect and added—"which is a solution." He associated each of Apple's publications with customers in varying states of anticipation and noted, "The average prospect walks into a store and takes five hours to make the connection between what he wants and what he should buy. Most don't care whether it's an Apple II or III or an IBM PC or a sack of walnuts. The dealer will grab anything that says apple, shove it into the prospect's hand, and hope he'll buy. They're not selling solutions. The literature has to start pulling the products together into solutions for people."

Joe Roebuck interrupted. "We're churning out requirements for literature like crazy."

"When I look at the business plan for the coming year," Roybal responded, "I find I'm running a shortfall of five writers a week. I can kill some projects or I can kill some writers."

THE BOZO EXPLOSION

Apple Computer started life as a business, not a company. The gradual change from a bloated garage operation into something resembling a corporation was arduous and protracted. Once Apple announced its disk drive in the summer of 1978, orders increased, the backlog of unsold computers disappeared, and the pressure to grow mounted. The headquarters was moved to a building fifteen times larger than the office Apple had occupied behind the Good Earth Restaurant. It was set among orchards a block or so from Stevens Creek Boulevard, and Apple's new neighbors were a plant nursery and a couple of wooden frame houses. When the ninety or so employees wandered around their empty new building, most were convinced that it would last, if not for a lifetime, certainly for several years.

Within three months the packing cartons arrived and again Apple commandeered a couple more buildings. The second shuffle was made in such a hurry that interior alterations were performed without any building permits and equipment was brought in over a weekend from trucks discreetly parked by some rear doors.

Packing cartons, new offices, fresh surroundings, and unfamiliar companions became a disconcerting way of life.

Over the course of about two years a sheaf of professionals arrived. For newcomers accustomed to the struts and underpinnings of a large company, the turmoil of a start-up was entirely foreign. There were few of the services most companies devise to make life easier. When a sink or lavatory got clogged, there was no maintenance department to call. When the telephones broke, no communications consultant came tripping down the hallway with a handpiece clipped to his belt. When somebody had to make a long business trip there was no travel department to look after the arrangements. Legal matters were handled by an outside law firm. Personnel problems were dealt with on the fly and raises were given at will. There was little time to relax and any sign of a casual air was a complete illusion. Above all, there was a relentless pressure.

Jean Richardson, who started as a secretary and eventually became Apple's advertising director, recalled, "For a couple of years the pace was awful. It was twelve hours a day and weekends. I knew if I took a drink at a water fountain I would miss a beat and slip a schedule. It was almost inhuman. I was at the burnout stage." As the professionals arrived, Apple was confronted with the problems of reconciling old and new, coping with the consternation and resentment provoked by the arrivals and accommodating the habits and influences they brought with them.

For a company growing as fast as Apple, hiring new employees was its most important task. In the long run this overshadowed everything else. People recruited one day frequently wound up hiring others within days or weeks of their arrival, so one early misjudgment could be amplified and have grave implications. For relative innocents running a small business, it was easy to be awed by the reputation of other companies, the length of a résumé, a string of advanced degrees, and the sound of a reputation. There was a conscious effort to hire people who were overqualified for the immediate job at hand but who would be able to cope with larger demands as orders increased.

Apple, like other companies before it, took to raiding established firms. Every major steal brought squeals of delight. Markkula couldn't conceal his glee when he lured somebody from Intel, Scott was just as happy when he snared a body from National Semiconductor, and Jobs interpreted a resignation from Hewlett-Packard as something approaching divine approval. When another company president called to complain about the way Apple was pinching his people, they chuckled some more.

Candidates for senior positions were usually interviewed by Markkula, Scott, and Jobs. The visible differences among the trio were enough to ring alarm bells in the heads of some who contemplated joining Apple. When, during interviews, Jobs insisted on putting his dirty feet on the table or when, at luncheon interviews, he returned a plate to a waitress informing her that the food was "garbage," he wasn't necessarily impressive. Though he tended to be swayed by reputations, Jobs distrusted résumés and preferred to rely on his instincts. He conducted many screenings at the Good Earth Restaurant or other nearby eateries, usually plumped for somebody he felt was right, and trusted his choices to be able to do what they said they could do.

In the summer of 1978, fifteen months after the announcement of the Apple II, the manufacturing department was fairly typical of the condition of the rest of the firm. Apple was building about thirty computers a day and managing to ship about fifteen disk drives a week. Twenty-eight people reported to one supervisor who, each morning, handed out instructions and doled out assignments. It was still a manual department. Purchase orders, inventory controls, and shipment rates were monitored with pen and paper. Half the manufacturing area was filled with a three-year supply of plastic that Jobs had managed to buy at a good price.

Roy Mollard, a ramrod-straight Liverpudlian, who had known Scott at National Semiconductor and Fairchild Semiconductor, was hired to direct manufacturing. He looked like a lean cotton-mill manager out of some D. H. Lawrence novel, and brought many of the tricks he had learned at National Semiconductor. He hired security guards, installed hidden microphones to trigger burglar alarms, and on the floor he appointed supervisors, scrapped the casual lunchtime Ping-Pong games, fired the quality-assurance manager, and insisted that there be no cupboards or drawers so that he could always see the inventory. His aim, as he put it, was "to hose out computers" and he wasn't prepared to tolerate nuisances.

He struggled to make the manufacturing area out-of-bounds for the rest of the company and made withering comments when people slopped into his bailiwick without shoes. "Steve Jobs didn't want to limit access. I said, 'Baloney!' I don't want my people in a goldfish bowl.'" Don Bruener, the high-school student originally hired to troubleshoot balky boards, observed the new tone. "At the beginning if you thought about a change in production you could talk to someone and get it changed. It became more of an assembly line and you had to go through channels and write up a proposal for change."

The same sort of shift occurred in the engineering laboratory. Rod Holt, the unwilling head of the department, found himself trying to guide the affairs of quality control, service, documentation, mechanical engineering, industrial design, and the work of the hardware engineers. "I stood up at a staff meeting," Holt recalled, "and said, 'If you guys don't square this around, I'm quitting.'" To solve the problem Apple overcompensated by chasing two candidates. One, Tom Whitney, had guided large calculator projects at Hewlett-Packard and was a college friend of the hardware engineer, Wendell Sander, and a former boss of Steve Wozniak. The other, Charles H. Peddle III, had managed the MOS Technology team that had designed the 6502 microprocessor that lay at the heart of the Apple II. When both men agreed to join Apple their decisions were greeted with enthusiasm. Each, however, was surprised to find the other present, and after a few weeks, Peddle left.

Whitney, a tall man with a studious air, sought to introduce some of the practices that had proved effective at Hewlett-Packard. He assigned project leaders, scheduled meetings on design specifications, and tried to sort through the heap of tasks that needed attention. A battery of forms with various Hewlett-Packard acronyms became part of the Apple vocabulary. ECOS stood for engineering change order, ERS for external reference specification, and IDS for internal design specification. One of the young engineers, Chuck Mauro, said that his colleagues greeted the new regimen with guffaws. "We thought, 'Here we go. Here comes red tape and forms to fill out and meetings every week.' Organization was just too hard to take."

The creeping professionalism was also reflected in the sort of software that was produced. Among the youngsters there was a strong allegiance to the BASIC programming language which had ruled strong at the Homebrew Club, was the lingua franca of the hobbyist community, and had proved more than adequate for games like Breakout—but it wasn't really suitable for more powerful applications. Jef Raskin, who wrote the first proper Apple manual, argued for the merits of the more powerful language, Pascal, and helped convince Jobs that he should at least give it a try. Bill Atkinson, a programmer who did much of the work on Pascal, recalled, "Mike Scott didn't believe in software. He thought we should put out hot hardware and people would supply software. Steve Jobs said, 'Our users only want assembly language and BASIC but I'll give you three months to convince me otherwise."

Jobs allowed his skepticism to be overruled by his natural inclination to find a better way to do things. Once Pascal was converted to run on the Apple, it gave the company a new language to sell, simplified development of new programs, and most important, boosted the company's reputation among experienced programmers who considered it a seal of respectability. Raskin and others continued to complain that Apple treated software as hardware's stepsister. "Software is the glass through which the majority of our users see the Apple. If it doesn't work right, the Apple isn't working right." Gradually his complaints, the arrival of some more graybeards, and the demands of the market helped nudge Apple away from a devotion to hardware.

A drive to introduce the ways and procedures of a larger company wasn't limited to recruitment or software. It extended to the invisible skein of systems that started to streak about the place. Scott found that his admiration for order and his interest in computers blended in a management-information system that linked most aspects of the company. At first Apple leased computers from an outside firm; then, when the monthly bills mounted, it bought its own minicomputers. The Management Information System was not glamorous and, for the most part, it was invisible. Yet it became one of the major reasons for the growth of Apple and was, perhaps, Scott's most important contribution. The system became Scott's pet delight. Sitting at a terminal he—and other top managers—had a birds-eye view of the entire company. He could punch in a code and find out how many resistors were in stock at a warehouse, which parts were running low, how new orders were piling up, and which customers weren't paying their bills.

One feature allowed Scott complete control. He could throw other users off the system, switch his terminal into lockstep with another to find out how someone was coping with the computer, and fire off messages to the hapless. It was an elaborate electronic toy calculated to appeal to his sense of whimsy and his passion for control. In a company where any number of programmers could wreak havoc with sensitive files, Scott's master password was changed frequently. His favorite moniker was adopted from his aptly named cat: Baal.

The appearance of managers with fringes of gray hair and business-school graduates with an ambitious glint raised eyebrows. The old-timers viewed the newcomers with increasing suspicion. They looked on them as arrivistes. When rumors started to trickle out about the stock options and incentive schemes used as enticements, the bitterness was given a sharper edge. They were classified as corporate parvenus willing to go wherever they thought they could make a killing. So a gap opened between the newcomers and those who had been around during the early months. It was a difference that amounted to a clash between notions of amateurism and professionalism.

Some of the fresh faces turned up their noses at most of the young programmers, dismissing them as "talented backyard hackers" who wouldn't bother to document their software and were only capable of writing "spaghetti code." One manager wrote a vitriolic memo dismissing a program written during the early months as "riddled with bugs the way an old log is full of termites." Tom Whitney summed up his attitude: "I wasn't interested in working for a game company. We needed to become more professional. Compatibility and providing support for the customer were more important than getting the new, whizziest features into a computer."

Some, usually the engineers and programmers who had been allied with the Homebrew Club, moaned that Apple had deserted its aim of making computers for all people and supplying free software. They found that designing the fastest version of *Star Wars* was no longer enough to gain a badge of honor and muttered that if they had wanted to make business computers they would have joined IBM. Youngsters like Chris Espinosa thought that the marketing types with their button-down shirts, ties, and neatly pressed suits should have stayed as "extras in Cary Grant movies of the sixties." Another programmer complained, "We started getting ad guys who used to sell shoes and thought it would be a good career move to get into personal computers."

When work started on computer systems to replace the Apple II, the young programmers found they weren't invited to contribute their ideas and were excluded from debates about what they felt was the essence of the company. Disenfranchised, they were understandably hurt and offended. Without degrees or doctorates they became something of an underclass and were acutely aware of the change. Randy Wigginton, one of the more abrasive of the crew, said, "The other guys thought small computers weren't useful. They thought, 'The Apple II isn't a real computer. It's a joke.' Their attitude was: 'You guys really don't know how to do a company. We'll show you how to do it right.'" A few of the programmers took to calling one of their new supervisors a Software Nazi because he was steadfastly opposed to revealing details about the internal mechanisms of the machine. But the complaints weren't limited to the engineers. When more experienced financial managers, lawyers, public-relations specialists, and personnel staff began to arrive, even the mild-mannered accountant Gary Martin was moved to note, "We started getting people who were trying to make Apple sound and smell like IBM."

As the employee count lengthened, it became increasingly difficult for Apple to tolerate quirks and idiosyncracies, although some of the demands were extravagant. (One employee, for example, was gravely upset when Apple failed to fulfill a promise to install his eighteen-foot-high, twenty-six-ring pipe organ in one of the office buildings.) In executive staff meetings Rod Holt came to be viewed by some as a disruptive influence while Steve Wozniak became the most notable casualty of growth. After he completed the controller for the disk drive, Wozniak worked on the design of a lower-cost Apple II but his heart wasn't in it. He didn't enjoy the tugs of management, the meetings, committees, memos, and long discussions. "I was lucky to have two hours a day to myself."

He still indulged in pranks and, at one time or another, covered other people's clothes in a soluble green slime, filled sodas with a fizzing compound, and pinned tablets of Alka Seltzer to the menus at a nearby Bob's Big Boy—accompanied by the message

"For your convenience." When mice started to invade the engineering laboratory he showed his colleagues how the creatures would always scamper into paper bags because they mistook the dark opening for the safety of a hole.

However, Wozniak's rebellious side began to emerge and he became a manager's nightmare. His position in the company and all the kudos and status that gradually came to be associated with the Apple II converted him into one of the corporate untouchables. Instead of pursuing an assignment he would find a more interesting diversion like computing *e* to one hundred thousand places. (He calculated that it would take three days to compute and four months to print.) For some weeks he tried to copy diskettes with an electric hand iron, hoping that the heat would cause the magnetic patterns to shift from one diskette to another. He also began to take long weekends to go gambling at casinos in Reno. Dick Huston, a programmer who had watched Wozniak cope with the disk drive, formed his own conclusion. "Woz lost the challenge. People stopped telling him that what he was doing was bullshit. He acquired the status of being a wizard and after a while he believed it. He knew better in his heart but he loved the role. So when someone got on his case he'd get temperamental." Randy Wigginton looked at his friend and thought, "He didn't have the same amount of individual importance. He preferred being the Messiah."

The newcomers brought their own strands and strains. During the first couple of years Apple recruited heavily from Hewlett-Packard, National Semiconductor, and Intel, and the habits and differences in style among these companies were reflected in Cupertino. There was a general friction between the rough and tough ways of the semiconductor men (there were few women) and the people who had made computers, calculators, and instruments at Hewlett-Packard. Part of this was simply due to the different nature of the business. The primary drive of the semiconductor men was to manufacture high volume at low cost. Hewlett-Packard, on the other hand, had not been in a high-volume business until its calculators became popular and even then had steadfastly refrained from chopping prices to gain market share. The recruits from National Semiconductor were more inclined toward sales and opportunism and came from a company that made a religion out of its disdain for luxury and comfort. The Hewlett-Packard crowd tended to favor planning and believed in serving the customer and in some of the statelier aspects of corporate life.

Some of the Hewlett-Packard men began to see themselves as civilizing influences and were horrified by the uncouth rough-and-tumble practices of the brutes from the semiconductor industry. They came to believe that semiconductor men were hopeless male chauvinists—an impression that wasn't dispelled when Markkula warmed up a managers' meeting with the rhetorical question "Why did God invent women? Because he couldn't teach sheep to cook." The knights from Hewlett-Packard muttered that Apple's directors were opposed to contributions to charities like the United Way, that the company had no commitment to affirmative action, underpaid its secretaries, and was, at least during the first two or three years, a difficult place for women to gain promotion. So it was no wonder that cartoons of Mollard, the one-time National Semiconductor manufacturing man, appeared with him outfitted in Gestapo regalia and armed with a swagger stick.

Those who were either from, or shared the sympathies of the people from, Hewlett-Packard were surprised at stories that some National managers bounced expense reports. One of the daintier managers looked at the pressures to ship that built up toward the end of every quarter as an effort was made to meet planned targets, have a "big push," and "make the number," and felt that the National managers kept their own code. "There was a real sense that they were going to ship this shit one way or another and they were going to get the dealers to fix it. They more or less said, 'We're going to ship this sucker, to hell with the customer.'" Another summed up the approach his National colleagues took toward suppliers and others who stood in the way, and talked of them as if they were hoods. "Their style ran like this, 'We'd like to kill those sonuvabitches legally if we can. But if we cannot we'll still have to kill 'em.'"

Many of the men from National Semiconductor and other stern backgrounds harbored a similar contempt for the Hewlett-Packard recruits. They came to look on them as prissy fusspots. They didn't question their professionalism; they just seemed to feel that they were too professional. Rod Holt felt, "The Hewlett-Packard types . . . spend more time writing down what they are supposed to do and what their subordinates are supposed to do than they do doing anything." Someone else characterized a colleague as "another one of those country-club H.P. types," and Michael Scott complained, "They're not penny pinchers. They gloss over things."

Though the differences were most pronounced between the men from Hewlett-Packard and National, others also brought the practices they had become accustomed to. When Ann Bowers, who had spent some years working at Intel and was the wife of one of its founders, was placed in charge of Apple's personnel matters, Sherry Livingston observed, "Everything had to be done the Intel way. She wouldn't go to the left or the right." Since Apple tapped companies like Hewlett-Packard, National, and Intel for particular strengths, and since some of the trailblazers were instrumental in luring others from their old stomping grounds, it was common for them to wind up working in small enclaves. This, combined with the ferocious pressure and the friction between young and old, tended to exaggerate the normal sorts of conflicts that spring up between departments of any company.

The engineers, for example, felt the manufacturing men were concerned only with eliminating bumps and swings to keep the line running smoothly and to meet production schedules. "The manufacturing people," Rod Holt insisted, "by and large have taken Apple for a ride." The feeling was mutual and certainly was not improved when the production people raided the engineering files and removed all the carefully plotted test procedures and descriptions of final assemblies. The production men tended to think that the engineers were treated too daintily and should have been disciplined with rigorous schedules and milestones. They cursed the aesthetes who wouldn't make compromises over things that would have made their life far easier—like the color of cases.

There was also, during the early days, considerable tension between the manufacturing department and the men who monitored the flow of materials and supplies. Mollard recalled that the enmity ran so deep "there were people almost coming to blows in the parking lot." The butt of the company, the publications department, couldn't complete manuals until engineers and programmers had stopped tinkering with a device or piece of software and was also battered by pressure from the marketing side who wanted to ship products quickly. For a time, while Apple was still very young, the technical writers developed their own little world. They arranged noon-time madrigal sessions, installed beanbag chairs in their offices, erected walls of cardboard boxes, and armed themselves with Ping-Pong-ball guns to fend off intruders.

By September 1980, three and a half years after the introduction of the Apple II, 130,000 had been sold. Revenues had risen from $7.8 million for the fiscal year that ended on September 30, 1978, to $117.9 million, and profits had risen from $793,497 to $11.7 million. And that fall, thirty-one months after the thirtieth employee had joined the company, and just twelve months after the three-hundredth employee arrived, Apple's payroll topped one thousand. The company occupied fifteen buildings in Silicon Valley, eleven of which were in Cupertino. There was some manufacturing in Cupertino and San Jose but large-scale manufacturing was conducted at a factory in Texas. Warehouses had been opened in different parts of the United States and in the Netherlands. Overseas there was a plant in Ireland (which was opened by an unemployed plumber, the mayor of Cork) and another was about to open in Singapore. The pyramidal structure was bulging and so Apple moved one step closer to convention and formed divisions.

There was nothing very surprising about the decision. It was one of those penalties of size that emphasized how fast the company had grown. The change in structure also reflected tacit admission that Michael Scott's hopes of keeping the company small had been scuttled. His dream of limiting Apple to between fifteen hundred and two thousand employees, and of running an enterprise that made only its latest product (while subcontracting everything else), disappeared. Divisions were formed for all the usual reasons: attempts to keep affairs manageable, to pinpoint profit and loss areas, and to delegate authority.

Before the divisions were announced some of Apple's managers went on inspection tours and tried to do their homework. They asked senior members of Hewlett-Packard and Digital Equipment Corporation how decisions were made in their companies and then returned to Cupertino to draw up battle plans. One division was formed as an experiment. Its charter was to take care of disk drives. In the fall of 1980 five others were added: the Personal Computer Systems Division to look after the Apple II and Apple III, the Personal Office Systems Division to design and nurse the Lisa system, Manufacturing, Sales, and Service.

There wasn't, of course, any particular time when the formation of divisions would have been comfortable. At Apple the formation of divisions occurred when there were plenty of other pressing distractions. The decision was made about the same time the directors decided that the company should make its first public stock offering and also during the weeks when a successor to the Apple II was being introduced.

Though most of Apple's top managers had worked within a divisional structure, none had managed a company that had divisions. There were scarcely enough middle managers to go around and nowhere near enough people to fill all the empty cubicles. The computer systems weren't installed and procedures weren't drawn out. It was hard to escape the impression that the creation of divisions was scarcely a masterstroke of planning.

The grand change and dislocation helped push into the background some of the conflicts that had resulted from mismatched corporate blood types. A growing fund of common experience tended to do the same thing. The divisions presented an entirely new set of tensions. Their physical separation led to a technical isolation. They created fresh allegiances and new lines of reporting. As the divisions started to flex their muscles Apple came to be divided by the pull of fashion and the movable squabbles of fiefdoms. The divisions were allowed, for example, to hire their own technical writers and order their own printed circuit boards, and on occasion, they tried to exercise control over what others were doing. The Peripherals Division, to cite just one case, wanted to set the standard for what should be plugged into peripherals. It didn't take a translation expert to understand that this amounted to an attempt to dictate corporate product planning.

More important the people working within the different divisions became aware of distinctions. The glamour of the hot divisions, where work proceeded on new computers, cast a pall across areas where the primary task was to support existing machines. The nature of the work appealed to different emotional and intellectual interests and attracted different sorts of people. Many of the engineers and programmers who had been caught up in the success of the Apple II preferred to work in the Personal Computer Systems Division (PCS). Others, who wanted a brighter future, respectability, and the opportunity to work with newer technologies, knocked on the door of the Personal Office Systems Division (POS), which was formed from a core of people developing the Lisa system.

The subtleties were subjected to microscopic inspection. Rick Auricchio was a programmer who worked in PCS. "We felt that the Lisa Division was full of prima donnas. They wanted a thirty-thousand-dollar laser printer and they got it. They went out and hired high-powered people. We didn't. Their working cubicles were bigger. They had more plants. Even though we were paying all the bills and pumping cash across the street, we were dull and boring and not doing anything. There was a perception that they would be nine feet tall, scowl at you, and turn up their noses. Without the right color badge and an escort, you couldn't get into the Lisa building. That was an insult. People started thinking that they didn't want to be cretins for the rest of their lives so they left PCS and joined POS." The people who worked in the Lisa Division returned the compliment. One said, "We took a look at the Apple III and didn't take it very seriously. We just took a look and said, 'They don't know what they're doing.'"

As the divisions solidified, a corporate bureaucracy began to emerge. Again, there wasn't really any way to escape the stultifying drag of growth. Coping with several hundred people (let alone several thousand) requires some codes if only to free managers from having to explain exceptions all day long. Some of this was reflected in companywide memos. Occasional bulletins kept employees posted on budgets "which reflect efficiency and frugality" and registered alarm when the phone bill topped $100,000 a month. Others provided information on FICA taxes, profit-sharing plans, stock programs, official company holidays, a new Xerox reproduction center, and insurance schemes. Performance reviews (scheduled every six months) came complete with a "review information matrix."

A memo from the legal department asked people not to abbreviate the name of the company to Apple Computer or Apple and stated: "The legal name of the corporation is Apple Computer,

Inc. (note the comma) . . . . Please don't hamstring our efforts by casually misusing the corporate symbols." Other notices kept people abreast of schedules of shuttle buses that ran between the Apple buildings, urged them to use up stationery supplies, drop by a corporate engineering library, or sign up for television classrooms that were connected to the Stanford instructional television network. There were other announcements that sought to differentiate among some of interoffice memos and in-house publications. "'Apple Bulletin,'" readers were told, "communicates information that has time value . . . . It is distributed by the mail room and telecommunications people to all Apple locations."

Even some of Apple's staunchest boosters, like marketing manager Phil Roybal, were forced to admit, after several years, a difference in tone. "The character has changed because the company has grown. There is more overhead, policies have been created, administrators have been hired, and there are rigidities. There is less whimsy. Now things happen pretty much as expected. It's more like an organized company." Others were less complimentary. Publications manager Jef Raskin, who eventually had a falling out with Jobs, said, "At first the company was run by a consensus, where a good idea had a chance of success. Afterward it was like standing beside a freight train and tugging it with a chain. It wouldn't move off the tracks." Some, like Roy Mollard, found that divisions, additional layers of management, and increased specialization meant that his influence was circumscribed. "My area of control was narrowed and the job became less interesting."

For outsiders like Regis McKenna, who had played a crucial part in Apple's formative stages, the arrival of a vice-president of communications meant that responsibility for public relations and marketing strategy was split. "You have to go through people to get to the very people you used to deal with one on one. You deal with corporate organization that wants to control everything." And for the newcomers, the presence of men like McKenna with established ties to the founders did not make life any easier. The uneasy truce was made clear by the way in which Apple came to handle some of its public relations internally while the McKenna Agency dealt with the rest.

However, the emergence of a bureaucracy was not a dull blanket that brought equality. There was a distinct and pronounced pecking order that was camouflaged by appearances. The carefully cultivated suggestions of equality were, in many ways, a mirage. On the surface Apple didn't bear much resemblance to pinstriped America. There were no reserved spaces in the parking lots. Jeans, open collars, and sneakers were an accepted form of dress. (In fact, they almost came to be a uniform.) There were no lavish office suites, just cubicles and shoulder-high partitions. The offices became a maze of Herman Miller open landscape furniture. Punching clocks was unheard of even on the assembly lines. Secretaries were called area associates and the head of personnel was known as the director of human resources. Business cards carried offbeat titles. For outsiders these unconventional appearances were deceptive. Insiders saw straight through them. Programmer Dick Huston echoed the sentiments of many of his colleagues when he remarked, "I have never thought of Apple as an egalitarian place to work."

Many of the ways in which employees came to tell each other apart were entirely conventional and bore more similarities to traditional industries and the industrial crescent than Apple's leaders were prepared to admit. Except at its Irish factory, Apple was not a unionized company. Jobs had all the ruffled pride of a founder who felt that the arrival of a union would mean that he had failed to care for his employees, and he also thought that unions were responsible for problems in some older industries. He promised to "quit the day we become unionized." But even if walkouts and pickets weren't part of the Apple vocabulary, there was still an enormous difference between the shop floor and the executive offices.

Don Bruener, who spent some time working in production, said, "People in production were afraid to deal with any people outside production. And the people outside production didn't care about production. It was workers against executives." After a time most of the executives took offices in one building and the senior officials were known as members of the executive staff. Once Apple started holding public stockholder meetings the same executives shared the front-row seats with the company's directors. Apart from the younger faces in the audience, there wasn't that much difference between early Apple annual meetings and ones held by Chrysler or Bank of America.

A young company like Apple also developed other signals of rank. The greatest distinction was based on wealth. For the disparities that existed at Apple, especially after it became a public company, were far larger than those that separate the chairman from the janitor in mature companies like General Motors and Exxon. The company also made loans to senior executives to help them buy stock or pay large income-tax bills, and profit-sharing was allocated according to rank.

There was never any mistaking who was the boss. The appearance of Scott or Markkula or Jobs could provoke a tightening in the muscles of underlings. A casual comment, a hint, an upturned eyebrow, a skeptical glance, a rise in the voice were all amplified and produced what one keen observer delightfully called "thunderbolt management." He explained, "Everybody knows who calls the shots. Somebody says something in a hallway or makes a passing remark and suddenly twenty levels below, it becomes law."

One of the most important signs of status was the numbers given to employees on the day they joined the company—which had caused Jobs such concern at their first appearance. Printed on the plastic identification badges, these numbers became a corporate version of the big-city social register. As Apple grew, the status of the employees with the lowest numbers rose. Though the badges often didn't match financial standing, they still provoked admiring glances. Some of the earliest employees could rattle off the names of the first fifty or so of their colleagues and others took to advertising their positions by having their employee numbers stamped on their automobile license tags. Another way in which the old-timers emphasized their difference was the Cross pen decorated with a small Apple that had been distributed to every employee on Apple's third Christmas. Eventually the pens were made available in the company store.

The social order was also visible in companywide messages. One sonorously proclaimed the difference between a monthly newsletter and a shorter corporate memo: "Recently promoted people deserve applause and recognition . . . 'Apple Times' will list newly promoted employees . . . 'Apple Bulletin' should not be used to announce promotions and other personnel changes below the level of division manager."

There was also a debate about the value of the technical writers. Jobs had always placed great importance on Apple's manuals, and there was a feeling that they formed an important part of what the company was selling. Some argued that if this was so, the technical writers deserved to be on a pay scale similar to that of the top-flight engineers. Eventually, however, Apple buckled to the notion of "replacement value" and paid its writers on the levels that existed outside the computer industry. One publications manager was not allowed to become a principal member of technical staff, according to a formal complaint that he lodged, because "doing an industry-leading job in publications just did not have the stature of 'designing a power supply or software system.'"

So with all these strains and pronounced stripings it was a dizzying challenge for the old hands, let alone the newcomers, to sort out where they fitted, what tasks to pursue, and precisely what it was that the company stood for. As the divisions were formed in the fall of 1980 those sorts of questions became even more baffling. For in the space of twelve weeks Apple went on a hiring binge and boosted its payroll from six hundred employees to twelve hundred: a period that some came to refer to as The Bozo Explosion. Some employees were snapped up from temporary agencies and squads of as many as sixty were gathered for orientation seminars.

For everyone the growth was unsettling. The rate of change was revealed in odd ways and in little household items like the corporate telephone directories that were kept in looseleaf folders and updated every few weeks. Managers found their schedules were slipping and paperwork was multiplying though the latter was partly due to a proliferation of Apples which spat out charts and graphs and reams of numbers. Some of the focus of the first few years disappeared, and there was a general sense that the company was sliding out of control. Even Markkula, never the corporate disciplinarian, was forced to admit, "We had trouble keeping the car on the track."

Layers below there was far less insulation from the rush of the new. In an engineering laboratory Chuck Mauro was startled by the speed with which fresh faces appeared. "It made your head reel, hearing about four new guys who were going to start on Monday. It was all you could do to keep up. It was impossible to even remember all their names."

Apple went to considerable lengths to preserve some sense of continuity, instill a form of community, conceal differences, and give the impression of stability. A large part of the effort was directed toward providing pleasant working conditions, a goal that sprang largely from Jobs and, to a lesser extent, Markkula. Part of the impetus was purely practical, for other companies in the area had gained a reputation for looking after their employees and Apple's management generally recognized that one way of keeping people, in an industry where companies were sometimes crippled by a sudden exodus, was not to skimp on the trimmings. Part sprang from the long benevolent reputation of Hewlett-Packard. Part was based on the unshakable conviction that people work harder and more efficiently when they are treated well and given decent surroundings. But running through all of this was more than just a gratuitous streak of altruism. Like the founders of many companies, Apple's were determined to improve on the deficiencies they saw elsewhere.

The picnics, parties, and presents that broke up the work week were larger versions of affairs that had sprinkled every stage of Apple's development. After the company shipped its first $100,000 worth of computers, the entire fifteen-person work force had gathered for a pool party at Markkula's house. When the manufacturing department had been spruced up, the rest of Apple was invited to an open house at which children, spouses, and "spouse equivalents" were made welcome. Succeeding milestones had almost always been celebrated with a party, a cake, or a bottle of champagne.

As the months lengthened into years, the parties got grander—extending to marquees and bunting and jazz bands. There were outings to specially arranged sneak screenings of movies like *Star Wars* and *The Empire Strikes Back*. A Halloween party that had been held during the first few months (where Jobs arrived as Jesus Christ) developed into an annual ritual and more or less turned into an unofficial company holiday. The scale of the celebration grew so large that a couple of blocks in Cupertino had to be cordoned off while employees paraded about in fancy dress.

Entertainment and the provision of creature comforts were taken seriously. Employees could join bowling leagues and aerobic dance classes. They could take out memberships at local health clubs. There were corporate scuba-diving classes and ski weekends in the California Sierras. Offices were provided with what many large companies would have considered expensive furniture and consultants were hired to give advice on topics like "Building Traffic Patterns" and the optimum amount of desk space for programmers. Employees were always given some form of Christmas present. One year most had received a hundred-dollar bill wrapped around a pen, and later, after an important sales goal was achieved, everybody was given an extra week's paid vacation.

Apple also started a program that gave employees, once they had demonstrated a minimal efficiency, their own Apple computers. There were computer classes for family members, and a company store offered large discounts on purchases of Apple equipment to relatives and close friends of employees. More important the programmers, engineers, and technical writers could work as efficiently at home as in their offices.

Despite these efforts Apple's identity must have seemed clearer to customers than to employees. By 1980 the company was too large and too scattered for any one manager to cover in a daily stroll to take the air and test the waters. So for most employees the corporate hand was invisible. To combat the uncertainty and provide a corporate manifesto and a coherent ideology, Apple established a committee which, with steadfast earnestness, set about trying to make some sense out of diffuse motives. It tried to reduce the abstract to the concrete and to codify all the conflicting impulses and intentions, the clashes between individual enterprise and teamwork, between autocracy and democracy, that make up a company. It was little wonder that the result, though full of good intentions, sounded banal, self-conscious, and hackneyed.

The general message of the committee was reflected in companywide memos that included lines like "Apple is more than just a company . . . it is an attitude, a process, a point of view and a way of doing things." But the committee's will and testament was embodied in a statement of corporate values that was heavily influenced by precepts Hewlett-Packard had distributed as a guide to its own employees. Apple's group fastened on nine commandments and made the general observation: "Apple values are the qualities, customers, standards and principles that the company as a whole regards as desirable. They are the basis for what we do and how we do it. Taken together, they identify Apple as a unique company."

As for particulars, the committee fastened on:

Empathy for customers/users (We offer superior products that fill real needs and provide lasting value. We deal fairly with competitors, and meet customers and vendors more than halfway . . .)

Achievement/Aggressiveness (We set aggressive goals and drive ourselves hard to achieve them. We recognize that this is a unique time, when our products will change the way people work and live. It's an adventure, and we're on it together.)

Positive Social Contribution (As a corporate citizen, we wish to be an economic, intellectual and social asset in communities where we operate . . . .)

Innovation/Vision (We accept the risks inherent in following our vision, and work to develop leadership products which command the profit margins we strive for . . . .)

Individual Performance (We expect individual commitment and performance above the standard for our industry. . . . Each employee can and must make a difference; for in the final analysis, individuals determine the character and strength of Apple.)

Team Spirit (Teamwork is essential to Apple's success for the job is too big to be done by any one person . . . . It takes all of us to win. We support each other, and share the victories and rewards together . . . .)

Quality/Excellence (We build into Apple products a level of quality, performance, and value that will earn the respect and loyalty of our customers.)

Individual Reward (We recognize each person's contribution to Apple's success, and we share the financial rewards that flow from high performance. We recognize also that rewards must be psychological as well as financial and strive for an atmosphere where each individual can share the adventure and excitement of working at Apple.)

Good Management (The attitudes of managers toward their people are of primary importance. Employees should be able to trust the motives and integrity of their supervisors. It is the responsibility of management to create a productive environment where Apple values flourish.)

Apart from issuing statements dripping with goodwill, the committee also nudged the company toward specific actions. Apple started holding weekly lunches where employees could meet senior managers and vice-presidents. And Markkula made a determined effort to let people know that they could come to him and air their grievances. He more than anyone listened to people far down in the company argue against managerial decisions. Other doors stayed closed. Jobs and Scott, some of their colleagues said in the unholy jargon of Silicon Valley, were not "people persons."

Trying to instill a system of values in a company where the spirit of the founders ran so strong was difficult if not impossible. Even if Apple was too large for the founders to be seen in every nook and cranny, it was small enough for rumor of their behavior, word of their performance, and their general reputation to have a profound effect on the corporate tone. They were mobile bill-boards. And when their deeds or their words failed to match the beatific standards preached by the culture committee, the entire effort was stymied.

Culture was not to be confused with democracy, and though certainly no one at the company said as much, Apple Values contained more than a hint of corporate totalitarianism. One of the most vigorous proponents of Apple Culture, Trip Hawkins, a Stanford Business School graduate in his late twenties, chose to explain the importance of corporate culture in military terms. "If you have a strong culture you don't have to supervise people so closely and you don't have to have so many rules, regulations, and procedures because everybody thinks the same way and they all react to situations in the same way. It helps you delegate more effectively. For example, you can put a bunch of marines on the beach under fire and they'll actually run up the beach. Companies that don't have strong cultures cannot do anything quickly."

Jobs certainly found the theory of a corporate culture alluring but he was more taken by actions that offered immediate, tangible results. He certainly wanted to make Apple a pleasant place to work. He would enthusiastically describe his plan for an updated version of a company town, which he called "Supersite," where offices and houses would intermingle. He hoped that it would help Apple hire young engineers who wouldn't be able to afford California housing prices, allow them to get their feet on the ground, and become familiar with the area. In dreamy moments he would paint a bucolic picture of a corporate park where meetings would be held, and programs written, in the shade of large trees.

Jobs had originally favored flexible hours that allowed engineers and programmers freedom to work at home or at the office. But when this failed to achieve the necessary results, he fired off a memo to a group he was heading that stated: "When I agreed to totally flexible hours it was with the stated assumption that it was the most efficient way to get a very professional quality of work done. This group has not demonstrated that quality in the last 60 days. . . . Effective tomorrow, everyone . . . is required to be in by 10:00 A.M. No exceptions."

Some who worked for Jobs found him difficult to tolerate. Publications manager Jef Raskin, who worked at Apple until April 1981, said, "He's extraordinarily seductive. He would have made an excellent king of France." In a four-page memo sent to Michael Scott and titled "Working for/with Steve Jobs," Raskin suggested that Jobs "get management training before being allowed to manage other projects." Raskin complained: "While Mr. Jobs's stated positions on management techniques are all quite noble and worthy, in practice he is a dreadful manager. It is an unfortunate case of mouthing the right ideas but not believing in or executing them when it comes time to do something." Raskin continued: "Jobs regularly misses appointments . . . . He does not give credit where due. . . . Jobs also has favorites, who can do no wrong— and others who can do no right . . . . He interrupts and doesn't listen. . . . He doesn't keep promises . . . . He is a prime example of a manager who takes the credit for his optimistic schedules and then blames the workers when deadlines are not met."

Apple Culture and the blanket of corporate goodwill could not conceal different levels of competence. A few weeks after the distraction of the public stock issue, problems arose with the Apple III. A general irritation with the company's performance bubbled to the surface and resulted in Apple's first widespread dismissals.

During the company's first few years, Apple's founders had been proud that they were able to avoid savage firings though they had certainly asked a number of employees to leave. The dismissals were usually cloaked beneath milky phrases like "leave of absence" or "vacation" but the artful guise didn't conceal reality.

Some considered that Apple was far too willing to forgive incompetence and a few, like Rod Holt, would complain, "If you get an engineer who engineers everything wrong and doesn't work and is screwed up one way or another, then you make a manager out of him. They won't fire people around here."

When Michael Scott, with the approval of Jobs and Markkula, decided to fire forty-one people three months after Apple went public, the ripples were immense. The firings were an expression of immense frustration and also a cost-cutting move. Above all, they were a public admission that there was a distinction between the competent and the incompetent, and that Apple had managed to hire laggards. It also brought a pronounced change in tone and some months of nervous fright. "All of a sudden," said Fred Hoar, vice-president of communications, "Apple values were tanked and in its place we had ruthlessness."

In the weeks leading up to the dank, rainy day that around the company quickly became known as Black Wednesday, Scott asked each department to provide him with a list of the people that were no longer wanted. He passed the list of eighty names around to see whether some should be retained. A few people were switched between divisions and the rest were summoned to Scott's office, given one month's pay, and fired. One group singled out for dismissal was the department that reviewed new products. Scott felt they caused too many delays. But there was a lot of confusion about many of the others. Some of the people summoned to Scott's office had slipped between the cracks because they had no immediate supervisor, and they were rehired. Others, just a few weeks earlier, had been given good performance reviews and bonuses.

The afternoon of the dismissals Scott held a company meeting in the basement of one of the buildings. Amid the beer and pretzels he made an awkward little speech, fielded some questions, tried to give a pep talk, but his tone only made matters worse. The effects of the firings went far beyond the deed. Chris Espinosa buttonholed Jobs and told him that it was no way to run a company. A glum Jobs asked, "How do you run a company?" Rick Auricchio, who thought he had been fired and later discovered he was still employed, felt that "it was like Walt Disney taking a walk around Disneyland and chopping off Mickey Mouse's head." Phil Roybal recalled, "A lot of people always assumed that sort of thing couldn't happen at Apple. This was the first sign of grim reality. People didn't know what the world was coming to. Their values had been turned upside down. Suddenly we were a company just like any other." Bruce Tognazzini thought Black Wednesday was like a divorce. "It was the end of a lot of things. It was the end of innocence. It was the end of loyalty. It ushered in an era of incredible fear."

In the weeks following Black Wednesday an anonymous memo, which many considered too savage, popped up on various notice boards: "We are forming the Computer Professionals Union (CPU) so that we can keep Apple's management in line. The thing they fear most is concerted employee action; the tactics they use are divide and conquer, and threats of economic reprisal. They can't get away with it if we unite! Apple was once a good place to work; management preaches to us about the 'Apple Spirit'; let's show them what a little bit of real spirit is like and ram it down their throats!"

For Scott, Black Wednesday brought disaster. He had gained a reputation for a ruthlessness that was almost physical. But behind his bullying demeanor was a kind, thoughtful, romantic streak that was hidden by a bruising shyness. He was a cross between Santa Claus and Spectre. Some of the old-timers at Apple thought that nobody cared more for them than Scott. He had a sense of the extravagant and tended to throw a party at the slightest excuse. On a couple of occasions he had rented a movie theater and mailed elegant cards to his friends and Apple employees inviting them to see a special preview of George Lucas space movies. At the theater, as his guests turned up, Scott stood by the entrance door handing out white roses. At an Apple Christmas party Scott chose a nautical theme and, to match the spirit of the affair, donned a tight-fitting white captain's uniform complete with peaked hat. On another occasion he dispatched a memo that summoned to the boardroom a couple of dozen people who had been working at a trade show and had missed a movie outing. Most, fearing the worst, arrived at the meeting in trepidation and found that Scott had something else in store. He ushered them to a bus which took them to a movie theater as waiters in red jackets doled out hors d'oeuvres and champagne.

But Scott's darker side and a macabre humor were more apparent. When a Digital Equipment Corporation computer, which was supposed to form the cornerstone of Apple's management-information system, failed to arrive on time, he dispatched a funeral wreath to the president of what was a far larger company with a card reading "Here's what I think of your delivery commitments." He had little patience with lengthy discussions in executive staff meetings about whether Apple should offer employees decaffeinated coffee as well as a regular blend. He was annoyed that salesmen drove full-size rather than compact cars and irritated that executives were allowed to fly first-class. To send a message to underlings and to show who was boss, Scott also delayed signing checks that urgently needed his signature. Landscaping wasn't high on his list of priorities nor were discussions about how many square feet each office should have. He wanted to impose his own brand of management and even asked all the vice-presidents to abandon their titles. His memos had an abrupt style. When he wanted to prove that the day of the computer had arrived, he issued a terse memo banning all typewriters. It was headed in capital letters: YOU ALL BETTER READ THIS. He posted another memo containing the orders: "No talking in aisleways. No talking standing up."

In the weeks that led up to Black Wednesday, Scott was working harder than ever. He was also troubled by a serious eye infection that his doctors feared might blind him, and his secretary, Sherry Livingston, was forced to read his mail aloud. After asking Apple's executive vice-president of engineering to resign, Scott had taken over responsibility for engineering and was also trying to keep his arms around the rest of the company. He began to mutter ominous threats, talked about "having more fun around here," and started saying, "I'm not going to put up with things I don't like." He strode around the company peering over the tops of cubicles and asking, "Are you working your ass off?" He ordered managers not to hire anybody else for the rest of the year and managed to terrify and intimidate most people he came in contact with. Jean Richardson recalled, "He was such a cold force. He'd sort of rampage through the halls and not speak to anyone." And another employee said, "You felt that he'd come down the aisle any minute and pick a fight."

Some of the executive staff, alarmed by Scott's behavior, by his peremptory dismissal of the second-most-important operating manager in the company, and by his ill-timed remark that the

Black Wednesday firings were "just the first round," started a whispering campaign. Ann Bowers, head of the human resources department, muttered her contempt for Scott. To people he humiliated in meetings, she dispatched mock awards from the executive staff headed "For valor and courage in the face of fire." Even one of his court of admirers said Scott enjoyed displaying force "in the way a gorilla enjoys raw, unabated power." Markkula quietly fielded the petitions of complaints that were spearheaded by Bowers and John Couch, both of whom had developed a reputation among some of their colleagues for being keen corporate politicians. Someone else who complained directly to Markkula about the difficulties of working for Scott was told, "Don't worry about it. You're going to have a great career here. I'm going to fix it."

For Markkula, Scott's frazzled edge was awkward. As the four years he had promised to devote to Apple drew to a close, Markkula was creeping toward hibernation. For the previous year he had been working in a staff position, taking longer holidays, and spending more time with his family. He did a lot of skiing, enjoyed flying in his new plane to places like Sun Valley, and, in his spare time, doodled with designs for vacation homes. He was preparing for a luxurious retirement. Apple had even gone so far as to pay a headhunting firm $60,000 to search for a replacement. When matters at Apple started to unravel at the beginning of 1980, Scott had asked Markkula to run half the company. Markkula had refused, but Scott's behavior now left Markkula with no alternative. Jobs wasn't old enough or experienced enough to run the company, there was no obvious outside candidate who could quickly step into the breach, and nobody else knew Apple as well as Markkula. So Markkula reluctantly accepted the fact that he would have to head an interregnum until somebody suitable to run Apple could be found.

Scott had no inkling of the whispering conspiracy. As matters came to a head, he took a long weekend in Hawaii, where he found relief from troubling sinusitis, entirely unaware of developments in Cupertino where Markkula had convened a meeting of Apple's executive staff. It was an odd meeting and some of the senior managers, including Scott's staunchest allies, were not invited. Markkula took a voice vote, working around the table from Scott's bitterest opponents to his supporters. When Scott returned from Hawaii he found a message on his telephone answering machine, asking whether Markkula could drop by and talk. That conversation ended abruptly after Markkula announced, "Scotty, the executive staff has voted to ask for your resignation." As Markkula made his way to the front door, he asked Scott to submit his resignation in writing the following morning.

None of the shrewder hands questioned Scott's contribution. He had within forty-eight months helped transform a garage operation, full of complicated headstrong individuals, into a publicly held, divisionalized, multinational corporation that was running at an annualized sales rate of $300 million. Some at Apple thought he was the victim of a raw deal and a bloody conspiracy. Wendell Sander, the hardware engineer, thought "he couldn't have done as well with hindsight as he did with foresight." The venture capitalist Don Valentine regarded Scott's management as the most successful of any of the seventy or so companies he had invested in.

For his part Markkula explained that Scott's dismissal was "a matter of management style. Scotty's management style is very dictatorial and was really good for the company in its early development and I had hoped he would modify his style with the growth of the company." When Scott departed he took with him the thread of discipline that had run through the company, what amounted to an eagerness to make tough decisions, and a rough relish for strapping Jobs into a corporate straitjacket.

A shallow glee spread among the whisperers at Apple—who never came close to understanding the scale of Scott's achievement. The scope of the change was concealed from outsiders by a vacuous memo that talked about a reshuffle. Markkula assumed Scott's duties as president while Jobs took Markkula's place as chairman. Scott was left with Jobs's vacated title of vice-chairman. "What we have decided to do," the memo announced, "is to rotate the responsibilities of those at the top of the organization, to capitalize in a fresh way on the capabilities and energies of each." The memo was so bland and the change so discreet that the venture capitalist and director Arthur Rock even complimented the vice-president of communications on the way matters were handled. After Scott was asked to resign, Jobs and some others tried to make amends by asking him whether he would mastermind Apple's change to a larger management-information system, and for a few weeks the cosmetic changes remained. Scott even made a presentation on the proposals for a new computer system, but he finally buckled and dispatched a final angry letter that announced his displeasure with "hypocrisy, yes-men, foolhardy plans, a 'cover your ass' attitude and empire builders."

But for Scott the parting was devastating. In his darkest moments, he contemplated trying to assert that his authority had been wrongfully usurped and dreamed about returning to Apple and firing every vice-president. Rod Holt recognized the degree of Scott's attachment to Apple. "Scotty had his whole life associated with Apple Computer. He didn't have anywhere else to go. Scotty was always working. It didn't leave him any margin for emotional distress, a drinking bout, or a hangover."

Even though he owned the fifth largest chunk of the company, Scott stayed at his ranch house a few minutes' drive from Apple, with the shades drawn. For a time he didn't answer his telephone. When people called he said he felt fine though he didn't bother to reply to some of the notes of sympathy that arrived. For months afterward when talk turned to Apple Scott's face looked glum and he became morose and listless. About the only time his spirits perked up was when he showed that he could still remember all the parts numbers of the Apple II. But mostly Scott slept late, fed his cats, sprawled on an enormous couch, and watched television on a screen that dropped down from the ceiling of his living room. He played the organ, listened to Wagner, fielded telephone calls from his stockbroker, and made occasional trips to a nearby garbage dump to launch model plastic rockets into the sky. "Apple," he kept saying at the time, "was my baby."

Among the people who knew Scott well, there was a mixture of embarrassment, distress, shame, and fury. Markkula took a few people aside and confided that firing Scott was the hardest thing he had done in his life but that Apple couldn't weather his personal problems.

Jobs probably understood better than anybody else the extent of Scott's humiliation. For months Jobs nursed a bleak, private, guilty fear, "I was always afraid that I'd get a call to say that Scotty had committed suicide."

THE PLATINUM CREDIT
CARD

Wealth complicates life. At Apple riches arrived more quickly, with a greater force, and in larger quantities than anybody had contemplated. The sums involved were so disconcerting and extraordinary that they meant nothing when measured against hamburgers, sodas, walkie-talkie radios, and the other everyday yardsticks of El Camino Real. One obvious comparison was with great American fortunes but the term itself had become frowzy. In the last quarter of the twentieth century Apple's founders and a few top managers became, in the malleable lingo of Silicon Valley, "zillionaires"—a perverse comment on inflation as much as language—and their portfolios assumed a distinctly Arabian flavor. They became young tycoons armed with a brute wealth that, at least on paper, was a match for most that had been made in the preceding one hundred years. Theirs were true fortunes which, on the occasions when the stock market treated Apple with reverence, came to dwarf the visible assets of the Prince of Wales, shade the tangible riches of the Catholic Church and make most of the captains of American industry look like paupers.

At the beginning of 1977, when Jobs, Wozniak, and Markkula had tried to place a value on the parts in the garage and the design of the Apple II, they valued the rump of the partnership at $5,309. A year later when the three venture-capital firms acquired some stock Apple was valued at $3 million. On New Year's Eve, 1980, almost three weeks after its shares were first publicly traded, the stock market gave Apple a value of $1,788 billion which was more than Chase Manhattan Bank, Ford Motor Company, and Merrill Lynch Pierce Fenner and Smith, over four times as much as Lockheed, and about twice as much as the combined market value of United Airlines, American Airlines, and Pan American World Airways.

During the first eighteen months of Apple's existence, monetary issues were obscured, thanks to a combination of circumstance and design. The sheer pressure of work provided enough distractions to fill a day while the financial maneuvers of a small private company offered far less opportunity for prying eyes than the visible transactions of a public company. Under California law all private stock transactions were subject to Apple's seal of approval—a procedure that ensured some discretion. Newly hired hands talked with Scott and Markkula about the possibility of buying stock but the details usually remained confidential. Markkula, in particular, kept a firm grip on the stock, politely telling the occasional outsider who inquired about the possibility of making an investment that the shares were for employees.

But gradually word of private sales, whispers of an engineer who had taken a second mortgage to buy more shares, rumors of stock splits, talk of changes in capital-gains tax rates, and discussions of the advantages of trusts crept into daily conversations at Apple until they became one of the staples of life. Rick Auricchio, a programmer who eventually left the company, said: "I learned as much about stock and taxes at Apple as I did about computers." Money was an uncomfortable topic that tripped a wide range of emotion.

Distribution of stock, or options to buy stock, became an intractable dilemma that led, in the eyes of Rod Holt, "to a reasonable amount of perfectly justified hostility." During the first couple of years the distribution of the discreet gray envelopes that contained stock options were accompanied by all sorts of warnings that the contents shouldn't be treated too seriously.

In the early days a few of the recepients were disappointed when they were given a couple of hundred options rather than a pay raise. But the cold force of arithmetic eventually removed any disappointment. For after three hefty stock splits, every share distributed before April 1979 was equivalent to 32 shares on the day that Apple went public, which meant that anybody who owned 1,420 of what were known as "founders' shares" and kept them until the morning of December 12, 1980, was then worth, on paper, $1 million.

Options to buy stock were assigned to most of the weightier newcomers on the basis of their past accomplishments and the possibility of what they might do for Apple. Some of the cannier recruits turned their job interviews into bargaining sessions and waited to shake hands until the promise of options had reached what they felt was an appropriate level. Others, more innocent in the ways of the corporate world, took a salary and a cubicle. For Apple the pool of options was a powerful recruitment tool and the options that were distributed from time to time were enormous incentives. Scott took particular delight in dangling the prospect of riches in front of people who weren't convinced that Apple was a worthwhile proposition. He was hard pressed to squelch his chuckles when he informed waverers, "We are making a massive change in people's life-styles."

When word of some of the arrangements seeped out, bitterness mounted. Fate and chance imbalance certainly played a part. Those hired within a few days of each other, but on opposite sides of a stock split, wound up with substantially different sums. However, some of the differences resulted from careful calculation. While Apple's salaried employees were given options to buy stock, the hourly employees were not. This, predictably enough, caused friction. In the laboratories, for example, engineers received stock while the technicians who worked at their elbows didn't. Some became convinced that they were the victims of injustice and even those who prospered, like Bruce Tognazzini, were aware of inequities. "The amount of stock that people were given had nothing to do with their ability to work. It had everything to do with their ability to get stock." Rod Holt was, at times, hard pressed to conceal his anger. "The fact that a turkey who is worth a million and a half doesn't deserve to have an office in the building is a quirk of fate."

Daniel Kottke remained a technician and wasn't given any shares before the company went public. Holt offered to make some amends by giving Kottke some of his own shares and proposed to Jobs, "How about we each chip in? You give him some stock and I'll match it." Jobs replied, "Great! I'll give him zero." Jobs, always more emotionally attached to Apple than Kottke, was torn. Part of him mourned the loss of a friendship but he also deeply resented Kottke's lack of visible appreciation. "Daniel generally tends to overrate his contributions. He just did a lot of work that we could have hired anybody to do and he learned an awful lot."

Bill Fernandez, the first person hired by Apple, was also disappointed, and though he later rejoined Apple, he quit in 1978. "I felt I was doing all the donkeywork and that I was going to be a technician forever. It didn't seem that I would get stock. I didn't think the company was loyal to me." Elmer Baum, who had lent Jobs and Wozniak some money while they were making the Apple Is, was informed that the company couldn't sell him stock. Chris Espinosa, by then a student at the University of California at Berkeley, also came up empty-handed. "We missed out on the American dream because we were too nice to grab a part of it. Kottke was too nice. Fernandez was too Buddhist and I was too young. Don Bruener was screwed twice. He was in manufacturing and also a college student. We all realized to some degree that we weren't heavy enough. We weren't obnoxious enough to make ourselves millionaires."

The size of stock distributions was distorted by gossip and scuttlebutt. A few bragged about the size of their holdings while others were embarrassed and tried to exercise their options discreetly. When freshly recruited middle managers discovered their subordinates were far wealthier, the jealousy wasn't easily concealed. Similarly Sherry Livingston found that other secretaries, who were paid by the hour, made her life increasingly uncomfortable after they discovered she owned some shares. One clerk who handled the paperwork for the stock options became so distraught at the size of the sums involved that she left the company.

Though Markkula fended off people who made it their business to speculate in private companies, it was certainly far easier for well-connected outsiders to obtain shares than it was for diligent workers. Knowing the right people, lunching with the proper crowd, placing the appropriate telephone calls, all paid off. The occasional privately arranged stock sale reflected the importance of personal contacts and the claustrophobic sense of community. The venture-capital firms that managed to get their hands on stock had usually done business together, were used to tipping each other off about hot deals, and were at pains to repay past favors.

The few individuals who acquired Apple stock before the company went public also had the proper pals. At the beginning of 1979, for example, Wozniak sold some stock to the Egyptian-born financier Fayez Sarofim, who had been a friend of Arthur Rock's since the early fifties when both had attended the Harvard Business School. Sarofim managed a portfolio worth well over $1 billion from an unmarked Houston office suite that was draped in modern art. Wozniak also sold stock to Richard Kramlich, a partner in Rock's venture-capital firm, and to Ann Bowers, the wife of the vice-chairman of Intel who became head of Apple's human resources department.

In the summer of 1979, when Apple raised $7,273,801 in what the venture capital community colloquially calls a mezzanine financing, connections once again paid off. Among the sixteen buyers who bought shares at $10.50 apiece were some of the best-known venture-capital firms in the country, including New York's LF Rothschild, Unterberg, Towbin, and the Brentwood Capital Corporation which was based in Southern California. One name on the list stood out: Xerox Corporation bought 100,000 shares though the company agreed not to buy more than 5 percent of Apple. The deal helped Apple gain access to Xerox's research laboratories though Scott recalled, "We were careful they didn't get a peek at our advance products," and, on later occasions, the Xerox representative was not invited to meetings where sensitive topics were discussed. Yet the biggest buyer was Arthur Rock's friend Fayez Sarofim, who bought 128,600 shares. Both Markkula and Jobs sold slightly over $1 million worth of stock.

During the following twelve months Arthur Rock kept a close eye on the vagaries of the new issues market and it was he, above all others, whose opinion and advice determined when Apple should brave the perils of a public stock offering.

Though most had recognized that Apple would eventually go public, the decision to abandon the relative tranquillity afforded private companies was made suddenly and unexpectedly. Among Apple's top managers, there was some reluctance to head a public company. Jobs, for a time, was enchanted with the notion of emulating the enormous, privately held San Francisco construction company Bechtel. He liked the idea of not releasing information that might help competitors, of running a multinational company without having to endure pressure from stockholders, and of avoiding taunts from the gadflies who make a pastime of appearing at annual meetings. Along with his colleagues, Jobs was aware of the distractions created by due-diligence procedures, the legal work involved in preparing the stock prospectus, and the drain of lengthy tours to explain the strengths of the company to bankers and investors in major American and European cities.

Michael Scott wanted Apple to grow into a large enterprise without help from outsiders and roundly cursed his betes noires: lawyers who hampered his freedom to maneuver, federal bureaucrats who would swamp him with documents, and journalists who would do nothing but turn his thoughts to pap.

Aside from personal preferences, there were compelling reasons for Apple to go public. The market for new stock issues, which had been torpid in the years following the 1973–1974 recession, regained some of its spirit during 1980. Some of that reflected the 1978 cut in the maximum long-term capital-gains tax rate from 49 percent to 28 percent which had led to an enormous increase in the amount of money flowing into venture-capital funds. And though Apple was in business before the tax cut, other companies that were beginning to emerge from obscurity owed at least part of their existence to venture-capital funds. Inside Apple, surveys also projected that the number of shareholders—thanks to the distribution of stock options—would soon top five hundred at which point all companies under the 1934 Securities and Exchange Act are required to file public reports. But most of all Apple was in the fortunate position of not really needing a large injection of money.

All Apple's founders and managers were aware that a public stock issue was an essential part of growing up. They heard, depending on the inclination of the speaker, the stock issue compared to a twenty-first birthday, the arrival of an heir, the betrothal of a daughter, or a bar mitzvah. So at a board meeting in August 1980, when Arthur Rock argued that a public offering was an obstacle that would have to be negotiated at some time or another, Apple's directors decided to heed his advice. The timing, rather than the news itself, took people by surprise. Apple's freshly hired vice-president of communications, Fred Hoar, had to draft a press statement before he was even given a desk. Meanwhile, Regis McKenna was asked to cancel advertisements that were running in *The Wall Street Journal* to prevent any accusations from the Securities and Exchange Commission that the stock was being touted.

The strength of Apple's bargaining position was reflected in the number of investment bankers who came knocking on the door trying to sell the virtues of their firms. Apple's stock offering promised to be one of the largest in years and the prospect of the commissions was enough to make even the most staid investment banker drool. The visitors left thickly padded brochures boosting the merits of having their firms estimate the value of Apple, and there was plenty of talk about "ongoing relationships," "after-market support," and "retail networks."

Among the callers were officers from the San Francisco investment and underwriting firm Hambrecht and Quist, which for about a decade had specialized in investing in young companies and underwriting technology issues. The men from Hambrecht and Quist had to make about ten visits and give presentations to Apple's top managers and its financial and legal staffs before finally winning the business. To balance Hambrecht and Quist's reputation among the freer spirits of the investment community, Apple arranged for the issue to be co-sponsored by the more stolid New York banking house of Morgan Stanley. When Morgan Stanley decided to seek the Apple business and, more important, when it accepted equal billing with an upstart invest-ment firm, it gave tacit notice that longstanding allegiances had given way to new. Almost immediately Morgan Stanley dropped its connections with IBM and started to be more aggressive in its quest for business from young companies.

An odd sort of relationship developed between West and East and between Apple's managers and the financiers. Jobs complained that the bankers weren't giving Apple enough attention, and Michael Scott, in particular, took every opportunity to goad the men with their monogrammed shirts and tiepins. When Apple's managers were invited to attend a briefing made to some investors by Genentech, a South San Francisco biotechnology firm that was also preparing to go public, Scott turned up wearing jeans and a cowboy hat and was sent out to buy a tie. At another meeting with the bankers he dressed himself and a couple of others in baseball caps, black armbands, and T-shirts stenciled with the slogan THE APPLE GANG. For their part some of the bankers found it hard to believe that Scott was the president of the company they had so eagerly embraced.

Few stock watchers needed to be reminded that Apple was going public. In the last half of 1980 the new issues market seemed almost like a throwback to the late sixties when the hot intersection had been in Beverly Hills at the corner of Wilshire and Santa Monica boulevards. As fall turned to winter Arthur Rock's hunch came to look better and better. When Genentech went public in October 1980, it was the cause of pandemonium. After opening at $35 the stock burst to $89 before retiring for the night at $71. With that display the interest in new issues spread like swine flu. Though the SEC forbade companies to give earnings forecasts or promote the stock in the weeks before the public issue, magazines and newspaper reporters did their own work. The publicity that Apple received in the weeks leading up to the stock issue was the first widespread national publicity that the company had received. It was partly generated by the prospect of the size of the issue but it was also the belated payoff for the way Apple had wooed, flirted, and dallied with the press during the previous years.

Apple was touted by investment analysts and portfolio counselors, by mountebanks who made their living dispensing tips, by the authors of stock guides and newsletters, digests and advisory columns. "Every speculator in hot new issues," *The Wall Street Journal* reported, "wants a bite of Apple—Apple Computer Inc.—but most will be lucky even to get a bit." Potential investors came out of the woodwork. The sacks of letters that arrived at Hambrecht and Quist's office in San Francisco included an appeal for stock from a seven-year-old boy.

In the weeks before Apple went public, the telephones in Cupertino also started to ring with alarming frequency. Callers wanted to know where they could buy stock or when it would split again. Strangers lurked in computer stores that Wozniak was known to frequent, and both he and Jobs received calls from people they hadn't talked to in years. School friends, distant cousins, and even the contractors who worked on their homes wondered whether they could lay their hands on a couple of shares. Other major Apple stockholders arranged private sales with British unit trusts and investment houses, Caribbean-based technology funds, the Hewlett-Packard pension fund, and with people who had either spotted Apple or maintained trading accounts with the underwriters. Some of the most persistent callers were professional investors who wanted to add Apple to the list of coups they had participated in over the last couple of decades. Charlie Finley, the controversial owner of the Oakland Athletics baseball team, arranged a sale with four officers despite Arthur Rock's objections, and then sued because he was dissatisfied with the price. Some doctors, dentists, and lawyers who served Apple's stockholders also managed to get their hands on a few shares. One Beverly Hills consultant bought shares, explaining that he was familiar with Apple because he had conducted "a workshop training the top management of the corporation in more effective communication skills."

At brokerage offices the prospect of the offering produced a frenzy. One customer at a San Jose firm offered to open a $1 million account in exchange for 3,000 shares of Apple. Around the country brokers tossed their names into hats to get a couple of shares for their favorite clients. One Merrill Lynch analyst said, "Even my brother who invests in the stock market only on Tuesdays in leap years called to ask what I knew about Apple Computer." An analyst with the Detroit Bank and Trust remarked, "It's safe to say that everybody is going to be able to find some money to buy Apple stock." Another observed the clamor and the news that a computer store intended to go public with the dry prediction that some owners of Apple IIs would soon try to issue shares. Apple employees found that the mere whisper of the company name brought clicks of attention. One youngster found stockbrokers hanging on his every word even though he still got carded when he entered a bar. Owning Apple stock, he decided, "was like having an American Express card made of platinum."

The fever also served to accentuate the resentments and jealousies that had built up within Apple. Wozniak dreamed up his own scheme to try to correct the lopsided stock distribution. He decided to sell some of his own holdings to colleagues who had either not received what they deserved or were victims of broken promises. The Wozplan, as it quickly became known, touched off a small stampede. Almost three dozen people snapped up close to 80,000 shares which, according to documents, Wozniak offered at $7.50 apiece. In answer to the formal questions posed by the California Commissioner of Corporations, the buyers explained their circumstances and how they learned about the offer. William Budge, for example, disclosed: "The amount of the proposed investment is in excess of 10 percent of my net worth and annual income." Jonathan Eddy revealed that his personal investment adviser urged him to buy. "She owns some herself." A few, like Timothy Good, resorted to familiar jargon: "I have interfaced with several officers on a professional level." Lewis Infeld said he had heard about the opportunity "from word of mouth within my working environment." Others, like Wayne Rosing, were blunt. "I am single, have no debts and more than sufficient net worth and insurance to provide for my needs." Meanwhile, Wozniak also sold another 25,000 shares to Stephen Vidovich, the developer of the DeAnza Racquet Club where Apple held a corporate membership: "Due to the fact that the founders were friends of mine I had made it known that I was interested in purchasing stock if it ever became available." Jobs observed the progress of the Wozplan and Wozniak's private sales and decided that his partner "ended up giving stock to all the wrong people. Woz couldn't say no. A lot of people took advantage of him."

Jobs meanwhile was harried by private worries that had been provoked by the birth of a daughter to his high-school flame, Nancy Rogers. The child was born on Robert Friedland's farm in May 1978 and Rogers was convinced that Jobs was the father. Jobs, who arrived at the farm a couple of days after the birth, helped Rogers settle on a name for the baby girl. They called her Lisa. After the birth Jobs and Rogers went their separate ways with the latter supporting herself and the child with the proceeds of a variety of waitressing and housecleaning jobs. Eventually she asked Jobs for a $20,000 settlement. Markkula, who thought this was too little, suggested Jobs pay $80,000. Jobs demurred and insisted that he wasn't Lisa's father. Absolutely convinced that he had nothing to do with the child, Jobs stopped making voluntary child-support payments on three occasions. "Each time we started to get a lawyer involved," said Rogers's father, "he started to pay."

In May 1979 Jobs startled the Rogerses by agreeing to submit to blood tests to determine paternity. The analysis conducted by the department of surgery at the University of California, Los Angeles, concluded: "The probability of paternity for Jobs, Steve . . . is 94.41%." Jobs wasn't swayed by the evidence and insisted that, thanks to statistical quirks, "twenty-eight percent of the male population of the United States could be the father." Eventually he came to grips with what was an immensely painful matter and agreed to a court-ordered settlement. "I settled because we were going public and it was consuming a ton of emotional energy. I had to get it resolved. I didn't want to defend a suit for ten million dollars." Within a month of Apple's stock offering, Jobs agreed to start paying Rogers $385 a month in child support, to cover the cost of the child's medical and dental insurance, and also to reimburse the county of San Mateo for the $5,856 that it had spent on public assistance to support the baby.

As Jobs battled with his own troubles, outside interest in Apple continued to climb. The head of steam kept pushing up the price of the stock. At Apple the eventual price became the source of furtive bets and sweaty speculation. The price climbed so steeply that in Massachusetts the secretary of state for a time banned citizens of the Bay State from buying the stock because Apple violated state regulations that required a company's book value to be at least 20 percent of the market value. During the first week of August 1980, Hambrecht and Quist (in which the Apple director and investor Arthur Rock was a limited partner) bought 40,000 shares for $5.44 each. When Apple's first stock prospectus was published on November 6 it was anticipated that the stock would be priced between $14 and $17. Even on the morning of December 12, 1980, the day Apple finally went public, when the stock was priced at $22, there were still signs that it had been underpriced because at the end of the first day of trading it closed at $29.

The day of the stock issue turned into an unofficial company holiday. For of the 237 companies that made initial offerings in 1980, Apple's was by far the largest and became the biggest initial offering since the Ford Motor Company went public in 1956. Apple's switchboard operators found that a few callers were complaining that they hadn't been warned about the actual day of the issue.

Around the company, computers were connected to the Dow Jones ticker and programmed to print the stock price every few minutes. There was a premature celebration when a few of the machines began spitting out the quotes for a company with the call letters APPL rather than Apple's AAPL. Some people wanted to erect a mock thermometer in the middle of the road that separated Apple's main buildings. Anticipating a surge in the price, they wanted to mark notches up the stem. Cooler heads prevailed.

Michael Scott hooked up a speaker phone to the New York offices of Morgan Stanley and at the end of the day carted in a few cases of champagne to help celebrate the $82.8 million that had been added to Apple's bucket of cash. Robert Noyce, vice-chairman of Intel, co-inventor of the integrated circuit, and husband of Apple's director of human resources, attended the small party while Jef Raskin surveyed the other guests and noticed that "all the people in the room were millionaires. The forceful thing was that the world had shifted. I hadn't seen that happen before."

It was natural to be overwhelmed since there were so few precedents. At the end of December 1980 the paper worth of a few individuals should have been etched in uranium. Jobs's 15 percent share of the company was valued at $256.4 million, Markkula's at $239 million, Wozniak's at $135.6 million, and Scott's at $95.5 million. Teledyne's Henry Singleton had a 2.4 percent stake in Apple that was worth $40.8 million. The venture capitalists' investments had also crept up. Venrock's initial $300,000 and its two subsequent investments had grown to $129.3 million, and Arthur Rock's $57,600 stake had turned into $21.8 million.

Meanwhile, Rod Holt found himself sitting on $67 million, Gene Carter on $23.1 million, and John Couch, the head of the Lisa Division, on $13.6 million. The head of engineering, Thomas Whitney, who had departed on what was politely called a "two week vacation" and whom Markkula uncharacteristically dismissed in private as "a burned-out case," found that his twenty-six months at Apple translated into a barrel of stock worth $48.9 million. Meanwhile, Alice Robertson, Wozniak's first wife, discovered that her share of the separation settlement was valued at $42.4 million, though she later complained she had been the victim of a raw deal.

After the company went public, there were other complications. Some of the executives whose names and stockholdings were revealed in the official prospectus and newspaper reports started to worry. They installed extra fences around their houses, bought faster cars, wired up elaborate security systems, and fretted about the possibility of kidnap attempts on their children. Leslie Wozniak, who had been given some stock by her brother, retired from her work as a journeyman printer and was overwhelmed. "It was hard to decide what to do with my life. Anybody who wins a lottery should get a year's free therapy."

At Apple people found that they couldn't sell the stock as soon as they had hoped because of legal restrictions. Others waited to cash in their three-year options and then retired, while many worried about the best timing for a sale. A sizable group even flew to Vancouver, Canada, on the day when 1980 income tax returns were due in order to qualify for an extension. Programmer Bill Atkinson complained, "Some people spent half their waking hours counting their stock options. Those who eventually sold their shares discovered that ownership was interpreted as a matter of loyalty. When Jef Raskin sold his stake, Jobs accused him of betrayal. Raskin countered, "I didn't want to have to open the paper each day to find out how much money I had." As a company Apple began to find it more difficult to recruit people because they couldn't be made wealthy with quite as much ease as before the offering. Charts that plotted every hiccup and lurch in the price were tacked to the outsides of cubicles and had a discernible effect on morale. When the stock fell, the charts disappeared. Bruce Tognazzini admitted, "I went through a year of being totally whacko because my mood was entirely tied to the Dow Jones."

For Jobs, Wozniak, and the other chief beneficiaries of the wealth created at Apple, the benefits turned out to be more mechanical than emotional. They, and others, learned that wealth and the prospect of leisure didn't suddenly bring happiness and, to some extent, confused everything. Jobs and Wozniak began to receive letters thanking them for what they had done.

Occasionally the envelopes contained photographs of houses which carried inscriptions like "This is the house that Apple built" and the painted spaces in the company parking lot began to be sprinkled with Mercedeses and Porsches.

Some of the wealthier individuals made larger purchases. Alice Robertson bought condominiums and a gold-colored Mercedes which she decorated with the vanity license plates 24 CARAT. Rod Holt eventually took up ocean-racing, ordered a yacht and had a large Apple logo stitched to one of the sails. Markkula took to the skies, bought a used Learjet, had it repainted, equipped it with a stereo system, videotape player and Apple II, hangered it at San Jose airport under the company name ACM Aviation, retained a pair of pilots, and used it to gad to a weekend home on the shores of Lake Tahoe.

Jobs was at one time going to share the jet with Markkula but decided that was too ostentatious and settled for a life of expensive austerity. "You run out of things to buy real quick." He was not sure whether to be embarrassed or coyly proud of the fact that he and Markkula had shared a $200 bottle of Sauterne at dinner one evening or that he had the means to contemplate buying (though he never did) a full-page advertisement in *Le Monde* to help track down a woman he had met fleetingly in Paris but who had failed to turn up for a date. He found that the wealth, and the notoriety that trailed in its wake, opened doors to a wider stage. Invitations started to arrive for dinner parties, politicians began to solicit contributions, charities with unfamiliar names mailed fund-raising letters, and when he was asked to give talks or speeches, Jobs became increasingly polished. As business started to take him about the world he found large cities like Paris and New York more diverting than Cupertino or Sunnyvale. His wardrobe also took on a worldly air. The jeans began to be replaced by elegantly cut two-piece suits furnished by the San Francisco outfitter's Wilkes Bashford.

When the San Francisco newspaper columnist Herb Caen, with a characteristic lunge for the jugular, referred to Cupertino as Computertino, Jobs must have been part of the reason. Before Apple went public, the young master of Computertino bought a quiet home set in the hills of Los Gatos which he shared, for about three years, with a girl friend who had once worked at the Regis McKenna Agency. There he demanded the same quality of workmanship from his contractors as he did at Apple. But he was too busy to bring his full energies to the house that stayed empty of furniture and full of echoes.

After his girl friend moved out, it became the home of a lonely soul. About the only furnished room was the kitchen, decorated in French peasant style, but with knives by Henckel and a coffee maker by Braun. The master bedroom contained an Apple II, a mattress, and a dresser on top of which stood an eclectic collection of photographs: the guru Neem Karolie Baba, former California governor Jerry Brown, and Albert Einstein. A half-filled lawyer's bookcase in another room stood guard over packets of shirts returned from the dry cleaner. Architectural plans stayed scattered on the floor of a downstairs room. There were no easy chairs or sofa.

Outside in the driveway a Mercedes replaced the succession of beat-up old cars and he would run his hands along the smooth, sleek lines, promising people that someday Apple's computers would look equally elegant. He bought a BMW R-60 motorcycle which he sometimes rode about the hills and a painting by Maxfield Parrish. Along with Robert Friedland Jobs bought some land in the Pacific Northwest and also helped to finance SEVA, an organization devoted to eliminating blindness in Nepal.

But he was much too introspective to find the wealth comfortable. He worried about some of the consequences, asked his parents to remove the Apple bumper stickers from their cars, wondered how to give them some money without turning their world topsy-turvy, worried that women might like him just because he was wealthy, and knew that his friends expected him to use his fortune wisely. He had become—in his middle twenties—a digitized version of Scott Fitzgerald's Monroe Stahr.

Wozniak, who seemed determined to follow Samuel Johnson's advice that it was better to live rich than to die rich, was always louder, splashier, and more cavalier about his fortune. As a student and an engineer he had always managed his financial affairs haphazardly and nothing changed as he grew wealthy. He could never keep track of receipts, for months didn't bother to seek financial advice, and made a habit of filing his tax returns late. Wozniak turned into an approachable teddy bear and a soft touch. When friends, acquaintances, or strangers asked him for a loan he often wrote out a check on the spot.

Unlike Jobs, who guarded his founder's stock carefully, Wozniak distributed some of his. He gave stock worth $4 million to his parents, sister, and brother and $2 million to friends. He made some investments in start-up companies. He bought a Porsche and fastened the license plates APPLE II to the car. His father found $250,000 worth of uncashed checks strewn about the car and said of his son, "A person like him shouldn't have that much money." After Wozniak finally did arrange for some financial advice, he arrived at Apple one day to announce, "My lawyer said to diversify so I just bought a movie theater." Even that turned into a complicated venture. The theater, located among the barrios on the east side of San Jose, provoked angry community protests after it screened a gang movie, *The Warriors*. Wozniak attended a few community meetings, listened to the concerns of the local leaders, promised that his theater wouldn't show violent or pornographic movies, and accompanied by Wigginton, spent a few afternoons in the empty, darkened theater screening movies and playing censor.

A few months before Apple became a public company, Wozniak took up flying, bought a single-engine Beechcraft Bonanza, and eight weeks after the stock offering, came close to fulfilling the last half of Samuel Johnson's adage. Wozniak embarked on a weekend flying expedition along with Candi Clark, the daughter of a California building contractor, whom he had first met during a water-gun fight at Apple and who was about to become his second wife. They were accompanied by another couple and were supposed to fly to Southern California to pick up Wozniak's wedding rings. Before setting off from Scotts Valley airport, located in the Santa Cruz Mountains, Wozniak was jittery. He complained about interference on his headsets and his companions were equally nervous. Their queasiness was justified. When the plane left the runway, it rose about fifty feet in the air, touched down again, bounced a couple of times, reared at an angle, barreled through two barbed-wire fences, careened up an embankment, and tipped on its nose about two hundred and fifty feet from a roller-skating rink crammed with teenagers. A San Francisco stockbroker who arrived on the scene switched off the plane's ignition and found Wozniak slumped in his fiancée's lap.

After an investigation the National Transportation Safety Board found no evidence of mechanical failure. Meanwhile, doctors examined the four injured victims. They found that Wozniak had bitten through his upper lip, smashed a tooth, fractured the orbital socket around his right eye, had double vision, and was suffering from amnesia. His fiancée, meanwhile, needed plastic surgery to touch up cuts on her face. Wozniak's accident prompted dark headlines in the local newspapers: COMPUTER EXEC IN PLANE CRASH, APPLE EXEC IN GUARDED CONDITION. In the days following the accident, Jobs rented a limousine to ferry Wozniak's parents to and from El Camino hospital. There in his bed Wozniak became frantic, refused food, and said that the government was plotting to blow up the hospital and take all his money. Though his doctors were divided on the issue, seven days after the accident Wozniak was released and six months later he ordered a brand-new single-engine Beechcraft Bonanza.

"He doesn't want photographs right now," she said.

The Stanford University dormitory lounge looked like a poorly lit set for a nineteenth-century Gothic romance. Imitation-marble plinths sagged above the radiators, gilt-edged chandeliers threw yellow shadows across a ceiling painted crème de menthe. Branches of trees, thinned by fall, brushed in a drafty dusk against the windowpanes. A hundred or so freshmen, most of whom seemed to possess an earnest desire to graduate, were folded in various states of repose. A couple were fidgeting with small tape recorders. They had come to listen to Steve Jobs. The informality did not extend to the three women from the Regis McKenna Public Relations Agency who perched at the rear of the room. They had helped select the students' invitation from among the two dozen or so requests that Jobs received every week. The youngest of the trio had not met Jobs before, but monitored him with marital familiarity and clucked to a magazine photographer, "He isn't in a good mood. He doesn't want photographs right now."

For the students the chairman of Apple Computer was a welcome break from the diet of familiar college administrators and professors they had been fed on previous occasions. Jobs was dressed with formal indifference in a well-cut cotton sports coat and jeans: chest courtesy of San Francisco clothier Wilkes Bashford, legs furnished by Levi Strauss. While a student made some introductory remarks Jobs shucked his jacket, tugged off a pair of worn corduroy boots which revealed a pair of argyle socks, and took up a lotus position on a coffee table.

The students seemed a touch intimidated but the line of questions quickly showed that the subject under inspection possessed, in their eyes, the same molecular structure as Apple Computer. Jobs used the questions to give a seductive talk which, with slight variations, served as his standard speech for magazine editors, congressional committees, state commissions, business school students, electronics conventions, politicians, and visiting academics. It explained part of the reason for Apple's popular appeal and why Jobs, some months before, had made the cover of *Time*. It was a cross between technological evangelism and corporate advertisement and Jobs busily juggled the roles of standard bearer and corporate promoter.

He told how Apple got started. "When we first started Apple we really built the first computer because we wanted one." Then he said, "We designed this crazy new computer with color and a whole bunch of other things called the Apple II which you have probably heard about." He added, "We had a passion to do this one simple thing which was get a bunch of computers to our friends so they could have as much fun with them as we were."

Suddenly the magazine photographer's light flashed and Jobs asked, "What's that?" and provoked a barrel of snickers. The photographer crouched near a pillar and raised her camera. Jobs paused and stared into the lens and said, "Hi!" and the questions stopped. When they resumed a student wanted to know when the company stock would rise. "I cannot talk about that," he said demurely. He said that he hoped Apple would someday sell half a million computers a month. "It's still kind of a pain in the ass to use a computer." He told the students about the company's Lisa computer, disclosed his dream of putting a computer in a book, and promised, "We won't put garbage in a book because our competitors will do that."

He proceeded to tell the students about his plan to give a compu- ter away to every high school in the country. Cynics said that it was a cold marketing ploy to produce generations of Apple users, but at the start it had been a romantic gesture. The plan was formally called The Technology Education Act of 1982, but at Apple it had become known as the "Kids Can't Wait" program and reflected Jobs's impa- tience to get things done. On his first serious excursion, he had spent a couple of months lobbying congressmen, hoping to get a change in the tax law that would give companies the same relief for donat- ing computers to schools that they received when they gave them to universities. Jobs had given senators and congressmen a standard twenty-minute pitch but the Reagan administration had been unwill- ing to bend the tax laws to help special cases. So when the students wanted to know what had become of the well-publicized plan, Jobs announced that Apple wasn't willing to support the amended legislation and that "the Senate has screwed it up."

Apple had received a warmer reception at the California legislature which had amended a local law, and Jobs said that the company would soon start distributing ten thousand computers throughout the state. "We're in the right place at the right time with the right people to give something back. That's kind of nice.

Computers and society are out on their first date so wouldn't it be great if we could make the date go great and blossom." He added, "The race is on to improve the productivity of the knowledge worker. The personal computer can generate—at a crude level—free intellectual energy but the computer will dwarf the petrochemical revolution."

In answer to some more questions he told the students, "The company that will most affect how we do is not IBM. It's Apple. If we do what we know how to do well, we'll leave everyone else in the dust." After a student asked what it was like to run an empire Jobs replied, "We don't think of it as an empire. We hire people to tell us what to do." He dismissed the Japanese quest for a new generation of computer as having "a very high bullshit content. They don't really know what they're talking about." He complained about the Japanese and the evils of protectionism. He also said it was no longer possible to start a computer company in a garage but suggested the students might still have a shot with a software company.

As the questions died down Jobs conducted his own informal poll. He asked what part of the country students came from and what they were studying. Most seemed to be enrolled in computer science. "How many of you are virgins?" he asked. There were a few giggles, but no hands were raised. "How many of you have taken LSD?" There were some flushes of embarrassment and one or two hands rose slowly. "What do you want to do?" he asked, and a student blurted, "Make babies."

There wasn't much hint that Jobs had acted through the script dozens of times, or had casually talked with friends about the possibility of running as an independent candidate for president. Jobs knew all the punch lines. It was the work of a corporate sorcerer with an actor's sense of timing. After Jobs's questions he was badgered again. A couple of students tugged at his cuffs. One just wanted to introduce himself as the owner of an Apple II, another wanted Jobs's autograph on one of the Apple annual reports that were spilling out of a couple of cardboard boxes. A tall junior wondered whether he could get a tour of an Apple factory. Most of the students seemed pleased with the evening. "Well, at least he's not a jerk," one brown-haired coed said as she, in her Lacoste shirt, carefully pressed jeans, topsiders, and companion made for the door.

WELCOME IBM, SERIOUSLY –

The stock market provided the loudest applause for Apple Computer but there was plenty from other quarters. Small newspapers tracked the progress of Apple IIs all across America and greeted the appearance of these personal computers with charming, goggle-eyed astonishment. This was an updated version of the gasps that had followed the arrival of automobiles in muddy country lanes and of radios in quiet living rooms. But now the photographs were not of a family sitting upright in stiff leather seats with hats poking over the brow of a windshield, or knitting and smoking around a fireplace while ears were tuned to the wireless perched in holy splendor on a mantelpiece. The new trailblazers were pictured in hunched positions around a screen that glowed, their hands perched on a keyboard, and the heads that tilted toward the camera seemed to be saying that the future had arrived.

As well as the photographs of the flash-stunned teenager in the family den, there were snapshots of Apples in libraries and class-rooms, banks and laboratories, mobile homes and airplanes, houseboats and music studios, and there were even a couple bracketed to electric guitars. Reports of these California curiosities slipped into papers like the *East Aurora Advertiser,* the *Geneva* (Neb.) *Signal* and the *Bristol Herald Courier.* The *Chaska* (Minn.) *Herald* marveled as BOY HANDLES COMPUTER PROGRAMS while the *Columbia Independent* in Ohio resorted to an apocalyptic tone: EUCLID JUNIOR HIGH SCHOOL ENTERS COMPUTER AGE. When an Apple arrived in Southern California, the *La Jolla Light* announced COMPUTER AGE COMES TO COUNTRY DAY and the *Star Press* in Blairstown, Iowa, told of a farmer learning to program an Apple and finding the experience "not nearly as tough as it is to teach a computer person how to feed cattle." Apples helped a belly dancer keep track of her Jezebel brassieres and monitored the temperature of mud around a semisubmersible oil rig in the Gulf of Mexico. A University of Virginia coach used an Apple to calculate the velocity of a football and a Boeing engineer programmed his to forecast four out of five winners at a Washington State racetrack— but admitted, "The more I refine this handicapping program, the worse the results." In Buffalo Grove, Illinois, a high-school senior organized a tennis tournament with an Apple and in Sarasota, Florida, a cerebal-palsy victim could communicate more easily after an Apple was connected to a speech synthesizer.

In Manhattan, a vice-president at W. R. Grace and Company programmed an Apple II to estimate how many sides of beef his company's restaurant chain should order, while the poet laureate of Florida wrote paeans with an Apple hooked to a large-screen television. His words sparkled, rotated, and grew on the screen in line with their importance and he took to calling himself "a solid-state balladeer." The Sunnyvale Police Department, working from physical descriptions, used an Apple to help search for the names of suspects. And in Santa Ana, California, a man was arrested for running a major prostitution ring with the help of an Apple that kept track of his four thousand clients, their credit history, and proclivities.

Overseas, Apples analyzed census data in North Africa, measured factors affecting crop yields in Nigeria, provided diagnostic assistance for eye disorders in Nepal, improved irrigation planning in the Sahara, monitored developing bank activities in Latin America, assisted a schoolteacher in Botswana, and in the darker reaches of the world like Cardiff, Wales, *The South Wales*

Echo reported that for a university lecturer an Apple provided "a hobby that became a way of life" though his teenage daughter complained the new arrival meant "we don't really talk to one another anymore."

The users groups that sprang up all over the world added further testimony to the reach of Apple. The envelopes that arrived in Cupertino might have been addressed to a collector of exotic postage stamps. There were letters from Grupo Usarios Apple de Columbia, Brazil Apple Clube, Jakarta Apple, Apple Club Zagreb, Hong Kong Apple Dragon, Apple Gebruikers Groep Nederland, Catalunya Apple Club and others from Sweden and the Philippines, New Zealand and Israel, Tasmania and Guam.

In the United States new clubs in different cities invented names with the gusto that editors of cookbooks reserve for fresh concoctions. There were Apple Peelers and Crab Apples, Green Apples and Applebutter, Applesiders and Apple Tart, Applepickers and Apple Jacks, Apple Pi and Apple PIE, Appleseed and Applesac, Appleworms and Apple Cart, but two with the nicest ring were Appleholics Anonymous and Little Rock Apple Addicts. Magazines with names like *inCider, Apple Orchard, Call Apple* and *Apple Source* were published to reach customers and dealers. Exhibition halls were rented to stage Appleexpos and Applefests that were undisguised celebrations of the company's computers.

Apple's founders were presented with Apples of various sizes, fashioned from so many materials that they must have wondered why they hadn't called the company Matrix Electronics. They were deluged with apples carved from koa, mahogany, cedar, and redwood, fired in porcelain and china, dried in papier-mâché, blown from crystal, melted in brass, and stamped in plastic. There was also a proliferation of memorabilia supplied by little companies that specialized in making corporate trinkets and icons. There were apple belt buckles and apple pens, apple doormats and apple goblets, apple notebooks and apple paper knives, apple calendars and apple paperweights, apple key chains and apple bumper stickers.

As Apple became a major computer company there were less convenient, more oblique compliments to the size of its success. There was, for a start, the irritating flattery of imitation. On the East Coast of the United States, Franklin Computer Corporation manufactured a machine very similar to the Apple, called it the

ACE 100, and in advertisements shamelessly touted it by placing an apple in a prominent position and declaring that it was "sweeter than an apple." (In federal court in 1983 Franklin admitted that it had copied Apple's operating system.) A computer from Commodore was boosted with a series of commercials saying that it was "the worm that ate the apple." In Taiwan and Hong Kong local knock-off artists made copies that were decorated with names such as Apolo II, Orange Computers, and Pineapple. A West German computer distributor manufactured still another look-alike, a small Italian firm designed a computer that bore a lemon logo, while a British firm decorated its machine with a rainbow-colored pear.

In California Apple was troubled by a local disease, becoming a carcass for headhunters to pick over. The more persistent got to be so well known that Apple's telephone operators were ordered not to forward their calls. Undeterred, the cunning "executive recruiters" simply resorted to false names. Apple was not immune to job-hopping and in time people started to leave. It was by no means a mass exodus but the dribs and drabs were enough to be irritating. The lure of other start-ups, the sight of the flaws and frailties of Apple's founders, and the fear of getting bogged down in a large company all helped to nudge the ambitious toward the door. Within two years of the public issue, four small companies had been started by one-time Apple employees, and even if the turnover was nowhere near as high as in some corners of Silicon Valley, it was also nowhere near as low as Apple's managers liked to say.

So with all these accolades—some overt and some opaque— the people working in the creamy shadows of the Cali Brothers grain silos in Cupertino had ample reason for pride. They could be excused if they sometimes dreamed that the world was no longer round but had assumed the shape of their corporate logo. However, as they started to believe that Apple was a top dog, the company also became intrigued with the notion of empire, and an aggressive conceit threatened to unravel much of the earlier success.

Outsiders who had followed Apple's progress spotted the danger signals. Hank Smith, the venture capitalist, began to warn the officers of other young companies about the penalites of success and he used Apple as his case study. Richard Melmon, who had worked on the Apple account for the Regis McKenna Agency and was later connected with a software company that sold programs for Apples, agreed: "Everybody at Apple sits around and says, 'We're the best. We know it.' They have a culture that says it and it starts from Steve Jobs and works on down." And Ed Faber, the president of Computerland, summed up Apple's swaggering demeanor: "The word that keeps popping up is 'arrogant.'" Arrogance seeped right through the company and came to affect every aspect of its business: the style with which it treated suppliers, software firms, and dealers, its attitude toward competitors, and the way it approached the development of new products.

From the outset, the shape and style of Apple's computers was Jobs's primary interest. Within months of the introduction of the Apple II, he became vice president of research and development and thereafter almost always had the final say in major product decisions. As the company grew, and Jobs's influence mounted, so did the force of the tactics he had used to push, goad, prod, cajole, and coax Wozniak during the development of the Apple II. He was always attracted to the latest, and brightest prospect, and in time the more interesting projects came to be associated with his presence.

Jobs had little interest in laborious research. There was nothing he believed in more deeply than his own intuition and his sense and touch for where the technology and markets would meet. Long-term product planning and a sense of how Apple's different computers would combine to produce a uniform lineup was a subordinate concern. With the continued success of the Apple II, Jobs developed what amounted to a religious faith in the strength of his instincts: "You make a lot of decisions based on the fragrance or the odor of where you think things are going." He was unwilling to let product planning become burdened with analysis, focus groups, decision trees, the shifts of the bell curve, or any of the painful drudgery he associated with large companies. He found Apple's prototype customer in the mirror and the company came to develop computers that Jobs, at one time or another, decided he would like to own.

Inside the company he gained a reputation for possessing a flair for getting things done, for having a gentle touch for the "soft side" of production. "He has," said Bill Atkinson, "a drive for excellence, simplicity, and beauty." And Tom Whitney observed, "One of Jobs's attributes is an infinite patience to make something better. It's never good enough for him. He always wants more features with less cost. He always wants to leapfrog the next natural step. A lot of the success of Apple is due to his damned stubbornness but it's also very difficult to work around because he always wants everything." Another who watched him closely was more skeptical. "He would have been happier as Walt Disney. One day he could have been working on rabbits' ears, the next day on Disneyland, the day after on movies, and the day after that on Epcot Center. The trouble with the computer business is that you don't get to change your mind a whole lot."

Jobs developed computers the way he improved himself. He had a knack for adopting other people's ideas when they suited his needs, discarding the aspects he found wanting, making subsequent improvements, and finally delivering opinions (or computers) with such conviction that it was easy to believe they were his entirely original contribution. But his strengths were also his greatest weaknesses. An ability to listen to convincing arguments provided an immune system against his snap judgments, but underlings came to be wary about speaking their minds. His optimism, what one manager called "the depth of his technical ignorance," meant that he underestimated how long computers would take to develop or what price they would sell for. Gradually the lineup of Apple's computers came to reflect Jobs's own temperamental, unpredictable, inconsistent streaks.

Yet his audacious, aggressive nature colored Apple's computers and was the spark that lit the company. Two years after the introduction of the Apple II, work was either starting or proceeding on five products which bore the code names Sara, Lisa, Annie, Mac, and Twiggy. Sara, named for the daughter of its chief hardware designer, eventually became known as the Apple III. Lisa was named after Jobs and Nancy Rogers's daughter. Annie was a low-cost Apple II which never saw the light of day. Mac was one person's favorite apple. A group working on developing a disk drive called their product Twiggy because, in its original incarnation, it was supposed to bear a physical similarity to the British model: It was going to house two diskettes and thus, one enlightened engineer decided, would come to resemble the fragile model whose figure was adorned with two mini-floppies.

One of the consequences of visible corporate glory was reflected in the ambitious schedules established for the Apple III. Those timetables reflected none of the perils of developing computers that had been carefully spelled out in numerous articles and books. "We were terribly optimistic about the schedules on the Apple III," said product designer Jerry Mannock. "The Apple II had been so successful that everybody was walking around thinking they could do anything." From the start the Apple III was supposed to be a stopgap product, a bridge between the time that Apple II sales were expected to drop and the day that Lisa was ready.

It also came to be seen as a test of Apple's ability to build a computer as a company. The circumstances had obviously changed since the days when Wozniak made gross modifications to the Apple I, and though Apple's payroll had lengthened so had the company's commitments. There was a growing band of customers who needed attention and support, there were the sundry distractions of corporate life, and there was also the need to have large numbers of the new computer ready to ship at the time of introduction rather than the dozens that were needed after the announcement of the Apple II. The schedule for the Apple III was the sort of timetable that might have been set by a hobbyist determined to show off a design at the Homebrew Club. It called for a computer that would be designed, tested, and ready for manufacture within ten months of conception.

Building a computer as a company, Apple soon discovered, was far more laborious than knocking together a machine in a garage. "The Apple III was designed by committee," Randy Wigginton complained. "Apple felt that was the way a proper company should design a computer. Everybody had certain ideas about what the Apple III should do and unfortunately all of them were included." The general plan was for a computer that contained all the features that were missing from the Apple II and to stretch the powers of the 6502 microprocessor since more powerful processors were not available at low prices. It was to have a larger memory, a built-in disk drive, a better operating system, a display of eighty columns that would be suitable for word processing and spreadsheet calculations, an upper- and lower-case keyboard, a keypad, improved color, and a faster microprocessor. It was also supposed to run all the programs developed for the Apple II and so become instantly useful in scores of different applications.

A fearsome pressure built up inside the company and helped promote stomach-contracting schedules. Some of this stemmed from marketing projections that repeatedly forecast imminent declines in the sales of Apple IIs. Wendell Sander, the chief hardware engineer on the Apple III, said, "We kept wondering when the bubble was going to burst on the Apple II. We could have done with more professionalism from the marketing side." Pressure also sprang from the commitments to ship the Apple III that were made in the prospectus prepared for the public stock offering. None of this was helped by Jobs who, a few months before the computer was announced, doled out some glossy posters carrying the line THE DECISION YOU'RE MAKING NOW HELPED SHIP 50,000 APPLE IIIS IN 1980. The combination of pressures was sufficient to squelch the cries of anguish and dam the stream of frantic memos that circulated among the people under the most strain. "It was the classic story," said Jef Raskin, "of people at the bottom saying, 'Things aren't working here. We're in trouble.' Then the next level up would say, 'We're in some trouble with this,' and the level above would say, 'We're getting around the trouble,' and the people at the top would say, 'It will be okay. Let's ship.'"

The rush to ship the computer resulted in an all-out scramble that was reflected most keenly in the publications department where the technical writers were again sandwiched between the changes being made on the laboratory bench and the implacable demands of the marketing department. The writers did not see the Apple III until nine weeks before it was announced, and the deadlines offered so little slack that the procedures for reviewing the manuals and the computer were all but ignored. Drafts of the completed manuals were sent to the engineering, marketing, and new-product-review departments on the same day they were delivered to the production department for paste-up. There the programmers worked two-hour shifts helping the graphic artists lay out the pages.

Meanwhile, Apple was also learning that there was nothing like software development to illustrate how quickly a year could slip by. Though the Apple III was supposed to run all the programs written for the Apple II, the improvements and modifications made adjustment of the Apple II software a complicated and tiresome venture. The programmers had to accommodate all the changes in the hardware: The computers started differently, the keyboards and disk drives were laid out differently, and the memory had been expanded. The programmers were also submerged beneath the sheer weight of the programming, which was ten times as much as for the Apple II.

Though the burden had increased Apple decided to try to develop as much software as possible inside the company. Little attention was paid to working closely with outside software houses, and there was a distinct effort to tighten up on the distribution of technical information about the intimate secrets of the Apple III. This made it almost impossible for independent software companies to develop programs for the computer. Two weeks before the announcement, a prototype machine was delivered to Visicorp accompanied by a request for a demonstration program of Visicalc. It was a year after the announcement before Apple's programmers had finished modifying the Pascal language so it would work on the computer and thus give independent software a way to write programs other than with BASIC or assembly language.

The Apple III was announced with great fanfare at the National Computer Conference in Anaheim in the summer of 1980. Apple rented Disneyland for an evening, distributed twenty thousand free tickets, and hired a fleet of red double-decker buses to ferry guests to the amusement park. The splash didn't deceive anybody in Cupertino. Sherry Livingston recalled, "They blew the Apple III and they knew it when they announced it." Once the public promises had been made, Apple was hoist with its own petard. The pressure to ship started backbiting between the competing interests of the engineering, marketing, manufacturing, and corporate sides of the company.

Problems with the design, some of which resulted from creeping elegance, made it impossible to squeeze the computer into its case. This resulted in a second, clumsy board which had to be piggybacked on the main printed circuit board. In addition Apple didn't pay much attention to testing quality. In the garage Jobs and Wozniak had performed their own crude, yet competent, tests, but as Apple grew no department had been formed to monitor the quality of parts. Wendell Sander said, "We didn't have any way of comparing the quality of components. We didn't have enough component-evaluation engineers to test the choice of connector. We listened to the salesmen and believed what they said." A chip from National Semiconductor, which was supposed to provide the computer with a clock, usually failed after about three hours, and though Jobs savagely berated the chief executive of the semiconductor company, that didn't solve the problem.

Lines on the printed circuit boards were too close together and that led to shorts. "We screamed that it shouldn't be shipped without new boards," said Rick Auricchio, "but the marketing people said it wouldn't be a problem. The engineers said it would be." The production team had its own gripes. Screws were so positioned that they pierced cables inside the computer. A heavy metal case was used because of uncertainty about some FCC regulations, but this made it unwieldy for many of the smaller women working on the assembly line. "It finished up as a mechanical nightmare," said Roy Mollard, the production man. "The engineers washed their hands of it and said it was a manufacturing problem." The connector between the two printed circuit boards didn't have enough plating and kept shorting; chips slipped from sockets and the cables to the keyboard were too short. As a test and to help fasten the chips into the sockets, the engineers suggested that the computer be dropped three inches. The shock of the fall, the engineers said, was guaranteed to coax the computer to life. The manufacturing men devised a more scientific test to see if everything worked: They started hitting the computer with rubber hammers.

By then the damage had been done. The Apple III was bollixed up at almost every stage of its development. What was shipped was unreliable and prone to failure. Visicalc was included in the early shipments because no other piece of software was ready. The Apple software that accompanied the computer was untested. The manuals looked shoddy and were accompanied by twenty pages of corrections. Word began to seep out when buyers discovered that the computer was full of startling surprises, SYSTEM FAILURE flashed in an aberrant manner across the screen. Damaging newspaper articles began to appear which wreathed the machine in a funereal cloud. Apple stopped advertising the computer, subjected the machines to arduous tests, redesigned the circuit board, readied some software, allowed early customers to swap their machines for ones that worked, and reintroduced the machine (with an expanded memory) a year later. What eventually became a sound, reliable workhorse and a capable business computer was ruined by the disastrous introduction and Jobs's optimistic poster became an embarrassing reminder of what might have been. For in the three years following its introduction only sixty-five thousand Apple IIIs were sold.

Jobs, who hopped away from the Apple III once the look and shape of the computer had been settled, was always more interested in the development of Lisa. Work had started on Lisa before the Apple III and from the start it was seen as a bolder, more ambitious project. In October 1978, or almost five years before the computer was shipped in any volume—at a price of around $10,000—Jobs had visualized what he wanted it to look like. He knew he wanted a computer that incorporated the disk drives and screen and also had a detachable keyboard. He knew too that he wanted it built around a sixteen-bit microprocessor rather than the eight-bit device that sat at the center of the Apple II. And he also had an inkling that word processing and a spread-sheet program like Visicalc would have to be included. A preliminary paper drawn up to accommodate most of these ideas bore out a colleague's observation that Jobs "decided what he wanted Lisa to look like before he was sure what technology would be in the machine." The original estimates for the computer called for shipment in January 1980, a retail price of $2,000, and a manufacturing cost of $600.

A small group formed to work on Lisa was quartered in Apple's one-time home—the office suite behind the Good Earth building—and began to grope toward a target that was, to say the least, hazy. For close to eighteen months the project floundered. Occasionally it was interrupted by hiccups and spurts, by the arrival of new managers or by politicking. But there wasn't all that much contact between the planners and the laboratory, or even between the software and hardware engineers. The general questions of who would use the machine and how it would blend with Apple's lines of distribution were, for the most part, sidestepped. Left to their own devices, the hardware engineers built a prototype around an eight-bit chip, the Intel 8086, that turned out to be slow and disappointing. Others started to inves-

tigate the possibility of using a competing eight-bit chip, the
Motorola 68000 (the successor to the eight-bit 6800 that Wozniak
had used during development of the Apple I).

Another prototype was developed under the guidance of
Ken Rothmueller, a one-time engineer in Hewlett-Packard's
Instruments Division. His computer was calculated to win the
hearts of the sort of people who ran data-processing departments
in large companies and those with a technical bent. It had a green
screen controlled in the same way as the screens on the Apple II
and III, a conventional typewriter keyboard, and an overwhelming
gray formality—and it by no means matched Jobs's aggressive
spirit. The cynics said that it was a dull, solid machine Hewlett-
Packard might have introduced.

Progress wasn't helped by the carping and clash of ideas that
developed between Rothmueller and John Couch, then the head of
the software department. Each man had, at various times, worked
for the other at Hewlett-Packard, and at Apple they both reported
to the same person. It was a battle for control of the computer:
a struggle for dominance between hardware and software. But the
critical importance of the software was emphasized by work that
was conducted, not by Apple, but at Xerox Corporation's Palo
Alto Research Center (PARC).

Xerox Corporation indelibly altered not only Jobs's picture of
the future but also the tone and nature of the computers that he
was later to say would last Apple through the eighties. It enlarged
his ideas and provided the specter of a competitor that, in the
laboratory, was working on ideas that were far more dramatic
than those being considered at Apple.

Set on a gently rising hill south of Stanford University, the
research center had been built by Xerox as an incubator where
young, bright sparks could dream up some grand new ideas that
would have the spectacular impact of the company's copiers.
It had opened in 1969, but researchers hadn't hatched any golden
egg by the last month of the seventies when a group from Apple
arrived to inspect the results of their work on personal computers.
Xerox had spent more than $100 million at PARC to fund research
on computers, semiconductor-chip design, and laser printers. That
sum was more than double Apple's total sales in 1979 but PARC

had managed to demonstrate the wide gap that exists between the laboratory bench and the shop window.

Xerox's substantial financial stake in Apple certainly smoothed the way for the expeditions of programmers and engineers that set out from Cupertino. But the curious didn't need the mind of Sherlock Holmes to figure out what was going on at PARC. The center was a showcase for Xerox and visits by outsiders were part and parcel of daily life. Even without knowing the details of how Xerox's prototype desk-top computers were designed, anybody who kept in touch with the field was certainly aware of some of the broader trends. A few well-placed telephone calls, a piece of cocktail-party chatter, or some interrogation of the bright high-school students Xerox was using as guinea pigs could shed light on the obscurer points. Computer journals had carried papers that reported on aspects of the Xerox research. A special 1977 issue of *Scientific American* contained an article by Alan Kay, an airy spirit and one of Xerox's principal scientists, that described the work in Palo Alto and amounted to an enthusiastic prescription for personal computers that were easy to use.

More than a decade of research by scientists like Douglas Engelbart at the Stanford Research Institute, by child psychologists, and at Norwegian universities had all, to varying degrees, influenced the work at Xerox. Indeed some of the most important principles had been published in the mid-sixties and had been displayed by SRI as early as 1968 with a demonstration of a system called NLS. Its chief thrust was to find ways to help people with no technical training control computers. In a way it was an academic extension of the general effort of the hobbyists: to make computers personal and then remove, or at least conceal, the mysterious and intimidating elements. Xerox's prototypes bore the traces of people who believed that computers were an entirely new medium, that they were far more than stolid, passive devices suitable for crunching numbers and editing prose. Some of the PARC researchers possessed the imaginative vision of flexible machines that would eventually combine the sensory charms of color television, stereophonic music, and finger paints. Like others before them, they said their eventual goal was to pop a computer into a case the size of a notebook or build a machine that businessmen could slip into their briefcases but use to communicate with other computers and people anywhere in the world.

In 1973 the PARC researchers built their first machine and called it Alto. Its chief virtues were a visual appeal and far greater flexibility than other computers of the time. It was supposed to simulate the sort of sights that people were already familiar with rather than boggling reels of numbers.

The Alto rested on advances in both software and hardware. Xerox developed a language called Smalltalk, which had similarities to Logo, a language that had been designed to help children program by moving and turning small, familiar objects without having to worry about codes and equations. For charts or memos that were too large to be displayed at one time, the Xerox computer simulated sheets of papers strewn on a desk and, in the jargon of the trade, called them "overlapping windows."

The clarity of the images was made possible by a process known as bit-mapping. The computer controlled each tiny dot, or pixel, on the screen. Text could be displayed in several typefaces and the computer could generate music. The Alto also used a mouse—originally developed at the Stanford Research Institute in 1964—to sidestep the codes of typewritten commands. By the late seventies, a hundred or so Altos were scattered about the White House and congressional offices as part of a splashy field test.

At first Jobs resisted the entreaties to visit Xerox, leaving others with the impression that nothing any other company was working on could possibly top some of the projects Apple had on the boil. A few of the Apple programmers familiar with the Xerox work kept pressing, and eventually he gave in to this own curiosity. With his impatience for anything but the practical and a willingness to admire anything with superior virtues, Jobs was enchanted by what he saw. He was as impressed as everybody else with the performance of the Alto and after seeing the combined effect of the mouse, the graphics, and the overlapping windows, turned to Bill Atkinson for some expert guidance. "Steve asked how long it would take to get the software up on Lisa and I said, 'Oh, six months.'"

The visits to Xerox became one of those few, crucial events that helped bring some clarity to the shape of Apple's computers. For a small company to even contemplate trying to match, let alone better, the Xerox work required something more than substantial confidence. But without a dose of audacity and a bolt of arrogance it would have been easy for Apple to play safe and incur the greater risk of doing nothing. The visits to Xerox also coincided with a hardening of the idea in Cupertino that Lisa would be the spearhead for Apple's attack on the office market. Businesses, so the argument went, would be able to afford to pay for machines that someday would be cheap enough for the general consumer.

The results of this flurry of activity were seen quickly enough. Within a few weeks Jobs managed to get hold of a mouse while the programmers started to delve into bit-map graphics and worked up some demonstrations of their power. The displays were so impressive that they prompted a palace coup. Most of the engineers turned against the stubborn bent of the chief hardware engineer, who was eventually replaced by the project's fourth hardware manager. It was also tacit recognition of the triumph of software.

So Apple's course was set by Xerox. A group of Xerox programmers and scientists eventually left PARC and joined Apple to work on Lisa and had a great influence on how the computer would appear to a user. For the three years following the revelation at Xerox, Apple's engineers and programmers edged forward. They didn't contribute any new, sweeping vision but they displayed a determination to improve on the work that had been done elsewhere. There were substantial enhancements in the software, and the grandest part of the enterprise was the way in which it was all squeezed into a desk-top system. They also practiced the message of one of Apple's earliest advertisements: SIMPLICITY IS THE ULTIMATE SOPHISTICATION and tried to remove any cause of confusion. After weeks of debate, for example, the buttons on the mouse were reduced from three to one. Features that had formed part of the original machine, like the "softkeys," keyboard buttons that concealed certain functions, also disappeared.

Jobs's contribution to the Lisa project oscillated between the inspirational and the destructive. One marketing manager recalled, "Pricing after pricing would come back with an absolute five-thousand-dollar minimum price. There were gut-wrenching debates with Jobs. He'd say, 'If I have to I'll bring Woz in. Woz could do it for less. If you were good enough you could do it.'" He also managed to undermine morale. According to one observer,

"The engineers would say, 'It doesn't matter if it's on time. We know Jobs. He'll change it anyway.'" But for all the commotion, Jobs also left his aesthetic touch on the computer. He left an overall style and shape and also helped with small details like the rounded edges on pictures of file folders, which he preferred to square corners.

The difference between Xerox and Apple was illustrated at the 1981 National Computer Conference in Houston. There Xerox announced the Xerox 8010 that colloquially was known as the Xerox Star. The computer had not been developed by the PARC group but nevertheless displayed some PARC hallmarks. It relied on a visual simulation of a desk top, a mouse, and bit-map graphics, but the execution was poor and the computer worked properly only when it was linked to a range of ancillary Xerox equipment. The software was excruciatingly slow and the execution of some novel ideas was generally considered rather clumsy.

There was far more patience at Apple. The miserable results of the Apple III served as a constant reminder of the penalties of rushing the development of a computer and releasing something that wasn't properly tested. There was also less inclination to forecast the imminent demise of the Apple II, which the people in Cupertino started to think possessed some of the durable virtues of products like the Volkswagen Beetle.

If the scope of the work on Lisa was one example of a corporate ambition, so was the development of a disk drive. When Apple decided to start a project to build its own disk drives, there were some perfectly sensible reasons. Sales of Apple II systems rested heavily on disk drives and Apple's one supplier, Shugart— by coincidence a Xerox subsidiary—was producing devices that in the opinion of some were unreliable. There was a distinct fear that Apple's growth was being limited by the scarcity of disk drives. Apple found another supplier to provide a second source of drives and then decided to start its own project. The motives were muddled by a desire shared by Scott and Jobs to humiliate Shugart.

Wendell Sander described the scope of the project: "The company didn't realize it was taking on a project that wasn't really a computer system. There's a closer affiliation between disk drives and integrated circuits than there is between disk drives and computers. They didn't realize it was going to be so big. They didn't appreciate the difficulty." Another observer said, "Steve really believed that Apple could build a floppy disk faster, for less money, and with more performance than anybody else without having any experience with products like that." The drive, code-named Twiggy, was originally supposed to be included in the Apple III but development problems soon ruled out that possibility.

The arrogant disregard for convention that proved so powerful when it came to thinking about new computers had less salutary results when it spilled over into the way Apple treated the outside world. It was an excruciating balancing act for Apple's managers to dally with the impossible inside the company and simultaneously cope with mortals on the outside. They were also confronted with the conflicting need to guard corporate secrets and maintain congenial relationships. Yet at times the corporate arrogance seemed to teeter on the brink of what amounted to a willful effort at self-destruction, and much of the goodwill that had been so carefully and laboriously built up between Apple and outsiders started to evaporate.

"Apple was uniquely aggressive," said Daniel Fylstra, chairman of Visicorp, once known as Personal Software, "about pursuing its self-interest." Fylstra had good reason to know, since the Visicalc program was instrumental in helping push Apples into offices. When Visicorp started to mimic Apple by retaining the same law firm, public-relations agency, accountants, and investors the amiable relationship began to sour. It deteriorated further when Visicorp decided to adapt versions of Visicalc for computers made by Apple's competitors and further still when it tried to increase the price of the program when it was made available for the Apple III. To keep Visicorp in its place, Apple's programmers were ordered to develop a spread-sheet program. The project kept slipping and was never officially released, but the relationship between the two companies became still sorrier.

The same was true of other software companies. The decision to develop in Cupertino most of the programs for the Apple III antagonized the smaller software companies. Apple wanted to maintain a tighter control over some of the programs—like word-processing and spread-sheet packages—that were becoming as important as the computer. But there was, as the Apple II had demonstrated, so many things that the computer could be used for that Apple had nowhere near enough programmers and nowhere near enough expertise to exploit all the opportunities. When Apple failed to provide the technical information and languages necessary to write programs, more feelings were hurt. Thanks to the premature introduction, the manuals explaining the software weren't even written. And when Apple then charged hefty admission prices to seminars explaining the innards of the Apple III, things took another turn for the worse. All the problems with the Apple III were certainly aggravated by the small amount of software that was available. When work started on Lisa, a similar attitude prevailed and outside companies weren't invited to contribute.

A tightening proprietary attitude was also displayed toward Apple engineers who wanted to pursue their own ideas. When Chuck Mauro decided to leave Apple in 1980 to start a company to make a peripheral that would convert the display of the Apple II from forty columns to eighty columns, Jobs wrote him a formal letter and wished him the best. Days later, as the possible consequences of the decision began to sink in, he changed his mind and argued vigorously with Mauro that the board had been developed on Apple's time and was therefore company property. "He invited me to lunch," said Mauro, "and as we were walking over to the restaurant he looked at me and said, 'You know, if we wanted to we could squash you like a bug.'" However, with the legal position murky, Jobs lifted the corporate heel and didn't provide any further obstruction and Mauro founded his own company.

The same sort of antagonism began to come between Apple and its dealers. To grow quickly Apple relied on a two-step system of distribution. Apple sold products to distributors who in turn resold the machines to dealers. After a time, the distributors weren't growing as quickly as orders and were restraining Apple's growth. Most of the distributors were small companies started by inexperienced businessmen who couldn't raise the local bank manager on the telephone and arrange for an increase in credit. As soon as any distributor showed a sign of weakness, Apple moved. When it became clear, for example, that Byte Industries was having trouble developing a nationwide chain of Byte Shops, Apple stopped supplying them. One Apple manager stated simply,

"Byte was floundering around so we cut the strings." So when in 1980 Apple was large enough and had enough money, it made a perfectly sensible business decision and decided to buy out its distributors and supply dealers directly.

From early days, Apple had cracked down hard on its dealers, and after a while, almost every senior Apple executive managed to upset or ruffle one of them. It was the sort of tussle that often exists between the factory and the field, with the former pushing as hard as it can to boost sales and the latter pulling as hard as possible to extract concessions and incentives. It was a cat-and-mouse game. Jobs, with his graphic sense of reality, explained, "We've got each other by the balls." The head of Computerland, Ed Faber, explained that Apple had, after a time, tried to "control dealers with muscle." Apple was quick to offer dealers discounts if they bought in quantity. The strategy was calculated to make dealers sell more machines by making sure they always had some in stock and weren't caught short. Dealers, who didn't want to bear the costs of financing, complained vigorously. One dealer explained, "There were too many semiconductor industry salesmen and not enough people with retail experience. They more or less said, If you don't want to do things exactly the way we want to do them, then screw you.'"

The head of Apple's sales, Gene Carter, countered dealers' complaints about pressure by issuing the sort of platitudes that might have come from a Detroit automobile executive: "Apple Computer, its distributors and retailers all want to make money and the way to make money is by selling the product." In the middle of 1982 he elaborated further: "We are the golden egg. Every dealer wants the Apple because it has a high profile. Dealers know if you don't carry the Apple there must be something wrong with your store."

In 1982 Apple also stopped supplying mail-order houses, cracked down on bootleggers who sold to nonauthorized dealers, and dumped Computerland which was once the mainstay of their distribution network and had once been such an object of desire that Apple had started some tentative discussions about a merger. Apple was trying to control which Computerland stores carried its products so they wouldn't interfere with other Apple dealers. At the time Ed Faber said, "We cannot say to people, 'You're at the mercy of this manufacturer.'"

*   *   *

The press also started to feel the results of the flush of power. When a trade newspaper, *Infoworld,* published a copyrighted story that was said to describe Apple's future product plan, the editor received several telephone calls from Jobs in which he successively argued that publication would severely damage Apple, called the story only partially accurate, denounced the reporter as "a criminal," offered a "real nifty two-page ad" if the story was held, and offered to pay the costs of stopping the print run. Apple's attitude toward the press was made clear in a memo that was circulated within the company. After a run of analytical stories that contained whiffs of criticism appeared in the months following Apple's public offering, a memo was distributed by Fred Hoar, the vice-president of communications. It complained that journalists often took matters out of context by misquoting executives and compressing what they had to say. The memo read in part:

> SUBJECT: ADVERSE PUBLICITY
>
> Recently Apple has been the subject of some stories in the press which cannot be considered "puff" pieces . . . i.e., they do a fairly negative job of reportage. . . . It is in the scheme of things that bad news makes better copy than good news, and also that many, if not most, reporters have trouble conveying subtlety and complexity, much less their editors.

If journalists were one focus for contempt, so were Apple's competitors. One by one other companies had muffed the development and introduction of their personal computers. Large companies like Hewlett-Packard and Xerox had stumbled and belatedly introduced machines that didn't match the Apple II. Firms with a reputation among consumers, like Atari and Mattel, had also missed the boat while the minicomputer makers like Data General and Digital Equipment were slow to realize the threat posed by microcomputers that were getting more powerful by the month. And Texas Instruments, the company that had once been the cause of such fear, flubbed its computer strategy so badly that Apple looked better with every passing day. The TI computer showed little attention to cosmetic details, gave low performance for the price, had thin distribution, and was received so poorly that within two years the price dropped from more than $1,000 to $100. So at Apple the arrival of a new competing computer had developed into a ritual. In the months leading up to a major announcement, there was a certain amount of trepidation at Apple. But after the announcements were studied and the UPS delivery trucks pulled up in Cupertino bearing the latest product, the machines inside the Styrofoam cartons were almost always greeted with derisive hoots.

Machines that carried the names of Japanese companies were given the same reception as American computers. Some of the statements that emerged from Cupertino sounded ominously like the confident claims which had once risen into the air of Detroit in the mid-sixties. At one time or another the Japanese were not supposed to understand the microcomputer market, had no experience with complicated electronic consumer items, wouldn't be able to master software, wouldn't find any room left on dealers' shelves, and wouldn't be able to build an image for their brands. "The Japanese," Jobs liked to say, "have come flopping up on our shores like dead fish."

This despite the fact that Apple came to depend on a variety of Japanese companies for a steady supply of semiconductors, monitors, printers, and disk drives. And while Japanese manufacturers like Hitachi, Fujitsu, and NEC designed and made almost every part needed in a personal computer, Apple was little more than an assembler of other people's work. The long-term challenge was stark: Apple had no alternative but to become the lowest-cost producer in the world and simultaneously offer the most value to its customers if it hoped, in the long run, to beat the Japanese. The extent of the Japanese threat was made clear not in the United States but in Japan, where within three years conditions had changed dramatically. In 1979 Apple and Commodore owned 80 percent of the Japanese market; by 1980 this had slumped to 40 percent and the November 1981 issue of the *Japan Economic Journal* reported: "The three leading American personal computer makers—Apple Computer, Commodore International and Tandy—have witnessed their combined market share in Japan plunge from 80–90 percent in 1979 to less than 20 percent at present."

*   *   *

There was, however, one competitor that everyone had expected to enter the microcomputer market once it was large enough to matter. That was the company with three of the most imposing initials in American business: IBM. It was easy to dismiss IBM as an old, lumbering, stuffy, East Coast company that could offer its engineers or programmers neither fame nor fortune and insisted that everyone wear white shirts and striped ties. In 1981 when IBM introduced its personal computer, its revenues were ninety times as large as Apple's. It made satellites, and robots, memory chips and mainframe computers, minicomputers and typewriters, floppy disk drives and word processors. At the Homebrew Club the Juggernaut of Armonk had always been the butt of jokes and engineers like Wozniak had always been more intrigued by the features of machines made by IBM's competitors.

Though the company had sold calculators, tabulators, cards, and accounting machines in the twenties, it switched direction after World War II when Remington Rand's UNIVAC machine was close to becoming synonymous with computing. In 1952 when IBM entered the computer business, its total sales were dwarfed by General Electric and RCA and smaller fry like Sperry Rand, Control Data, and Honeywell, all of whom thought they could beat IBM. Some of the computers were superior. But for all-round strength, for profit margins, earnings growth, sales force, reputation for service and reliability, nobody could match IBM. By 1956 IBM owned more than three quarters of the computer market in the United States and one weary competitor exhaled, "It doesn't do much good to build a better mousetrap if the other guy selling mousetraps has five times as many salesmen."

A decade later IBM was virtually rebuilt around a family of computers given the number 360. In the late 1960s, after leasing companies sprang up to serve as middlemen between the factory and customers, IBM helped savage them. At the start of the 1970s when the so-called plug-compatible manufacturers started to chip away at the market for peripherals, IBM responded aggressively. In the mid-1970s when other mainframe companies introduced powerful machines, IBM cut prices and changed the price structure of the industry.

There were only two conspicuous exceptions. IBM had failed to match Xerox when it tried to sell copying machines and had also played second fiddle in the minicomputer market which was dominated by companies like DEC, Data General and Hewlett-Packard. It was those two examples, the exceptions to IBM's general ferocity, that offered hope for personal-computer makers. But the moral was plain: Anytime the managers of IBM felt that other companies were threatening their business they retaliated savagely and with a ruthlessness that was hidden behind a benevolent facade. In every decade of its history, when IBM had been threatened by other companies, it had always eventually competed and it had almost always won. IBM had made an art of defying the past and none of its victims ever accused it of playing fraternal games.

So it was with IBM's personal computer. It was not novel but it was impressive. The Apple II, even as a four-year-old computer, was more elegant than the IBM machine. The Apple was cleverer, it occupied less space on a desk, was nowhere near as heavy, and didn't need a fan. Thanks to the passage of the years IBM's had a better keyboard and more memory. It copied some of the features of the Apple II like expansion slots and graphics.

The most impressive feature of IBM's introduction was not the computer but the nimble way this enormous company had moved. IBM had established a small group to do in thirteen months what Apple had so conspicuously failed to achieve with the Apple III. IBM relied heavily on outsiders. Outsiders were brought in to help plan the product and outsiders supplied software. Microsoft, the company that had licensed a version of BASIC to Apple for the Apple II, developed IBM's operating system. Personal Software adapted Visicalc to run on the IBM, and the men from staid America even dealt with a convicted felon in the shape of retired phone phreak John Draper, who converted his Easywriter word processing which he had originally written for the Apple II. Outsiders supplied the microprocessor, which like those in the Apple II and III (despite IBM's assertions to the contrary) was an eight-bit device. Outsiders supplied the memory chips and printer and disk drive.

IBM, which had always relied on its army of salesmen, also announced that it would sell the personal computer through stores like Computerland and Sears Business Machines stores. The computer base price was between the Apple II and Apple III. As the electronics analyst Ben Rosen remarked, "It seems to be the right system at the right price with the right marketing approach for the right markets."

*   *   *

Neither precedence nor presence seemed to matter at Apple. The company greeted the arrival of the IBM Personal Computer with a full-page advertisement which reeked of earnest goodwill and, some said, condescension: "Welcome IBM. Seriously. Welcome to the most exciting and important marketplace since the computer revolution began 35 years ago. . . . We look forward to responsible competition in the massive effort to distribute this American technology to the world." (It was a politer version of an advertisement that the minicomputer company Data General had contemplated running when IBM entered the minicomputer market in 1976. That advertisement—which never saw the light of day—had read: "The bastards say, welcome.") Some days later Jobs received a letter from IBM chairman John Opel, which thanked him for the greeting and made an oblique reference to the fact that such friendly gestures might cause a cocked eye at federal agencies.

In Cupertino Markkula and Jobs elaborated on their advertisement. Markkula said during the week IBM announced its computer, "We don't see anything out of the ordinary. There are no major technological breakthroughs and there isn't any obvious competitive edge that we can see." Even at the time it was clear that the leaders of Apple were grievously underestimating the power of their new rival. Markkula could barely contain his irritation when asked how Apple planned to respond to IBM. "We've been planning and waiting for IBM to get into the marketplace for four years. We're the guys in the driver's seat. We're the guys with one third of a million installed base. We're the guys with a software library. We're the guys with distribution. It's IBM who is reacting and responding to Apple." He added, "They'll have to do a lot more reacting and responding. IBM hasn't the foggiest notion of how to sell to individuals. It took us four years to learn about it. They must learn about distribution structure and independent dealers. You cannot reduce time by throwing money at it. Short of World War III nothing is going to knock us out of the box." Jobs had his own, clipped appraisal of the IBM announcement and predicted, "We're going to outmarket IBM. We've got our shit together."

"Paradise is a cheeseburger," Jimmy Buffet said.

Like a nervous spinning top Apple's hot-air balloon bobbed alongside an enormous stage. When its gas-burner flared, the balloon tugged at its moorings and the generous Apple logo, stitched on the side, glowed. The balloon was the most visible sign of Apple Computer in the place where Stephen Wozniak was promoting what he wanted to be the largest rock concert ever held. At the end of the summer of 1982 Wozniak financed a grotesquely magnified version of what could have been an outdoor party at his split-level home. His Labor Day weekend rock concert turned into a Disneyland version of Woodstock and had little to do with either computers or companies. It dealt with the thin look of fame, the tinny sound of legend, and with billboard America.

Wozniak erected his rollicking, collapsible monument in a scrofulous desert bowl at the edge of the largest suburb in the world. Here on the doormat of Devore, a little town that nobody noticed apart from its 372 inhabitants, a colony of nudists and drivers who dropped off the freeway for gas or a hunk of watermelon, Wozniak chose to stage his first three-day rock 'n' roll festival.

From the start the concert was a tribute to Wozniak's generous innocence and his steadfast belief in the pleasures of the more abundant life. He had drifted away from Apple, enrolled again at Berkeley, and remarried. He puttered about the Berkeley campus or his shingled home in the Santa Cruz mountains, with its psuedo-wooden turrets and glorious view of Monterey Bay, that he shared with his second wife, four llamas, two donkeys, three Siberian huskies, four mutts, an Australian shepherd and a red-tailed hawk. He equipped the house, which his friends took to calling Woz's Castle, with the amenities of life: a video-game room, wide-screen television, ceiling-high stereo system, and what seemed like an example of every personal computer and peripheral ever made.

Nevertheless, he was bored. The idea for an enormous rock festival offered some distraction. He said that he first thought of it while driving around in his car and listening to a parade of hit records from major rock groups. "I wanted to do something good. I thought, 'Wouldn't it be neat if all these groups could be in one place and play together?'" But he also explained this new venture to his family as a moneymaking enterprise and predicted to his sister that the rock festival would turn a $50-million profit. So Wozniak chose to abandon the comfortable certainty of El Camino Real for the reptilian world of Hollywood Boulevard.

Wozniak rented a plush office suite in a glass building in San Jose and recruited an unlikely team. The man he chose to organize the festival offered credentials that included some references to management consultancy and experience of *est*. Before long they were spitting out press releases announcing the formation of the UNUSON Corporation, an acronym for "Unite Us in Song," and took to preaching a loosely woven gospel that sounded as if it had been lifted from some freshman papers turned in for Mod Psych 101. They said the purpose of the festival was to "refocus national attention on the power of working together." For this, they observed, marked the change from the Me decade to the Us decade. They promised a large technology fair that would show how man and machine could work together.

Wozniak took a small office for himself where he installed an Apple II and some game paddles. Every now and again his hired hands appeared and addressed him in the tones of older brothers arranging a birthday treat for the youngest, slightly spoiled member of the family. He invariably nodded or agreed to their requests. As the US Festival organizers started to place orders for equipment, the only numbers they seemed familiar with ended in strings of zeros. The concert soon turned into a sump for—depending on the month and the mood of the speaker—$8 million, $10 million, or $12 million of Wozniak's Apple fortune.

The people who knew Wozniak treated the US Festival with everything from sadness to alarm. Jobs, who was fond of repeating that it was easier to make a dollar than to give away a dollar, talked about setting up a charitable foundation and did little to conceal his contempt for the enterprise. Jerry Wozniak watched some of his son's television interviews and said that the figure on the screen struck him as "manic." Mark Wozniak treated the shenanigans skeptically: "My brother gets attracted to people who play up to him. People are using him. He'll get screwed over and over. It's the story of his life. Most of the people he gets involved with wind up screwing him." Wozniak's friend Chris Espinosa thought, "As a child and student he was innocent and isolated from the ways of the world. As an adult and millionaire he's still isolated."

For months yellow bulldozers and earthmovers scraped and crushed the mesquite near Devore into a gentle hill. A couple of streams were diverted and underground pipes turned part of the desert bowl into green palmetto. Landfill for parking lots was poured onto the laterite riverbed. Nearby canyons were organized into 100,000 campsites. Scores of turquoise-colored portable toilets were trucked in to serve as mobile sewers. Shower trucks, with boiling water and little shelves for the shampoo, were brought in for the press.

Tiger-striped marquees crammed with army cots housed security guards and the concession-stand workers. By the time the festival got under way and thousands of cars and buses began to peel off the specially constructed freeway exits, there was an example of every means of locomotion that had ever been seen on El Camino Real. Apart from automobiles—heavy on the Hondas, Datsuns (the official car of the US Festival), and Toyotas—there were motorcycles, sidecars, two-wheel dirt bikes, three-wheel dirt bikes, Cushman golf carts, flat bed trucks, Winnebagos, six-pak vans, Airstream caravans, bulldozers, backhoes, tractors, forklift trucks, semis and water dumpsters.

From the start Wozniak wanted to make sure that nobody had to wait more than five minutes for food. So the grounds were turned into an outdoor suburban shopping center. Beer gardens were stacked with brown bags of ice and canisters of bottled air. There was an official domestic beer and an official imported beer. Concession stands had munchies: M&M's, granola bars, trail mix, gum, and smokes. There were watermelons, pineapples, strawberries, nuts, cookies, New York-style pizza, hamburgers, chili dogs, hot dogs, Polish dogs, burritos, tacos, soda, lemonade, 7-Up, Coca-Cola and Pepsi-Cola. "Paradise," as Jimmy Buffet, one of the performers, observed, "is a cheeseburger."

The suburban shopping-center pharmacy also moved in. The thousands of concertgoers could buy toothpaste, soap, sunglasses, insect repellent, and sunscreen from the back of rental trucks. It took sunscreen to conjure up the ghost of another decade. For when the rock producer urged the crowd to be generous, he resorted to that deft friendly phrase of the sixties: "If you've got some sunscreen, share it with your brother and sister."

There was also a bumpy pyramid of law and order. Signs at the entrance gates were darn right upright: NO DRUGS,

BOTTLES, CANS, WEAPONS OR PETS ALLOWED. NO TENTS, SLEEPING BAGS OR LAWN CHAIRS. ALL PERSONS SUBJECT TO SEARCH. Dozens of men from the San Bernardino County Sheriffs Department (in helicopters and patrol cars and on horseback and motorcycles) kept an eye on things. One of a team of policemen from Southern Pacific explained that he was "here to protect the railroad." Scores of hastily recruited blue-shirted security guards, the neighborhood vigilante gang, enforced their own amateur brand of justice and guarded the strategic gates in miles of chain-link fences. All the emphasis on security had its drawbacks—a shifting, baffling collection of carefully colored and painfully coded security badges and laminated passes. The passes Wozniak programmed on his computer for his friends weren't even recognized.

There was more lavish treatment for the rock bands and the press than for the teeming masses. The bands—over twenty by the time all the contracts were signed—had quibbled about terms and demanded extraordinary sums when word trickled out that Wozniak's pocket was well-nigh bottomless. Most said that it was another date, another gig, another day, and giggled at the mention of the US decade. Behind the stage the bands stayed in air-conditioned trailers hidden by varnished lattice fences. Their names were carved in Gothic script on wooden nameplates that hung on each door, and their needs were catered to by a squad of runners working out of another trailer marked AMBIENCE CONTROL which was a glorified room service. Outside the trailers, crowds of press agents, managers, business managers, personal managers—every sort of manager—fussed, complained, and argued.

Even the sky was for sale. A makeshift air-traffic-control tower ordered an eclectic collection of aerial objects to fly in counterclockwise circles. Some ultragliders putt-putted like underpowered motor scooters with wings. A couple of parachutists dropped in. At noon on the opening day of the festival five Mosquitoes ripped five white tubular trails across the sky. Little planes coughed and towed banners touting automobile insurance, sweat shirts, and cheap air fares to Honolulu. Below the busy air lanes a sheriff radioed to his pal in a helicopter, "There's a low-flying fixed wing in the bowl area. Just want to make sure you're aware of it." At night the Goodyear blimp, in a mosaic of lights, winked WHAT A BIG TIME, THANKS WOZ. Twenty-four hours a day helicopters officiously ferried the rock stars and their groupies from a soft, steaming patch of blacktop to hotels that lay west of Rancho Cucamonga and Cucamonga.

The technology fair fell victim to the heat and the dust. It was no traveling Homebrew Club or West Coast Computer Faire. Some exhibitors failed to show; others found that their machines weren't designed to cope with the full might of Southland weather. Many of the visitors seemed to be as interested in the heaving air conditioners that struggled to cool the marquees as in the exhibition. There were some cheap examples of the power of technology, like the banks of telephones and the Walkmans and the women plugging their curling tongs into the electric cables that ran inside some of the theater-sized marquees.

But the triumph of technology was displayed late one night when three men were setting up a demonstration of a television satellite dish. They used a microcomputer to calculate the pitch and tilt needed to find a satellite floating twenty-five thousand miles high and monitored the results of their efforts on a color television. They adjusted the dish, skipping from one invisible satellite to another, until they found what they wanted: a Los Angeles porn television channel bouncing a signal more than fifty thousand miles so that three men in the California desert could watch a naked black woman perform cunnilingus on her equally bare, white, female partner. It was, at least, a marriage of community and technology and the festival organizers would not have been surprised to learn that the women worked well together.

Many of the two hundred thousand or so people (nobody was all that sure of the numbers) who spilled into the beer gardens, soaked under outdoor showers, sprayed each other with plastic mister-bottles, and wallowed in the drenching drafts of a water cannon, seemed to enjoy themselves. Those who had a way with words called the US Festival one big party, though they made it sound like *purdee*. Those who liked adjectives thought it one big, fuggin purdee. Many said they had come to purdee, to have a good time, a ball, and a blast. The US Festival was: Neat. Great. Incredible. Fantastic. Unbelievable. Amazing. Like Wow.

The altar of this vast affair was a stage cast in empyreal proportions that would have done justice to Cecil B. De Mille. A pair of three-story-high video screens served as the outer panels of the tryptych. The crowning glory was another screen, the sort used for instant replays in baseball stadiums, perched half a skyscraper high above the well of the stage. In the bowels of the stage roadhands and stage crew operated elevators and movable platforms and bounced up steep flights of steps tugging racks of guitars, portable wardrobes, and steel trunks crammed with the paraphernalia of rock groups. Out in the desert bowl, black banks of loudspeakers sent four hundred thousand watts bouncing around the San Bernardino and San Gabriel mountains, and cameras filmed the action for cable television syndication. Laser beams struck across the night sky, arrogantly sketching electronic patterns across sleepy black clouds. All the gadgetry and noise seemed like cosmographic versions of the videotape recorders, wide-screen televisions, stereo systems and video games that had crept into Wozniak's own home. Wobbling alongside the stage was the Apple balloon that in the hubbub looked strangely innocent and quietly forgotten.

Presiding over the entire concert was Bill Graham, a San Francisco rock promoter: a chunk of irascible threats who, dressed in denim cutoffs, T-shirt, and basketball boots, yelled until the veins in his neck bulged and the spittle in his throat dried but comandeered the festival. He jabbed the air with his fists, flexed his muscles, and later said that Wozniak was a tragic figure. When he slipped on stage between acts he asked for a big welcome for a grrrrade, grrrrade band, for a grrrrade artist, a grrrrade rock 'n' roller and hailed these three grrrade days of grrrade, grrade rock 'n' roll.

All the virtues Wozniak had combined in the Apple Computer were absent. This was sledgehammer action and there was no hint of obscurity, no sense of subtlety and little discrimination. Perhaps the festival sprang from some desire to amuse and entertain; perhaps it was nothing more than a spectacularly conspicuous expression of vanity. It was certainly a freeze frame of celebrity-riddled America. In a white press tent two hundred reporters, photographers, and television cameramen waited for Wozniak. There were journalists from the television networks, cable television stations, dozens of radio stations, daily newspapers, weekly magazines, rock 'n' roll journals, and the computer trade press. They represented a mad welter of well-known names, and while they waited for a press conference they poked at trays of food, phoned reports to friends and editors, and swatted at the wasps that hovered around soft-drink cans, garbage pails, and trays of half-eaten food.

They waited for Wozniak to descend from a house that he had rented on a hill overlooking the festival grounds and used as a base for excursions in a long, black limousine. The journalists all waited for a line, a quote, a picture, or a close-up. They ruffled through steno pads, tightened tripods and monopods, and fiddled with cassette and microcassette recorders. A stream of leads led to a hedge of microphones and tape recorders, and when Wozniak arrived, ducking under a canvas flap, the tent ballooned to life. A bowl of Nikons, Canons, Pentaxes snapped and clicked. There was pushing and jostling and elbowing. The curved wall of cameras slid forward. A table collapsed and there were loud shrieks. The motor drives whirred, slapping image after image onto roll after roll of film. There were shouts and whistles. "Keep it down. . . . For chrissake, shuddup. . . . Quiet. . . . Quiet. . . . Woz! . . . Woz! . . ."—and all the while there was pushing and elbowing to get better pictures and angles. Sitting behind a table between the rock promoter and the graduate of Erhard Seminars Training, Wozniak wore a baseball cap that was set at a cockeyed angle, a T-shirt, shorts, and socks and grinned like an admonished schoolboy. He was spattered with a sad, repetitive, empty loop of questions: "How much money you lost? . . . How many people are here? . . . Why d'you do this?"

EPILOGUE

More than a quarter of a century has passed since I wrote the previous page on an Apple III computer. In 1984, as the first edition of this book made its way to the press, I received several letters from the publisher—those being the days before email had become the universal telegraph system—expressing anxiety that Apple's day in the sun might already have passed. The apprehension was understandable. The hullabaloo surrounding the introduction of the Macintosh—trumpeted with an Orwellian television commercial on Superbowl Sunday 1984—had evaporated, and the notices had turned sour. IBM's personal computer business was gaining strength. Compaq had reached $100 million in sales faster than any previous company and Microsoft's operating system, DOS, was winning licensees by the month. There were plenty of reasons to think that Apple was teetering.

Twenty five years later, when people are as familiar with the names iPod, iPhone, or Macintosh as they are Apple, it is hard, particularly for those reared on cell phones and social networks, to imagine a time when the company appeared to be just another technology firm that would be snuffed out or absorbed by a competitor.

Since 1984, there have been plenty of technology companies that have faded to grey or gone to black, and it's remarkably easy to come up with an alphabetical list for these casualties that runs from A to Z.

The letter "A" alone includes Aldus, Amiga, Ashton-Tate, AST and Atari. As for the rest of the alphabet there's always Borland, Cromemco, Digital Research, Everex, Farallon, Gavilan, Healthkit, Integrated Micro Solutions, Javelin Software, KayPro, Lotus Development, Mattel, Northstar Computers, Osborne Computer, Pertec, Quarterdeck, Radius, Software Publishing, Tandy, Univel, VectorGraphic, Victor, WordPerfect, Xywrite and Zenith Data Systems. The large technology companies that have weathered these decades—IBM and HP—have done so in areas far removed from personal computing. IBM, once the company that others in the personal computer industry feared, has even surrendered its franchise to the Chinese company Lenovo.

The mortality rate makes Apple's survival—let alone prosperity—even more remarkable. I've watched Apple, first as a journalist and later as an investor, for most of my adult life. Journalists suffer from the malady of not forgetting a topic that once interested them. I'm no different. But a couple of years after I finished writing this book I found myself, thanks to some twists of fates, working at Sequoia Capital, the private investment partnership whose founder, Don Valentine, had helped assemble some of the formative blocks on which Apple was built. Since then, as an investor in young technology and growth private companies in China, India, Israel and the U.S., I have developed a keener sense for the massive gulf that separates the few astonishing enterprises from the thousands that are lucky to scratch out an asterisk in the footnotes of history books.

In 1984, if most consumers had been asked to predict which company—SONY or Apple—would play a greater role in their lives, I wager most would have voted for the former. SONY's success rested on two powerful forces: the restless drive of its founder, Akio Morita, and the miniaturization of electronics and products consumers yearned for. The Japanese company, which had been formed in 1946, had built up a following as a designer and maker of imaginative and reliable consumer electronic products: transistor radios, televisions, tape recorders and, in the 1970s and 1980s, video recorders, video cameras and the WalkMan, the first portable device to make music available anywhere at any time of day. Like the iPod, a generation later, the Walkman bore the stamp of the company's founder. It was created in a few months during 1979, it built its following largely by word of mouth and in the two decades prior to the advent of mp3 players sold over 250 million units. Now, as everyone knows, the tables have been turned and some years ago a cruel joke circulated which spelled out the change in circumstances, "How do you spell SONY?" The answer: "A-P-P-L-E."

This begs the question of how Apple came to outrun SONY, but the more interesting topic is how the company came to rattle the bones of mighty industries and has forced music impresarios, movie producers, cable television owners, newspaper proprietors, printers, telephone operators, yellow page publishers and old line retailers to quaver. None of this seemed possible in 1984 when Ronald Reagan was President, half of American households tuned into the three television networks, U.S. morning newspaper circulation peaked at 63 million; LPs and cassette tapes outsold CDs by a margin of ninety to one; the Motorola DynaTAC 8000x cell phone weighed two pounds had thirty minutes of talk time and cost almost $4,000; Japan's MITI was feared in the West; and the home of advanced manufacturing was Singapore.

Three mighty currents have flowed in Apple's favor, but these waters were also navigable by other crews. The first swept electronics deeper into every nook and cranny of daily life so that now there is almost no place on earth beyond the reach of a computer or the bewildering collection of phones and entertainment devices with which we are surrounded. The second has made it possible for companies born in the era of the personal computer to develop consumer products. It has been far easier for computer companies with refined software sensibilities to design consumer products than for those whose lineage was consumer electronics and whose expertise lay largely in hardware design and manufacturing prowess. It's not a coincidence that some of the companies with the acutest envy towards Apple have names like Samsung, Panasonic, LG, Dell, Motorola and, of course, SONY. The third current was "cloud computing"—the idea that much of the computation, storage and security associated with popular software sits in hundreds of thousands of machines in factory-sized data centers. This is the computer architecture that, in the mid 1990s, supported services such as Amazon, Yahoo! eBay, Hotmail and Expedia and later came to underpin Google and the Apple services that light up Macs, iPods and iPhones. Today, for the first time, consumers—not businesses or governments—enjoy the fastest, most reliable and most secure computer services.

In 1984 more immediate and mundane challenges confronted Apple. Faced with the challenge of managing a fast growing company in an increasingly competitive business, the Board of Directors of Apple, were faced with the most important task that confronts any board: selecting a person to run the company. Mike Markkula, who had joined Jobs and Wozniak in 1976, had made no secret of the fact that he had little appetite for life as Apple's long-term CEO. Thus the Board, which included Steve Jobs, had to decide what course to take. This decision—and three similar decisions over the ensuing thirteen years—shaped Apple's future.

Only in retrospect have I come to understand the immense risk associated with hiring an outsider—let alone a person from a different industry—to run a company whose path has been heavily influenced by the determination and ferocity of its founder or founders. It is not an accident that most of the great companies of yesterday and today have, during their heydays, been run or controlled by the people who gave then life. The message is the same irrespective of industry, era or country and the name can be Ford, Standard Oil, Chrysler, Kodak, Hewlett-Packard, WalMart, Fedex, Intel, Microsoft, NewsCorp, Nike, Infosys, Disney, Oracle, IKEA, Amazon, Google, Baidu or Apple. The founder, acting with an owner's instincts, will have the confidence, authority and skills to lead. Sometimes, when the founder's instincts are wrong, this leads to ruin. But when they are right, nobody else comes close.

When corporate boards start to have misgivings about the condition of a company or the ability of the founder and have no plausible internal candidate, they will almost always make the wrong move. They usually need to make a decision about a CEO when a company is barreling towards a fall, emotions are raw, testosterone levels are running high and, particularly in a company as visible as Apple, when every employee, analyst, smart-aleck and naysayer is ready to dispense advice. At Apple in 1985 the Board's decision was complicated by the fact that there was no obvious successor within the company. Jobs was considered too young and immature, and for his part, he knew that he needed help if Apple was to achieve the $10 billion sales level he had already started to dream about. The oppressive weight of conventional wisdom tilted the quest towards a résumé dripping with impressive-sounding titles and credentials. But experience—particularly when it's been acquired in a different industry—is of little use in a young, fast-growing company in a new business that has a different pulse and unfamiliar rhythm. Experience is the safe choice, but is often the wrong one.

After a lengthy search, Apple's board announced that John Sculley would be the company's new Chief Executive. Sculley was unknown in Silicon Valley, which was hardly surprising since he had spent his entire business career at Pepsi Cola where, in his final job, he had run its soft-drinks business, PepsiCo. Sculley's arrival in Cupertino was greeted with the demeaning commentary that Apple (and Jobs) "needed adult supervision." This is the very last thing that rare and wonderful founders need. These rare sorts of people may require help, they will certainly benefit from assistance and there may be plenty of things that are new or foreign to them. But the appearance of a boss, particularly one with little experience of technology and the brutish rough and tumble of a company in its formative years, will almost certainly end in misery.

At Apple, Sculley was greeted like an archangel and, for a time, could do no wrong. He and Jobs were quoted as saying that they could finish each others' sentences. In hindsight it is fairly easy to say that it would be almost impossible for a man like Sculley, reared within the confines of an established East Coast company selling soft drinks and snacks, to flourish in a business where product life cycles are measured in quarters, if not months, and where cowing to convention marks the start of the death rattle. It is easier for a founder, particularly when surrounded by people with different experiences, to learn about management than for a manager from a large company to master the nuances and intricacies of an entirely new business—especially if that happens to be a technology company.

Within less than two years familiarity began to breed contempt—a situation complicated by the fact that while Sculley bore the CEO title, Jobs was the Chairman of the company. Disagreements occurred. Sniping and backbiting broke out and the dissension became so intense that in 1987 Sculley, disgruntled, displeased, exasperated and exhausted by Jobs, orchestrated the latter's dismissal from the company. Sculley's tenure at Apple lasted until 1993, and for part of that time the external reviews, at least as posted by Wall Street analysts, were favorable.

In the decade Sculley spent at Apple sales grew from less than $1 billion a year to more than $8 billion a year. On the surface, this looks like a wonderful record. But the reality was far different. Sculley benefited from a powerful force—the massive demand for personal computers. This sort of market growth conceals all types of shortcomings, and it is only when the rate of change slows or the economy contracts that the real cracks become visible.

During Sculley's time at Apple, the company was outgunned by the brute force of IBM, then by the cunning maneuvering of the industry's arms merchant, Microsoft, which made the operating system that it had licensed to IBM available to all comers. This led to a proliferation of what were labeled "IBM compatibles"—some made by startups like Compaq, others by established players like DEC and still more from cost-conscious Taiwanese companies such as Acer. These machines shared two traits: the hardware was built around microprocessors from Intel, and their operating systems were furnished by Microsoft. Apple, in the meantime, counted on chips from Motorola (and later IBM) and had to labor hard to convince programmers to write software for the Macintosh, whose market share dwindled as the years slipped by. Apple was fighting on two fronts with weak allies against the vast budget of Intel—in an industry where engineering and capital counted for a lot—and the legions of programmers who had discovered they could build a business atop Microsoft DOS and its successor operating system, Windows. Part of Sculley's response was to gradually increase Apple's prices in an effort to maintain profit margins—a ploy that propped up earnings for a while but eventually foundered.

While pesky newcomers attacked, inventiveness withered inside Apple. The company that had led the industry with color on the Apple II, a graphical user interface with the Macintosh, desktop publishing and laser printing, integrated networks, and stereo sound stopped leading. As Sculley departed, amidst a flurry of recrimination prompted by his affection for the limelight and dalliance with the national stage, the cupboard was bare. The spark of imagination, or, more particularly, the ability to transform a promising idea into an appealing product, had been extinguished.

Apple introduced no meaningful new products in the decade
Sculley spent at the helm. The computers that did appear bore
sterile names such as Performa, Centris and Quadra. Computers
with more memory, larger screens and bigger disk drives do not
count for lifetime achievement awards. The Newton, a small,
digital organizer championed by Sculley in his self-appointed role
as Apple's Chief Technology Officer, amounted to little more than
an expensive doorstop. In an autobiography, published in 1987,
Sculley—in what now seems like a very accurate assessment about
the gulf between his capabilities and the Founder he displaced—
savaged Jobs' ideas of the future by writing, "Apple was supposed
to become a wonderful consumer products company. This was
a lunatic plan. High tech could not be designed and sold as a
consumer product."

When Sculley was fired, Apple was in peril. Windows 3.0,
introduced by Microsoft in 1990, was not as elegant as the
Macintosh software, but it was good enough. As Sculley returned
to the East Coast, Apple's market share had eroded, its margins
had collapsed; the best young engineers were inclined to apply for
openings at companies such as Microsoft, Silicon Graphics or Sun
Microsystems.

By the time Sculley departed, Apple's board had degenerated.
The people who had been major owners of the company and had
a vested interest in its success had been replaced by an odd cast.
This troupe was almost certainly bolted together by a nominating
committee eager to demonstrate political correctness by assembling a board composed of people with different experiences and
backgrounds. Over the course of forty-eight months in the mid-
1990s, the Board included the company's own Chief Financial
Officer, a person who had built a riverboat gaming company, the
CEO of an enormous European packaging company, the head of
National Public Radio, and an executive from Hughes Electronics
and StarTV. None of these people had experience in the personal
computer industry, none had worked for any time in Silicon
Valley, none knew the others well and none, with the excep-
tion of Markulla, had a major economic or emotional interest
in Apple. It is hard to imagine that they thought of themselves,
let alone acted, as owners. If there were any bond tying them
together it was probably the desire to avoid embarrassment.
It's little wonder they made two terrible selections, each of whom

was more suited to be a corporate undertaker than an imaginative leader.

The first, Michael Spindler, was a European whose business life, prior to Apple, had consisted of stints at DEC and Intel, where he had been a marketing strategist. As CEO he continued efforts begun by Sculley to sell Apple—with IBM, Sun Microsystems and Philips as his principal targets—and debating whether to license the Macintosh operating system to other manufacturers. An alliance with IBM and Motorola—the sort of convoluted corporate lash-up which in the world of technology never amounts to anything—was supposed to slow Microsoft by marrying Apple software to microprocessors made by the other two companies. In 1996, after less than three years as CEO, Spindler was ushered to the exit. The eight-person Board, without surveying outside candidates, turned to a fellow director, Gil Amelio, and charged him with rejuvenating Apple. Though Amelio liked to be referred to as Doctor (for his PhD in Physics), it was obvious, even before his appointment, that he was not the sort of medicine-man the patient needed.

While Apple shriveled, Steve Jobs endured his wilderness years—an arduous, painful journey that, in retrospect, was probably the best thing that ever happened to him. After being banished from Apple, he sold all but one share of his stock and, aged 30, cast about for a new beginning. In 1986 he bought Pixar, a 44-person company which was owned by the creator of Star Wars, George Lucas, and had developed a small reputation for making computer-aided animation systems. Jobs was largely interested in the influence Pixar's technology could have on personal computers. But for Jobs, Pixar was not the main event. In 1985 he formed a new computer company which, with characteristic elegance and symbolism, he named NeXT. There began a tortured tale which culminated at the end of 1996 with the most unlikely of endings: an acquisition by Apple.

Between NeXT's formation and its sale lay many sagas. The company showed how difficult it is for anyone to start another company after enjoying extraordinary success with a first. Jobs was a victim of his fame and notoriety and, instead of recalling all the lessons of Apple's first year (when money was tight, resources strained, survival always a question, and a workbench in his parents' garage the production line) his first acts at NeXT seemed like a continuation of life at a $1 billion company.

Paul Rand designed NeXT's corporate logo just as he had done for IBM, ABC and UPS; I.M. Pei, the high priest of modernist architecture, was commissioned to build a floating staircase (echoes of which showed up years later in many apple stores), and Ross Perot, Stanford University and others (including Jobs) supplied the start-up capital at a valuation roughly equivalent to what was awarded Microsoft at the time of its 1986 IPO.

As NeXT evolved into a maker of corporate workstations, Jobs was taken out of his natural milieu. Instead of conjuring up ideas for products millions of consumers could use, he found himself consigned to a market in which purchasing decisions are made by committees who aren't rewarded for making adventurous choices; where competitors such as Sun, Silicon Graphics, IBM, Hewlett-Packard and, of course, Microsoft wasted no opportunity to heap scorn; and where an expensive sales force is required to make inroads into customers. The black, cube shaped computer, which fell victim to terrible delays—one of the many curses that imperil an over-financed start-up—soon found itself along other Jobs-inspired products in New York's Museum of Modern Art. Customers were less impressed. NeXT's founding team gradually got burned out by the strain and the scent of failure. In 1993, Jobs threw in the towel on the systems business and attempted to convert NeXT into a software business—a strategy that invariably is the harbinger of doom for any computer company.

By 1996, both NeXT and Apple had petered out. Jobs had been relegated to a cameo act in the computer business, although his tenacity and patience at Pixar had paid off. Nine years after his purchase of the company, the release of the animated picture *Toy Story* and a subsequent IPO gave the company the financial staying power to cope with the muscle of its exclusive distribution partner, Disney (which, a decade later, bought the company for $7.4 billion, thereby making Steve Jobs its largest individual shareholder since Walt Disney himself).

Then, almost like a chapter out of a nineteenth century Victorian romance, Jobs, getting wind of Apple's interest in purchasing Be, a company started by a former Apple executive, convinced Amelio that he was better advised to purchase NeXT and use its prowess with the UNIX operating system as the software foundation of Apple's future. Amelio voted for NeXT, bought the company for $430 million in cash, gave Jobs 1.5 million shares of stock and thus, unwittingly, issued his own exit visa. There followed an awkward period during which Jobs announced that he was only interested in advising Amelio and taking care of Pixar. His sale of all but one of his recently awarded Apple shares registered his real opinion of Amelio. Less than three quarters after NeXT became part of Apple, Amelio was replaced by Jobs, who was appointed interim CEO. This provoked cackling and headlines that sounded like obituary notices: "How did this mess happen? The untold story of Apple's demise" and "Rotten to the Core" were just two of the messages splattered across the front of national magazines. Michael Dell, then one of the darlings of the personal computer industry, posed a rhetorical question about Apple in the fall of 1997: "What would I do? I'd shut it down and give the money back to the shareholders."

Steve Jobs had been weathered by his years in the wilderness. His battle with NeXT had taught him to to cope with dire circumstances and his experience in the animation business at Pixar was as the CEO of the world's most technologically advanced creative company. The Apple he inherited in the fall of 1997 had lost its creative zest and leadership position in the technology industry, was almost out of cash, was unable to recruit bright young engineers, was drowning in inventory of unsold computers and had nothing imaginative in the works. Jobs was unromantic. The marketing department, eager to announce a change for the better, wanted to run ads that said "We're back!" Jobs would brook none of it.

Instead, he rolled out an advertising campaign labeled, "Think different," based on a series of black-and-white photographs of remarkable individuals. A couple of iconoclastic businessmen were billboarded, but they were heavily outnumbered by the artistic and inventive. There were musicians (Bob Dylan, Maria Callas and Louis Armstrong), artists (Picasso and Dalí), an architect (Frank Lloyd Wright), charismatic leaders (Mahatma Gandhi and Martin Luther King), scientists (Einstein and Edison), movie makers (Jim Henson), dancers (Martha Graham), and an adventurer (Amelia Earhart). The campaign was a rallying cry, but it was also a keen expression of the artistic, sensuous, romantic, mystical, inquisitive, seductive, austere and theatrical side of the Jobs—adjectives not usually associated with the leader of a technology company. It was these attributes that eventually came to be expressed in Apple's products, which Jobs turned into objects of desire.

The advertising campaign was simple and direct, which perhaps had more significance inside the company than outside. It said, in plain terms, that the company could not afford to mimic others but needed to forge its own path. Jobs also forced the company to act differently. He cut costs, forced substantial layoffs, killed entire product lines he deemed worthless, undifferentiated or insipid, such as printers or the Newton. He stopped licensing the Macintosh operating system to other manufacturers, limited the distribution of Apple products to all but the most rabid of its dealers, installed five of his executives from NeXT as pillars of his management team while keeping Fred Anderson as Chief Financial Officer, jettisoned most of the discredited board of directors and replaced them with practical, hard-knuckled people he trusted, engineered a $150 million investment from Microsoft (that simultaneously ended years of legal bickering between the two companies, beefed up Apple's cash position, and ensured the Internet Explorer browser a prominent place on Macintosh computers) and, within ten months, introduced a fresh line of Macintosh computers with his customary flirtatious flair. One year later, in the fall of 1998, Apple reported annual sales of almost $6 billion and a profit of more than $300 million, compared to sales of $7.1 billion and a loss of $1 billion at the time he took the helm.

Despite Jobs' helmsmanship, the pop of the dotcom bubble, the recession of 2001 and the Mac's small market share meant that Apple was still battling against the tide. Leaks had been caulked, useless crew members had been made to walk the plank, worthless cargo had been tossed overboard, but the vessel's course had not been altered. This was reflected in the losses of 2001, the first red ink in three years. It was against this perilous backdrop that the iPod and Apple's stores were birthed—both born of necessity and the sense that the company could not count on the kindness of others to foster its growth. Independent software developers, including companies such as Adobe, which had helped Apple create the desktop publishing market, were beginning to abandon the Macintosh; retailers, particularly the large stores, were either ignoring or neglecting Apple's products. Jobs and his management team resisted the temptation to make large acquisitions—the normal way that large companies tend to try to escape testing times and which, almost always, starts with slide presentations promising the moon but ends with write-offs and recrimination.

If Apple's leaders uncovered a small product or promising team that could be quickly made productive and folded into an existing or nascent effort, they pounced. But for real growth they relied on their own wit and ingenuity.

The first example of Apple's desire to fend for itself came with iMovie, software designed to help consumers manage and edit video, an application that, hitherto, might have been supplied by Adobe. Jobs' conviction that video was the company's freedom ticket meant Apple was almost blind-sided by the dawn of the digital music business. While Apple was presenting consumers with video software, tens of millions of people were discovering that music was available all around the internet. Websites such as Napster and Kazaa roused the ire of music publishers and record companies, but these spots on the internet, when combined with hundreds of models of portable mp3 players, spelled a new chapter for the distribution of entertainment.

It was against this change in consumers' habits that the iPod was conceived and rushed to market at a pace similar to the manner in which Sony's Walkman had arrived a generation earlier. It went from start to store shelves in less than eight months—a madcap effort to buoy Apple's flagging sales during the 2001 holiday season. The iPod, which at first only worked with Macintosh computers, had a novel user interface—a dial that helped people sift through their music libraries—and a much longer battery life than most mp3 players. Buried inside was its most important feature: a compact version of a UNIX operating system that meant this innocent-looking device contained as much computing power as many laptops. In 2003, while the music labels bickered and dallied, Apple introduced the first legal music online service and replaced the notion of an album with the reality of a track.

In the same year in which the iPod was introduced, Apple opened its first retail store a few miles from the Atlantic coast in Tyson's Corner, Virginia. Later that same day, the second store opened near the Pacific Coast in Glendale, California. The stores were another expression of the need for Apple to take charge of its destiny. For most, this looked like a desperate measure, particularly since there were so few examples beyond the worlds of fashion or cosmetics of manufacturers becoming successful retailers. Apple's approach to retailing was influenced by the success of another Northern Californian company, The Gap.

Jobs had become a director of the company and, in turn, Mickey Drexler, the merchant who led The Gap during its decade-long rise, joined the Apple board. The first Apple store revealed a merchant's virtuosity. Computers, software and consumer electronic devices were displayed in an atmosphere that was like a breath of fresh, California coastal air.

The iPod and Apple's stores struck chords with consumers, and the company's management pounced on the opportunities with the thirst and relish of indefatigable and experienced travelers finally reaching an oasis. Variants of the iPod were introduced as quickly as possible and within forty-eight months it had been transformed from a 5GB monochrome device to a 60GB color player. When any model showed signs of wear, Apple's management resisted the opportunity to milk the last drop of sales and, instead, replaced it with something better.

The same sort of touch was applied to the stores with their Genius bars and roving sales assistants armed with wireless credit-card terminals. Apple's U.S. flagship store, which opened on Manhattan's Fifth Avenue in 2006, five years to the day after first two stores opened, was the apogee. Here, on the plaza in front of what was once another symbol of American success, the GM building, floated a glass cube in which Apple's illuminated logo was suspended. The frame for the cube was made from hand-blasted Japanese steel, pietra serena stone lined the floors and there, twenty-four hours a day, throngs of people of all ages and backgrounds came to wander, ogle, browse and shop. Apple's stores reached $1 billion in retail sales faster than any other company and by 2007 its sales per square foot—the shorthand measure of any retailer's health—was more than ten times larger than Saks, four times greater than Best Buy, and even handily outstripped Tiffany.

Inevitably, Apple's progress was marred by blemishes. There were the occasional product miscues: a Macintosh housed in a clear plastic cube that developed hairline surface cracks, lame versions of the iPod introduced with Motorola and Hewlett-Packard, battery packs in laptop machines that over-heated and an occasional product, like the first version of Apple TV, that fell far short of expectations. Later a contretemps erupted over stock options, in particular, two large grants made to Steve Jobs in 2000 and 2001 and which he surrendered in 2003. These, and some more made to other executives, attracted the attention of the SEC, stirred up the whiff of impropriety and occupied the business press. But nothing came to threaten Apple as much as Steve Jobs' health when it was disclosed in 2004 that he had been operated on for pancreatic cancer.

Rumors about Apple's encore to the iPod had been in the air long before Steve Jobs used one of his hallmark solo shows in San Francisco in 2007 to introduce the company's riff on hand-held computing. Though it was dubbed the iPhone, the device Jobs introduced was not a conventional cell phone or mp3 player, was far removed from a personal digital assistant and did not bear too many resemblances to a portable game device. The same day the iPhone was introduced, the word "computer" was dropped from the company's name, which was shortened to Apple, Inc.—a sign of how far the company had traveled in the previous years.

The iPhone was a glorious expression of Apple's approach to product design. It did not start with laborious research, focus groups or the acquisition of another company with a hot product. It began with a few people trying to design a product they would want to use and be proud to own. Like many previous products conceived under Jobs' leadership, this required taking a close look at the short-comings of existing products, adapting ideas from others and melding them into something that, by 2007, could only have come from Apple. Such was the allure and romance of being associated with Apple that AT&T management signed up, on draconian terms, to be the exclusive U.S. distributor for the iPhone with barely a glimpse of the product. While the advertisements, commercials or press reports would frequently employ the term "revolutionary" to describe the iPhone and other Apple products, they were *evolutionary*—exquisite refinements of the half-baked ideas and products full of compromises and shortcomings that other companies had prematurely rushed onto store shelves.

The iPhone appeared simple. It fired up immediately. It was housed in a case less than 12 millimeters thick and could connect to any machine—from a supercomputer to a smoke detector—that was hooked up to the internet. But simplicity, especially elegant simplicity, is deceptively difficult. Jobs' magisterial achievement, one that has few, if any, precedents, was to ensure that a tech-nology company employing tens of thousands of people could make and sell millions of immensely complicated yet exquisite products that were powerful and reliable and while also containing a lightness of being. This is Apple's triumph. It is one thing for an individual—Matisse with a line, Henry Moore with a shape, W.H. Auden with a phrase, Copland with a bar, Chanel with a cut—to express themselves. It is another matter entirely for the germ of an idea to be developed, refined, reshaped, molded, tuned, altered and rejected again and again before it is considered perfect enough to be reproduced in the millions. It is another matter too to steer, coax, nudge, prod, cajole, inspire, berate, organize and praise—on weekdays and weekends—the thousands of people all around the world required to produce something that drops into pockets and handbags, or in the case of a computer, rests on a lap or sits on a desk.

The iPhone, in some respects, came to be a throwback to the beginning of Apple and the way in which software developers all over the world had been encouraged to write programs for the Apple II. In a fashion that had not occurred since Microsoft had developed an army of software mercenaries trooping after its DOS and Windows operating systems, the iPhone ignited an explosion of interest from programmers around the world so that now tens of thousands of applications, from the life-saving to frivolous, can be bought with the tap of a finger from Apple's AppStore.

Sales of Apple's Macintosh computers are now outstripped by products that were not even imagined, let alone conceived, at the turn of this century. The popularity of the iPod and iPhone and the accessibility of Apple's retail store have rejuvenated sales of Macintosh computers, which were also helped by a shift to Intel microprocessors and the constant refinement of its operating system, which has developed a reputation for being more stable and secure than Windows. The overall results are extraordinary, testament to perhaps the most creative industrial turnaround in the history of America. At the end of Jobs' decade running Apple, an era during which the growth of the personal computer industry had slowed to a pedestrian pace, its sales had risen from $6 billion to $32.5 billion and the price of its stock had, at its peak, multiplied forty-fold.

During a period when so much was fictitious, when there were so many empires built on air and when frauds were uncloaked, Apple stands is an emblem for daring, ingenuity and enterprise. When so much was piled atop mountains of debt, it is reassuring to know that real earnings and tangible profits can be used to invest in the future. When weak companies scurry to Washington to bleat for Federal bailout money, it is a tonic to realize that nothing is more effective than the spirit of a restless company threatened with extinction. When so many mathematicians and scientists caught the scent of Wall Street and used their skills to construct futile risk models, it was delightful to know that some of their contemporaries had spurned the lure of Manhattan high-rises and, instead, had chosen to write code or program chips, without which Apple's devices would never have materialized. When entry visas and work permits were being refused to the brightest from overseas, it was all the more meaningful to see that Apple's engineering ranks were teeming with immigrants and first-generation Americans. When other companies had rushed new products into the market with scarcely a nod to design and finish, it was a relief to see a demonstration that aesthetics and attention to detail really make a difference. If ever there was a company that demonstrated an application of the exhortation "Yes we can," it was the Apple of the last ten years.

As with all books about business, this has been a tale of yesterday and today. And, as with all stories of success, this has been a triumph of human will. Now lies tomorrow. No technology company has ever been able to consistently produce great consumer products for half a century. So for Apple there is the inevitable question, *what comes next*? Can it continue to produce encore performances? Will the corpus always think and act differently? At a time of fears and concerns for Steve Jobs' health following the disclosure of his liver transplant, it's natural to wonder who might someday succeed the man whose identity and fate is so closely tied to the company? How will Apple avoid the fate of SONY following the retirement of Akio Morita? Will Apple's next chief possess enough of an owner's instincts not to keep stopping in his tracks and wondering, "What would Steve do?" Finally, there is the ultimate barometer reading for any technology company—whether it can stay youthful in spirit. This means answering the most testing question of all. What will keep the scintillating twenty-three year old engineers in the world's greatest colleges and universities yearning to hear word that they have been offered a job at the company formerly known as Apple Computer, Inc.?

INDEX

X

Z